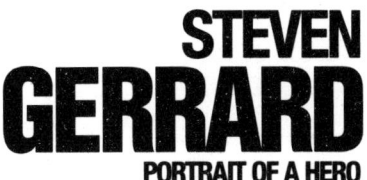

STEVEN GERRARD
PORTRAIT OF A HERO

ADAM COTTIER

JOHN BLAKE

Published by John Blake Publishing Ltd,
3, Bramber Court, 2 Bramber Road,
London W14 9PB, England

www.blake.co.uk

First published in hardback in 2006

ISBN 1 84454 208 4

All rights reserved. No part of this publication may be reproduced, stored in a retrieval system, or in any form or by any means, without the prior permission in writing of the publisher, nor be otherwise circulated in any form of binding or cover other than that in which it is published and without a similar condition including this condition being imposed on the subsequent publisher.

British Library Cataloguing-in-Publication Data:

A catalogue record for this book is available from the British Library.

Design by www.envydesign.co.uk

Printed in Great Britain by Creative Print & Design, Wales

3 5 7 9 10 8 6 4

© Text copyright Adam Cottier

Papers used by John Blake Publishing are natural, recyclable products made from wood grown in sustainable forests. The manufacturing processes conform to the environmental regulations of the country of origin.

Photographs courtesy of Getty Images, Clevamedia, Empics, Mirrorpix, Rex Features, ActionImages and Sportsphoto

Every attempt has been made to contact the relevant copyright-holders, but some were unobtainable. We would be grateful if the appropriate people could contact us.

Contents

1	Keeping it 'Pool	1
2	Born Red	11
3	From Bambi to Bison	25
4	Allez Gerrard and Houllier	35
5	Country Boy	61
6	Triple the Glory, Minus the Injury	75
7	Heartbreak High	129
8	Tough at the Kop	153
9	Captain's Honour	181
10	Stevie Wonder	209
11	Turkish Delight – The Champions League Final: 25 May 2005	247
12	Personal Professional	265
13	A Story Only Half Told	275

Chapter One
Keeping it 'Pool

'I love Liverpool so much. This is my club. My heart is with Liverpool,' were the sincere words of Steven Gerrard following his decision to end weeks of torment for Liverpool fans and sign a lucrative new contract with his hometown club in July 2005. Less than two months earlier, the inspirational captain, adored by so many, had lifted the European Cup after leading his side to the most unbelievable footballing comeback of all time. However, in the weeks to come, all the joy and jubilation from that incredible night in Istanbul were overshadowed by an episode in Gerrard's career that saw his lifelong ties to Liverpool FC come perilously close to being severed forever.

Gerrard is irreplaceable to Liverpool. He is their modern-day link to the golden age of the 1970s and '80s where home-grown heroes and sparkling silverware ornamented the great football arena that is Anfield. But it is because he is so good and so adept in everything he does, that almost every football team in the world covets his services. However, most simply could not afford to match his near-priceless value. That was until Roman Abramovich, the Russian billionaire, bought Chelsea in 2004. His arrival signalled a frenzy of multi-million-pound transfer activity at Stamford Bridge and almost all of the world's best players were either linked to, or signed for, the Londoners. Almost inevitably, they courted Liverpool's captain. In 2004, Gerrard turned them down, deciding instead to remain with his beloved, although underachieving, team. And his desire for silverware duly ended, with an unlikely European Cup-winners' medal. However, Liverpool still failed to gain any ground in their bid for an illusive Premiership title. It was only then that Gerrard was forced to think long and hard about leaving Anfield, knowing that if he did so, he would break the hearts of the fans he had made so happy.

Rick Parry, the Liverpool chief executive, frequently affirmed his desire to keep Gerrard on Merseyside and open contract talks with him immediately after Liverpool had returned from the Champions League final. 'How could I leave after this?' the Liverpool captain had said after leading his hometown club to glory on the biggest stage possible. The answer was simple: he would leave if Liverpool wanted the immeasurable amount of money that Chelsea were willing to pay for him.

A year earlier, Michael Owen had left in similar circumstances to sign for Real Madrid – albeit not after winning the Champions League – but Liverpool fans still feared the worst as Gerrard holidayed in Portugal with his girlfriend and his baby daughter amid rumours that the Reds were not about to offer him a new contract.

KEEPING IT 'POOL

Liverpool dawdled portentously. So much so that Gerrard came to the point, barely a month after he had experienced the proudest night of his life, where he believed the club he loved so dearly no longer wanted him. Before lifting the European Cup, Gerrard had warned Liverpool that, as much as it would hurt him, he would seek a transfer should the club fail to meet his expectations. He was certainly not expecting to win the Champions League. However, the magic of that triumph had alleviated any doubt as to whether Anfield was the place where he could realise his childhood dreams.

Gerrard's ongoing contract riddle was not the only concern Liverpool had after winning the Champions League. They were initially told that their achievement would not warrant them automatic re-entry into the competition and that they would only feature in the UEFA Cup, as they had finished outside of the Champions League qualifying positions in the Premiership. To the club's relief, however, UEFA decided to allow them back in, but only if they could overcome three allotted rounds of qualifying which would begin in mid-July. That meant that Liverpool had to return to pre-season training early, barely six weeks after the previous season had ended. With increasing doubt surrounding Gerrard's situation, Liverpool fans held their breath as their side began preparations for their first qualifying match.

'The ball's in Liverpool's court now,' said Gerrard, frustrated by the breakdown in communication on the club's part. 'I'm ready to talk and to sort everything out. I'm just waiting for them to give me the nod about where and when, and me and my advisers will be there... Of course, I want to stay at Liverpool. We haven't spoken about a new contract yet, so I don't know how long the talks will go on for. The sooner we get under way the better, because I want my future sorted out before the season starts.'

Most of Gerrard's unhappiness stemmed from Liverpool's lightning-quick ability to hand Dietmar Hamann a new contract and to tell Vladimir Smicer that he could leave the club, while failing to open contract talks with him before he went on holiday. British newspapers speculated about his future on a daily basis. Real Madrid became the Fleet Street favourite to land the talismanic maestro, closely followed by Chelsea. One story suggested that Madrid were all set to launch a £20 million player-plus-cash bid as well as offering the England star a staggering £150,000 a week for his services. A move to Spain to join David Beckham and Michael Owen looked increasingly likely as the ink pot began to dry up on the Liverpool contract table, until Madrid decided to bolster their star-studded staff with little-known Uruguayan midfielder Pablo Garcia, a player said to possess the same dynamic and industrial abilities of Gerrard. Garcia's arrival at the Bernabeu immediately suggested that Madrid had lost patience with Liverpool.

Gerrard's link to Madrid had emanated due to his ties with SFX, his powerful advisers who had already orchestrated the deals that had taken Michael Owen, Jonathan Woodgate and David Beckham to Spain.

Inevitably, though, it was Chelsea who came the closest to acquiring Gerrard's services in those dark, agonising weeks of uncertainty. The Londoners launched a sizable bid to land the midfield ace amid newspaper rumours of training-ground spats and a tarnished relationship

KEEPING IT 'POOL

between Gerrard and his manager, Rafa Benitez. The Champions League final seemed light years away – certainly for Liverpool fans – as their captain seemed increasingly destined for the Anfield exit door.

Benitez himself, desperate to preserve Liverpool's future and to allay rumours that he wanted Gerrard to leave, issued an impassioned plea for his captain to remain on Merseyside. It had been thought that, following Gerrard's unerring post-match declaration in Istanbul and Benitez's insistence that he wanted to build his team around his inspirational captain, contract negotiations were just a formality. However, Gerrard and his SFX agent, Struan Marshall, had found Liverpool's hesitancy intolerable. The English midfielder had become convinced that he was unwanted by his employers. Then, on Monday, 4 July 2005, the news arrived that Gerrard and his advisers had called a halt to contract discussions. All of a sudden, the Liverpool heart had stopped beating.

'The last six weeks have been the toughest of my life and it's the hardest decision I have ever had to make,' said Gerrard. 'I fully intended to sign a new contract after the Champions League final, but the events of the last five or six weeks have changed all that. I have too much respect for the club to get involved in a slanging match.'

There seemed to be no way back as Chelsea waded in for the kill with their long-standing target now fully in range. They launched a staggering £32 million bid that same July evening. Rafael Benitez and Rick Parry held an emergency meeting with Gerrard and his agent at the club's Melwood training ground in the hope of reviving discussions over a new contract. Despite their willingness to offer Gerrard a new deal worth more than £90,000 a week, the discussions ended with Anfield officials finally conceding that they had lost the battle to keep their now-want-away captain. An acrimonious separation loomed large with a British record transfer fee set to test the Merseysiders' resolve.

The Reds' only hope of keeping Gerrard rested with the England man himself. The midfielder spent hours mulling over his future and agonising over his decision on Liverpool's contract offer. Newspapers revealed that he had confided in friends that he desperately wanted to stay at Anfield, but that he was concerned that the club wouldn't be strong enough to compete for honours in the forthcoming season. Gerrard was also said to be worried that by signing a deal reportedly worth £100,000 a week, he would consume most of Rafa Benitez's transfer budget and that the club would, therefore, not be able to challenge for the Premiership title. With that the only major honour left for him to accomplish at club level, Chelsea offered an appealing alternative.

Liverpool fans gathered outside Anfield, with some of them even burning shirts to express their disgust at Gerrard's apparent disloyalty. Meanwhile, Chelsea's initial bid was rejected as a sense of urgency encroached on Liverpool's hierarchy to resolve the matter swiftly. The thought of Gerrard returning to Anfield the following season in a blue shirt was, as the *Liverpool Echo* put it, 'too hideous to contemplate.'

Gerrard's close family and friends had persuaded him to stay with Liverpool following the European Championships the year before and, one year on, they would have to win him over again.

'When I last spoke to him a couple of days ago he seemed as happy as Larry,' revealed Gerrard's grandad, Tony. 'There

KEEPING IT 'POOL

was no indication that he wanted to leave, so when I heard the news on the radio it came as a complete surprise. But he's twenty-five, a grown man with a baby daughter and he knows what he is doing. His family will support him in whatever he decides to do next.'

Threats of a fans' backlash haunted Gerrard. A relationship between football supporters and their heroes treads a thin line between love and hate. These were the fans that adored him – if he turned his back on them, he knew now that he would lose his iconic status and with it everything that he had ever dreamed of. And why move to Chelsea anyway? What fulfilment would he get from winning the Premiership title with them?

Gerrard, who has always been a family orientated man, was talked out of signing for Chelsea in the summer of 2004 by his father Paul. Although he would have doubled his £60,000-a-week wages, Paul reportedly told his son that if he left Liverpool, then life would become intolerable for the family. The same plea worked again.

On the morning of Wednesday, 6 July, the national newspaper back pages were decorated with talk of Gerrard's imminent transfer to Chelsea. However, by lunchtime, it became very clear that the Liverpool captain had, instead, made an incredible U-turn to remain with the European champions. Merseyside's evening papers broke the news.

'I had the whole of yesterday to think about my decision and what I was doing. I turned off my phone and my television and went through it all in my head again,' revealed Gerrard defiantly, in a press conference. 'I just couldn't leave the club I love'.

In the aftermath, Liverpool and Gerrard himself admitted that they had made mistakes. The twenty-five-year-old had been convinced that Rafa Benitez had secretly wanted to sell him and that that was the only reason why contract negotiations had gone on for so long. Gerrard pleaded for forgiveness for his part in the saga:

> In my heart, this is my club. I want to help bring success here for them and, for their sake and my own, I never want to go through this again. The last five or six weeks were the hardest of my life, because I wrongly believed the club didn't want me... Now I know how much the club want me... I've only one medal left to win at Liverpool and that's the Premiership. That's what I want more than anything and Liverpool is the only place where I've ever wanted to win it.

Liverpool fans were left stunned: once again they had seen their side come back from the brink of losing something very important. As far as they had been concerned, the divorce papers had been signed and their love affair with Gerrard was over. Instead, the romance was back on and both parties got the chance to renew their vows as Liverpool faced Wrexham in a hastily arranged pre-season game at the Racecourse Ground with the ink still drying on their hero's new contract. It was hardly St Paul's Cathedral, or even Istanbul's Ataturk Stadium for that matter, but it would do for now, as Liverpool put their troubles behind them and embarked on a new season.

Gerrard had committed himself to Liverpool until 2009. Thus, the Reds' heart began to beat again as all speculation surrounding the midfielder's future came to an abrupt end. Chelsea's 'consolation' prize came in the form of Manchester City sensation Shaun Wright-Phillips. Had

KEEPING IT 'POOL

Liverpool lost Steven Gerrard, if Liverpool ever do lose Steven Gerrard, there would have been no consolation – his remarkable talent is unique.

The extraordinary transfer saga was cast aside by the Liverpool fans, who were simply relieved that their most integral player had decided to stay. Gerrard paraded the Champions League trophy to the crowd before the Reds' game with Wrexham alongside Jamie Carragher, who had also joined him in penning a new deal.

Soon after, Liverpool and their fans were given a timely reminder of exactly how valuable Gerrard was to them. Making his 284th appearance in a Red shirt, Gerrard found the perfect solution to eradicate the demons of the summer by scoring his first-ever hat-trick for Liverpool in a Champions League qualifying tie against Welsh minnows Total Network Solutions at Anfield. In doing so, he put his beloved side back on the long road to success and set about writing another chapter in a truly extraordinary career.

Chapter Two

Born Red

The city of Liverpool will never forget 1980. It was, of course, the year in which legendary Beatle John Lennon met his untimely death. Yet it was also the year that a small community of Merseyside welcomed a new arrival – a person who would, one day, realise the same kind of iconic status that Lennon had embraced on Merseyside.

Steven George Gerrard was born on Friday, 30 May 1980 at Whiston hospital in the borough of Knowsley, on the eastern outskirts of Liverpool, the second son of Paul Gerrard and his wife Julie.

That same month also saw the birth of two other individuals who would go on to become sporting champions in their own right. Both tennis heroine Venus Williams and Brazilian football superstar Ronaldinho were born within days of Gerrard. Indeed, there was a champion feeling in the Liverpool-mad Gerrard family. The Reds, led by Bob Paisley, had just been crowned title winners in England for the twelfth time.

STEVEN GERRARD: PORTRAIT OF A HERO

You see, football has always been an innate passion on Merseyside – a welcome escape from the working-class world that encompasses so many of Liverpool's inhabitants. Almost from the moment they are born, children are laden with the dilemma of which one of the city's' two big football teams to follow. It's either Liverpool or Everton and, in the 1980s, that was no easy decision to make. Naturally, young Gerrard chose studiously.

Whether it is a pop star, a television personality or a footballer, every child has a hero; somebody to look up to; someone who can fuel their dreams. For Gerrard and his contemporaries, that person was always going to be a footballer. In the mid-1980s, Everton had stars, but it was Liverpool who had the superstars that youngsters saw as their idols. If the radiant abilities of Kenny Dalglish and Graeme Souness didn't sway Gerrard, then the timing of Liverpool's triumphs did.

Everton were successful in the 1980s – the most successful they have ever been – but in Gerrard's lifetime, Liverpool were the first to win a European trophy. The Reds were domestically dominant throughout the decade; they were unequivocally the best team in the land. And it was their European Cup success of 1984 that probably swung Gerrard in the red direction, igniting a love affair that would last a lifetime. The Rome final fell on what was his fourth birthday – Wednesday, 30 May 1984. How his infant eyes must have sparkled that night as Graeme Souness, the Liverpool captain of the time, inspired the Reds to beat Roma on penalties and then lift the giant, gleaming trophy.

It was on the tainted playing fields of the Bluebell estate in the football-mad suburb of Huyton that Gerrard fully realised his love for the game. Untamed dreams of playing for his hometown club, winning trophies and starring in Merseyside derbies were played out avidly, every single day. And there could not have been a greater influence on any young aspiring footballer than Liverpool's all-conquering side of the time.

The son of a garden-fence erector, Gerrard possesses an old-fashioned footballer's background – the two jumpers and a tin can, 'anything will do as long as we can play football' kind of background. That's what Gerrard did. Football was his, and many other children's, only method of escapism from a testing early life. As the likes of Ronnie Whelan, Steve McMahon and John Barnes graced Anfield in the late 1980s, Gerrard was mimicking them just a few miles away on the streets of the Liverpool council estate he lived on.

'I grew up on a council estate and I loved every minute of it,' Gerrard told the *Sunday Times*. 'I used to hang around lads who were two or three years older than me, because my brother, Paul, is that age. They were the ones who always seemed to be playing football and I played with them... We had a car park outside our house and we put a goal up at one end of it and played every second we could. It was great growing up with my mates there, but a lot of them are unemployed now, so I do think about what I might have been doing without football.'

Football in Liverpool in the 1980s was an adhesive bond, helped by the success of both the top clubs on Merseyside – it served a solid purpose in a society that would otherwise have been blighted by crime and poverty. Talents were nurtured and spotted early. Children focused solely on improving. Practice, practice, practice. It was that kind of dedication – the desire to be better than their mates – that spurred the likes of Gerrard on. Despite their impoverished roots, children would steer clear of crime thanks to football. It is the reason why so many young players who grew up at the same time in Liverpool have made it as footballers on a grand scale. Gerrard's exact contemporary and close friend, Michael Owen, is also enjoying an illustrious career. Then there are the likes of Jamie Carragher, Joey Barton, Kevin Nolan and Danny Murphy – all Scouse, and all successful Premiership stars.

Even one of Gerrard's family members has endeavoured to follow his lead and become a professional footballer. His younger cousin, Anthony Gerrard, came through Everton's academy prior to joining Walsall in the summer of 2005. Another cousin, Joe Coogan, is a talented player for the same primary school side that Gerrard graced as a child.

Whatever the inspiration that has led so many Merseyside youngsters onto the practice fields of England's top football clubs, Gerrard's was unquestionably the team he fell in love with at a very young age.

His earliest Anfield memory was when Liverpool played Coventry in a League Cup fourth-round replay on 26 November 1986. You can imagine a fresh-faced Gerrard, wrapped up in a red scarf and a red bobble hat and, hand in hand with his father, marching through the famous Bill Shankly gateway on a cold winter night and gazing up at the magnificent stadium for the first time. It would have been a feeling worthy of inspiring any six-year-old. Anfield was only half-full that night, but it didn't stop Gerrard from cherishing such a special moment. A crowd of just over 19,000 accompanied him in watching Liverpool progress in the League Cup courtesy of a 3–1 victory.

BORN RED

Midfielder Jan Molby, whose key attribute was his fine passing ability, scored a hat-trick of penalties. The Dane was always a prominent spot-kick specialist: in his Liverpool career he scored forty out of forty-two attempts, which by anyone's standards is fairly phenomenal. The inspiration was there for Gerrard to seize upon.

If you can't imagine Gerrard attending his first Liverpool game, then you must be able to imagine him in the school playground the following day, striking a ball as hard as he could against a brick wall marked with chalk in imitation of his new hero.

Liverpool won the league in 1987, and once again in 1988, before they were spectacularly humbled by Wimbledon in the FA Cup final later that same year. In 1989 tragedy struck at Hillsborough, before Michael Thomas' extraordinary late winner handed Arsenal the league title at the expense of Liverpool. That moment sparked a decade of relative anonymity by Kop standards, one that was only boosted by their 1992 FA Cup final victory under Graeme Souness and a League Cup final victory under Roy Evans in 1995. While taking a firm interest in Liverpool's trials and tribulations, Gerrard paid added attention to England's exploits at the 1990 World Cup in Italy. He has since openly admitted to jumping and leaping around his house with his family, watching the penalty shoot-out in the semi-final that saw England get knocked out by Germany. Gerrard watched, and admired, the midfield heroics of England's talisman of the time, Paul Gascoigne – the player who he would go on to emulate on the international stage some ten years later.

At the same time as witnessing and learning about the joys of British football, as well as coming to terms with the end of Liverpool's domestic dominance, Gerrard was also learning the ways of the world at his first school – St Michael's Primary School in Huyton – now called Huyton-with-Roby Primary.

Back then, the other boys towered over Gerrard. However, the youngster's fragile-looking appearance was deceptive. When Gerrard was in possession of a ball on the school's bumpy playing fields, his footballing abilities became instantly obvious – he looked more able than players twice his age.

'I just couldn't believe he was so good, because he was one of the smallest boys in the class,' Mike Tilling, Gerrard's tutor of the time, told the *Liverpool Echo*. 'I started him off as a striker and it honestly seemed as if he had been playing for years – he was so good with the ball at his feet.'

Gerrard played for his primary school football team from the moment he moved into year three. Incredibly, most children would not even be considered to take part until year six. He had what could only be described as an extraordinarily precocious talent. What he lacked in mass, he more than made up for in character and strength. Even in class, away from a football, Gerrard was the cream of the crop.

'We used to run a little business in the class,' explains Tilling. 'It was owned by the children and Steven would always win hands down when we voted for who the manager would be.' No matter how comfortable Gerrard was in the classroom, his outstanding talent was football. In 1990, Gerrard won his first piece of silverware, when he led his primary school team to the Huyton Under-11s Schools' League Title.

When Mike Tilling left the school to take up a new

teaching post elsewhere, all the children in his class signed a card to say thank you. Gerrard wrote his name in huge letters across the middle of the page. Perhaps that served as a symbol of what he was going to become – a midfield giant and the centrepiece of a team. What it definitely symbolised was an amiable young man's gratitude for the first person that had helped him outside of his family. It was the first measure of a true champion schoolboy.

While at St Michael's, Gerrard was invited to play for a Sunday league side called Whiston Juniors by George Hughes.

'Even as a nipper Steven was streets ahead of all the other lads,' Hughes told the press. 'We knew he was special straight away. He could take the opposition on by himself – he was that good.'

Hughes was so impressed with Gerrard's abilities that he alerted friends at the Liverpool School of Excellence, run by Reds' legend Steve Heighway. A guided tour of Anfield, followed by a successful trial, propelled the eight-year-old into the cradle of the world's most famous football club and his engagement to his first love was confirmed. 1988 may have seen Liverpool reduced to tears by Wimbledon, but it was also the year that a future European Cup winner began his Anfield affinity. Gerrard trained twice a week there up until the age of sixteen, when he signed professional forms. Gerrard's friendship with Michael Owen also blossomed while he was there, despite the fact that the pair had very different domestic backgrounds.

Away from the schoolboy set-up at Liverpool, Gerrard continued to play for Whiston Juniors, where he spent seven years. When that time ended, he moved to the Denburn Park Boys' Club before his graduation at Liverpool.

Gerrard's progress in his early teenage years was hampered, however, by something that could so easily have brought a heartbreakingly premature end to his football career. He suffered from Osgood-Schlatter's disease, a bone condition that meant that he was seldom fit for more than a week at a time. Had Gerrard himself been any less motivated by his dreams, then the growing pains he had to endure would almost certainly have beaten him, but he has always been a fighter and a winner – especially in the face of adversity. The condition he had meant that his muscles were outgrowing his bones and, subsequently, he was constantly sidelined with niggling muscle strains and pulls.

Whereas Michael Owen is estimated to have played around ninety games in two seasons at Under-13 and Under-14 level with Liverpool, Gerrard managed barely thirty outings. Such infrequency meant that he missed out on selection for the national football school at Lilleshall in Shropshire, where fellow future England stars Owen and Alan Smith went to have their talents primed for success. Jamie Carragher also made it to the national football school, but Gerrard, then twelve years old, was left behind in Liverpool. The legacy of that traumatic period in Gerrard's life lived on. Even when his Liverpool career was taking off a few years later, he was still visiting an osteopath in Paris on a regular basis.

Wrapped in cotton wool by Liverpool, Gerrard emerged, from what is now only seen as a minor blip on his career, triumphantly. Such was his undoubted ability at the age of thirteen, he was picked a year early for the Liverpool schoolboys' team. This gave him the opportunity to play against some of his future Anfield team-mates, including Jamie Carragher, who played for the Sefton schoolboys' team. From the moment Gerrard appeared for his hometown club, his dedication and love for it became evident.

Gerrard frequently impressed his coaches with both his commitment and his willingness. One such coach was Tim Johnson. 'I remember the first round of the English Trophy, which was the schoolboys' equivalent of the FA Cup,' Johnson told the *Liverpool Echo*. 'Steven scored the winner against West Lancashire and it was at the time of Jurgen Klinsmann, so when he scored he dived into the corner on his stomach. There was a lot of tut-tutting on the sidelines, but he really played his heart out for Liverpool schoolboys.'

Gerrard and Michael Owen were the cornerstone of their schoolboy side and their mutual respect for each other kindled a kindred footballing friendship that seems destined to last a lifetime. Back then the pair were very similar in terms of physical stature and their coaches were eager to nurture their abilities. In one instance, Gerrard and Owen were the only two Under-14 players taken on an Under-18 tour of Spain – taken not to play, but to learn. It benefited them greatly.

Three years after joining the Liverpool School of Excellence, Gerrard switched primary school for secondary when he made the move to the Cardinal Heenan Roman Catholic School in West Derby. It was there that his sporting skills bore even more fruit, as it quickly became clear that his profound abilities weren't solely harboured with football.

Gerrard was an expert in athletics: a natural at throwing the javelin and also the shot-put. He was also the best in his age group at 400-metre running, but his sporting utility did not end there – Gerrard was the school's tennis champion for fully four years.

Football, however good he was at tennis, was Gerrard's only real love. He scored a hat-trick in his first game for Cardinal Heenan in an 8–0 win over Savio High, the school that Jamie Carragher attended. Better things were to follow. At the end of his first year, an extraordinary event took place when Gerrard donned the captain's armband for his first ever cup final at the school. Playing against the renowned Bluecoat High School, Cardinal Heenan found themselves 3–0 down at half-time and it was the Merseyside Under-11s Cup final – to any eleven-year-old boy, absolutely massive. Half the Cardinal Heenan side were already resigned to losing, but not Gerrard – he was different to his team-mates; an inspirational leader, even then. He became almost solely responsible for a remarkable comeback that bears so much resemblance to the European Cup final which took place some fourteen years later.

Gerrard, as he did against AC Milan, proceeded to pull a goal back early in the second half. He went on to score again and, before he knew it, his side had won 4–3. There were no penalties that day, but Gerrard deservedly took the plaudits. Maybe it was divine intervention, maybe it was something else; maybe Gerrard was just destined for stardom. It was Captain Fantastic in the making.

Steve Monaghan, his coach and head of year at Cardinal Heenan, remembers that amazing afternoon with great fondness. 'Steven brought the team all back with him that day and you could see that something was building,' Monaghan told the *Liverpool Echo*. 'It was typical of his attitude. Even as a young lad he was good at rallying his team; he led by example and had that tremendous commitment. He always had the ability to say "no, we're not beaten here".'

Monaghan, who oversaw five years of Gerrard's development, played an important role in his education both on and off the field. 'All I had to do was try and keep his feet on the ground because, basically, he had all these adults fawning over him and I was the one who treated him like a normal child. I had him from the age of eleven and he was signed to Liverpool then but, because there were no academies at the time, he was still able to play for the school without any restrictions. I think that benefited Steven, because he was well liked in his peer group.'

Monaghan is also convinced that Gerrard could have been a champion of a different kind had he not pursued his footballing dream so fervently. 'Steven was a good all-rounder. Although he concentrated on football from being a teenager, he could have made a fantastic tennis player and one with a better attitude than some of our professional players now. His vision, his co-ordination and his awareness were just so good; they were ideally suited to tennis. It really is no exaggeration to say that we could have been seeing him at Wimbledon by now.'

Gerrard was not only a role model to his fellow pupils on the sports field. According to Monaghan, he was a model class-member.

'He was a little angel-faced blonde. But he was a good pupil, there was never a discipline problem and, although his exams did take second place later on, he didn't give up like some lads do, thinking he was definitely going to make it as a footballer.'

STEVEN GERRARD: PORTRAIT OF A HERO

Eric Chadwick was the PE teacher who, alongside Steve Monaghan, had the pleasure of nurturing Gerrard. He, too, could see the talents that the young boy from Huyton possessed every time he went near a ball.

'He was naturally gifted,' Chadwick told the *Liverpool Echo*. 'Steve was brilliant at any sport he touched, but if you lined him up against the playground wall with the rest of the football squad, you wouldn't have picked him out as the superstar... But, despite his size, he was a bit special with undeniable talent. I knew then that this thirteen-year-old had something more than any other of our football-daft youngsters.'

Gerrard's love and hunger for football and, perhaps more evidently, his desire to win was not reserved for the school playing fields. He often accompanied his father, who he still calls his greatest influence, to watch school matches all over Merseyside. More often than not the team Gerrard wanted to see were Cardinal Heenan's next opponents. After meticulously examining his future opponent's strengths and weaknesses, Gerrard would return to his teacher's office with a detailed report on the team they were about to face. It is no surprise then, that Gerrard remained unbeaten as captain of his school football team for three years. His final act for Cardinal Heenan was to lift the Royal Mail Trophy in his final game as captain before he joined the Liverpool academy. He left a lasting legacy on those who ever had the opportunity to be alongside him on and off the pitch.

'Steven was different class,' one of Gerrard's former school-mates, Ben Chadwick, told the press. 'He could do everything. I don't think I ever saw him lose a tackle and his passing was unbelievable. If he didn't know you he was quiet and shy, but once you gained his confidence, he was a typical Scouser with a great sense of humour.'

To this day, Gerrard has refused to forget his modest football roots and he remains ever proud of them. He regularly visits Cardinal Heenan school and has opened its sports centre and appeared at prize-giving presentations. It was on those rough edges of Liverpool that Gerrard's true talent came to the fore and he remains eternally grateful to those who taught him and encouraged him to follow his dreams.

Chapter Three
From Bambi to Bison

Gerrard signed professional forms at Anfield upon leaving Cardinal Heenan High School shortly after his sixteenth birthday. It was 1996, and the majority of Gerrard's friends from Huyton were leaving school to become electricians, plumbers or call-centre workers; some even ended up on the dole. However, the school-leaver with a true, sparkling ability moved a giant step closer to realising his childhood dream under the wing of Liverpool legend Steve Heighway. Another teenager with an abundance of talent, Michael Owen, also graduated to the youth-training scheme alongside Gerrard. The pair were the only two players to be kept on Liverpool's books. In the capable hands of one former Reds hero, both Gerrard and Owen progressed at an astonishing rate.

As a sixteen-year-old, Gerrard still had the same slender, injury-prone frame that had hampered him during his school days. He certainly didn't have the physique of a future Liverpool captain. Fearing a wasted talent, Mother Nature decided that things needed to change. In just over a year, Gerrard went from being a pint-sized 5ft 4in nipper to being a 6ft 1in midfield maestro. Gerrard's size and proportion had always been a worry for his coaches in terms of whether or not he could make it onto the big stage. The transformation left them stunned.

'Young Stevie had the most amazing growth spurt,' recalled Tim Johnson, Liverpool schoolboys' coach, in the *Daily Star*. 'I was at the academy some eighteen months after he had finished playing for me and this colossus appeared in the doorway of the sports hall. I just couldn't believe my eyes. I couldn't take it in that it was the same Stevie Gerrard. The Bambi that had left me had turned into a bison. It was some change in the lad, I can tell you – he was a lot stockier and bigger. The boy became a man at the Anfield academy. God knows what they fed him or did to him physically, but Liverpool clearly brought the best out of him.'

In that year or so of transformation, Gerrard's near-telepathic on-the-field relationship with Michael Owen also grew stronger. He often played at right-back during his initiation and it was from that position that his now-trademark pin-point long passing and extraordinary vision came to fruition, helping Owen bag the goals that propelled the prolific striker into the first team. Disciplined and refined, together the pair encroached on Liverpool's failing senior side that had been bereft of major silverware for almost a decade. It was Michael Owen who made it there first; partly aided by the fact that he had played for England at schoolboy level whereas Gerrard had not.

Owen made his first-team debut as a second-half

replacement for Patrick Berger in Liverpool's away defeat to Wimbledon on 7 May 1997. Fourteen minutes into his professional career, the seventeen-year-old took Stig Inge Byornebye's pass in his athletic stride and guided home his first Liverpool goal. In the season that followed, Owen rose to prominence as Liverpool's main marksman, taking that particular mantle away from Liverpool's original 1990s protégé – Robbie Fowler. At the 1998 World Cup, Owen announced himself to the world with an incredible goal in his country's second-round tie against Argentina.

In the meantime, Gerrard waited patiently for his chance, relentlessly striving to make an impression on the velvet training pitches of Liverpool's new academy facilities at Kirkby, which opened in 1998. Owen had made a telling impression with his electric pace and exceptional eye for goal. It wasn't as easy as that for Gerrard, but a managerial change at Anfield proved decisive.

Gerard Houllier's arrival at Anfield in July 1998, initially to become joint-manager alongside Roy Evans, brought fresh hope to the long-suffering fans of Liverpool and, no doubt, to the eager young stars of the brand-spanking-new academy. The Reds had finished third in the Premiership in the previous season, but having witnessed Arsene Wenger's success in leading Arsenal to their Double triumph of that year, they set about their own French revolution – believing that Houllier would have the same effect.

Houllier's arrival heralded a new dawn at Anfield, although many questioned the Liverpool board's decision to make him a joint-manager alongside Evans. Other managers that had tried and tested the method warned Liverpool of their peril but, nevertheless, the unique double act led Liverpool into the new season with expectations rocketing. Robbie Fowler was in the midst of a long injury lay-off, so the onus was on Michael Owen to make an even bigger impression than the one he had already made the previous season. He started as he meant to go on; hitting the winner as Houllier's new charges came from behind to beat Southampton at the Dell on the opening day of the 1997–98 season.

The return of Jamie Redknapp from a cartilage problem that had ruled him out of the 1998 World Cup was hailed by Houllier as the key ingredient in Liverpool's drive for success. After a devastating Owen hat-trick away at Newcastle and a 2–0 defeat of Coventry, the Reds were on top of the table. But an away defeat at West Ham followed, and cracks in an obscure managerial marriage began to show.

By early November, having won just one game in eight, Liverpool were fast becoming mid-table nonentities. Roy Evans' future hung precariously in the balance as Liverpool succumbed to Derby at Anfield. The fireworks exploded on Evans' thirty-three-year Anfield residence when a home defeat to Spurs prematurely ended the Reds' challenge in the League Cup on 10 November 1998. Gerard Houllier was left in sole charge of arresting an alarming decline that seemed to be spiralling out of control. His intended renaissance began as Phil Thompson, a former Liverpool European Cup-winning captain, stepped up to become assistant manager.

Despite Thompson's appointment, rumours of a player revolt, coupled with a crushing 3–1 home defeat by Leeds, failed to lift the heavy clouds above Anfield. However, it was that home loss that suggested to Houllier that he should look further inside the ranks at Liverpool to find an answer to his troubles. One of Leeds' three goals that day

FROM BAMBI TO BISON

was scored by a fresh-faced, home-grown eighteen-year-old by the name of Alan Smith. Having risen through the Leeds' youth set-up with dreams of playing for the club, the former England schoolboy struck within three minutes of making his debut. Houllier's inherited Liverpool side were bereft of the youthful spark that Leeds had found. Only the emergence of Jamie Carragher had given Liverpool fans hope for the future and, with the Reds floundering, drastic action was required. Houllier took a leaf from Leeds United and set about finding homegrown talent of his own.

The Liverpool team of the time were being branded as egotistical and narcissistic. Houllier would not have that – he believed in firm discipline – and some of the players he had in his squad did not meet the criteria. He told the *Sunday Times*:

> I don't believe in fines. I believe in individual responsibility. For ten years, players have got to live for the job. After that, they will live thanks to that job. But for those ten years they have got to commit themselves totally to what they are doing. If you get the right people, they will do that. At twenty, players are well rewarded. They are millionaires, so whether they win or lose means nothing financially. But if you look for them, there are still players around who, whatever wages they are on, will fight for you once they are on that grass. I'll name you one – Jamie Carragher. What a professional. He might have a niggly injury, but he'll always be out there giving you some of this. Yes, you need to have talent, but you also need winners. Players who hate to be defeated, who hate to lose out in the tackle.

STEVEN GERRARD: PORTRAIT OF A HERO

With those comments in mind, it is easy to see why Houllier chose to spend a little extra time at Liverpool's Melwood training ground, running the rule over the club's crop of youngsters. He wanted more players like Carragher – Liverpool through and through – and that had the added advantage of allowing him to steer clear of an inflated transfer market.

'This is not the best time to sign quality players,' said Houllier in a press conference. 'The best are involved in European ties, or their clubs are going for UEFA [Cup] places. We will have to wait, maybe until the end of the season. We have a good striking force, but we need to help them more. At this moment we are very low. We need to come back, gradually at first, to a better level, with the playing staff we have. They can get us to an ordinary level, but I'm aware that such a level is inferior for us, so we need better players to improve that level again.'

Houllier had been critically acclaimed for launching the careers of a medley of players during his time as technical director with the French Football Association. Emmanuel Petit, Patrick Vieira and Nicolas Anelka had all benefited from Houllier's shrewd coaching methods. The French manager was, evidently, no stranger to picking out young talent from a crowd of hopefuls. And he was no stranger to Merseyside either, having started his working life there in the 1960s as a teacher tutoring school children and college students. With big-money transfers ruled out, Houllier had to use his old skills again to find the most talented pupils in his new school.

In the weeks leading up to Liverpool's UEFA Cup third-round tie against Celta Vigo, Houllier decided to take in some Under-19 games at Melwood in search of a solution.

FROM BAMBI TO BISON

The Frenchman was still barely a month into his term as the sole manager at Anfield, but he was in desperate need of a bright spark to lift the Anfield spirits. On one particular afternoon, having been alerted to two players that the Liverpool youth coaches thought may be ready to advance into the first team, Houllier sat down to watch. There was, however, only one player who caught the manager's imagination that day – it was Steven Gerrard. In an obscure footballing sense, it was lust at first sight. Houllier will never forget the day he first laid eyes on his future captain.

'I could see very quickly that he was something special, that he was a special talent,' said Houllier, speaking at a press conference. 'It was a funny situation, really, because he was thought to be too young at the time and I was supposed to be looking at other players, but he was the player I saw. I knew straight away that he was the one I wanted. He was a different class.'

Three days after Robbie Fowler announced his return from injury with a sensational hat-trick as Liverpool thumped Aston Villa at Villa Park, the Reds headed for Spain for their UEFA Cup tie in confident mood, having seen off another Spanish outfit, Valencia, in the previous round of the competition. An unfamiliar face sat among Liverpool's tracksuit-clad warriors bound for Europe. Gerrard, at just eighteen years of age, had been invited to accompany the senior squad for the first time.

Although he didn't feature in Liverpool's 3–1 defeat to Celta Vigo, it was a valuable tutorial for Gerrard as he rubbed shoulders with his future team-mates for the first time. The following Sunday, as Liverpool prepared to entertain struggling Blackburn Rovers, Gerrard – having shown Houllier that he was ready for his big moment – was named among the Reds' substitutes. In the 90th minute of that match, which Liverpool won 2–0, Gerrard tore off his tracksuit and ran onto the Anfield turf for the very first time as a direct replacement for Norwegian right-back Vegard Heggem. The new kid on the block could barely catch his breath as the full-time whistle resonated around Anfield, but he was at the beginning of a breathtaking Liverpool career.

Gerard Houllier was encouraged so much by his performances in the youth set-up that, when the moment came to hand him his full debut, Gerrard was given almost incomprehensible responsibility. It was a true measure of just how much an impression the eighteen-year-old had made in such a short space of time. The responsibility was to mark David Ginola, the flamboyant Frenchman blessed with sublime skills, as Liverpool took on Tottenham Hotspur at White Hart Lane.

It turned out to be an experience that Gerrard did not enjoy, as he was substituted in the second half after an unbridled and inspired Ginola had handed him a torturous Premiership baptism.

'I didn't enjoy the experience,' Gerrard later told the *Sunday Times*. 'I remember travelling home thinking, "It's not my game, this. I'm getting out of it." Immediately I'd noticed the difference between playing at reserve level, with the pace of the game and the strength of the players, as much as their extra ability in the Premiership. The boss said I'd done all right and that he was always going to take me off because he'd just wanted to give me a taste. He played me in the next game and I got Man of the Match. It was then that I started to believe that I could play after all.'

FROM BAMBI TO BISON

That 'next game' was Liverpool's UEFA Cup third-round second-leg tie with Celta Vigo at Anfield. Gerrard took his place in a youthful Liverpool line-up that included fellow academy graduates, David Thompson, Jamie Carragher, Michael Owen and also Danny Murphy, who appeared as a substitute. Even if Liverpool's frailties were exposed that night as the Spanish side progressed with a 1–0 victory, Gerrard announced himself to the Kop with an assured and exemplary performance; one that was beyond his years. Liverpool may well have been dumped out of the UEFA Cup, but Reds fans could walk away from Anfield hailing a youngster that had emerged from their gloom.

Gerrard was understandably stunned at the ferocity of his transition from the training pitches of Melwood into the cauldron of the Anfield anarchy. He was grateful to Gerard Houllier for putting faith in him, where Roy Evans had not.

'Roy had told me I wasn't ready,' Gerrard admitted to the *Sunday Times*. 'He just told me to keep training and playing the way I was and it wouldn't be long before I made the step up. Then, as soon as he left, Steve Heighway really pushed my cause, getting me a regular game in the reserves. That's the way it works. If you're doing well at the academy, you get put in the reserves, who are run jointly by the whole of the coaching staff. That way they all get to see you. I did quite well in a few of the reserve games, and that's when I got moved from the academy to train full time at Melwood.'

Later, Gerrard also revealed that he had felt instant unity among the Liverpool players, which he believed to be a direct result of Houllier's arrival. 'After only a couple of weeks I felt I was part of one big, happy family,' he said.

And had the dressing-room atmosphere been any different at that time, Gerrard's steady rise into the senior ranks may not have run so smoothly.

During his debut season, Gerrard made twelve appearances in the first team – making four starts and featuring eight times as a substitute – while Liverpool limped to a seventh-place finish in the Premiership. He was even invited to experience life with Kevin Keegan's England squad preparing for their European Championship qualifier against Poland in March 1999. Despite that honour, undoubtedly the highlight for him that season came in his first-ever Merseyside derby a month later.

With Liverpool leading 3–2 inside a packed Anfield, Gerrard, playing at right-back having come on as a 71st-minute substitute for Vegard Heggem, showed his fighting, never-say-die attitude to react tremendously and repel a goal-bound shot from Everton's Danny Cadamarteri right on the goal-line. It effectively won Liverpool fans the Merseyside bragging rights for that year and also earned Gerrard a rousing ovation from the Kop.

Notwithstanding that victory, Liverpool had endured another wretched season by their own high standards; they didn't even qualify for Europe. At least they seemed to have a bright future – led by a local teenager who had grown from being a mere pint-sized prospect into a potential Anfield stalwart. For Liverpool and Gerrard, the only way was up.

Chapter Four
Allez Gerrard and Houllier

The 1999–2000 season saw Gerrard make his outright indelible mark on the Liverpool senior side. With Gerard Houllier stamping down his authority at Anfield in the summer of 1999, the teenager could only have been relieved that his name didn't appear on the long list of players that the manager saw as unfit to take part in his revolution.

David James, Paul Ince and Steve McManaman were the high-profile players among a mass exodus from Anfield that summer; McManaman moving on a free transfer to Real Madrid. The exodus was replenished with the arrival of, among others: goalkeeper Sander Westerveld; midfielder Vladimir Smicer; defenders Stephane Henchoz and Sami Hyypia; striker Titi Camara; and Newcastle's German midfield star Dietmar Hamann. The manager spent £21 million on new talent that summer in an attempt to put Liverpool back on track. Jamie Redknapp was also handed the captain's armband as the Reds began the Houllier era for real.

Hamann's arrival, in particular, seemed set to scupper Gerrard's dream of moving into a central midfield role from full-back – the role he had been given so far by Houllier. The youngster's prospects looked bleaker when he wasn't even named among the substitutes as Liverpool, minus an injured Michael Owen, opened the new campaign with a 2–1 away victory at Sheffield Wednesday. However, only 24 minutes into that game, Hamann, Liverpool's £8 million summer acquisition, had to be withdrawn, suffering from ankle ligament damage. The tenacious David Thompson, another product of Liverpool's academy, replaced Hamann that day and, although his appearance had no bearing on the result at Hillsborough, he was not seen as the ideal partner for Jamie Redknapp in Liverpool's midfield.

Michael Owen, who missed the start of the campaign with a hamstring injury, had already chosen his preferred replacement for Hamann – he wanted Gerrard.

'Steve will be our star man this season,' Owen had exclaimed before the start of the season. 'I am not just saying that because we are good friends – he is brilliant.'

Indeed, as Liverpool prepared to face Watford, the press were in agreement with Owen's counsel. Gerrard's chance to take firm hold of his Liverpool career for the first time had arrived. Sure enough, he returned to partner Jamie Redknapp in midfield for the first time as Liverpool's squad lay threadbare. Newly promoted Watford proceeded to stun the Kop with an unlikely 1–0 victory. With the Reds lacking bite in midfield, Gerrard's future in the first team looked to be in jeopardy when he was replaced midway through the second half. David Thompson, who replaced him, and Danny Murphy, were both baying for that particular midfield berth alongside Jamie Redknapp. Gerrard had a real fight on his hands if he wanted to hold down a regular place.

Questions continued to be asked of Gerard Houllier's tactics, as Liverpool fell to defeat in their next game away at Middlesbrough. Paul Ince, who had left Anfield for Teeside the previous summer, inspired his new club to a 1–0 win with Kevin Keegan, then the England boss, looking on. Gerrard was picked for his country later on in the season, although a needless booking, after an ugly fracas with Middlesbrough's Phil Stamp, could hardly have endeared the youngster to Keegan – it would certainly not have been the love at first sight that Gerard Houllier had experienced when he had seen Gerrard play for the first time.

Houllier, pleading for patience to allow his newly assembled side to gel, took Liverpool to Leeds for their next outing. Keegan was back at Elland Road and, this time, Gerrard and company made amends for their reprehensible reverse at Middlesbrough. Liverpool out-muscled their Yorkshire opponents to win 2–1, with Gerrard a telling influence on the game.

Growing in both confidence and esteem, Gerrard was even more of a significant influence as Gerard Houllier claimed the finest win of his managerial reign to date as Liverpool beat Arsenal 2–0 at Anfield. If, up to that point, Gerrard had yet to pass a stern examination in the infancy of his Liverpool career, it was in this game that he passed with flying colours and, what's more, he did it in front of Kevin Keegan while up against the imperious Patrick Vieira for the first time. The Arsenal captain was run ragged by a ravenous Reds midfield, led by Jamie Redknapp and invigorated by Gerrard, and was simply not allowed to play. How impressed Keegan must have been that night as Gerrard's prolonged job interview for the vacant central midfield role in the Liverpool team took a turn for the better.

A frenetic encounter with Manchester United followed for Liverpool, but the Reds found the Treble winners a tougher nut to crack in front of the Sky television cameras. Gerrard was chosen to face a United side missing Roy Keane, but the young star had little affect on the outcome, as two own goals from Jamie Carragher set United on their way to a 3–2 victory. Gerrard was replaced midway through the second half, as Gerard Houllier attempted to combat a dominant midfield display from the visitors.

From the embers of that fire came the return of Michael Owen from injury and he hit his first goals of the season in a 2–2 draw. 'Gerrard: Puts himself about seven,' read the *Sunday People*'s rating of a midfielder that was fast becoming a permanent fixture in the Liverpool side. Even if he wasn't yet being earmarked for iconic status, he was quietly making an impression that would last a lifetime.

Gerrard's breakthrough into the Liverpool first team exploded into life when Liverpool met Everton at Anfield on 28 September 1999. Dietmar Hamann made his comeback from injury and replaced Gerrard in Liverpool's starting XI, but this particular Merseyside derby was war – not even the substitutes were safe from the firing line of bad temper that ensued that evening. Kevin Campbell put Everton ahead inside the first five minutes of the contest, but that was barely half the story. Midway through the second half, Everton's young forward, Francis Jeffers, clashed with Sander Westerveld, the Liverpool goalkeeper. The pair exchanged slaps and Westerveld grabbed Jeffers by the neck. The severity induced a red card for both players from referee Mike Riley. Liverpool's ignominy was enhanced as defender Steve Staunton was forced to take the gloves of Westerveld with the three allocated substitutions having already been made. But this, the 161st Merseyside derby, didn't end there. Liverpool pressed forward in vain, searching for an unlikely equaliser. It never came and, to make matters worse, Gerrard, who had entered the battlefield as a 64th-minute substitute for Robbie Fowler, was sent off after delivering the final bruising blow. A waist-high, two-footed lunge on Kevin Campbell saw him see red for the first time in his Liverpool career. Gerrard trudged off disconsolate; he was facing a three-match suspension. However, in public, Liverpool's manager refused to be over-critical of him after the game.

'Steve has to learn; he is still learning the game,' said Gerard Houllier to the waiting press. Away from the microphones, however, Houllier was less lenient and laid down the law by not speaking to the nineteen-year-old midfielder for a full week. Gerrard later told of this particularly poignant learning curve.

'The manager had a bit of a go at me over the suspension, but I have taken on board everything the gaffer told me,' he said in the *Daily Mail*. 'He told me I needed to be more composed in my play and that he wanted me on the pitch, not on the sidelines. I was a bit disappointed not to have started that game against Everton and I admit my head was not right for the bench.'

Gerrard was not the first of Liverpool's fresh crop of young players to face the wrath of the French disciplinarian. David Thompson had already been warned about his demeanour and was ordered to train with the youth squad after being sent off in a reserve match. Danny Murphy had also been cited for having the wrong attitude by Houllier. It was the kind of hard-line approach that would pay rich dividends for Liverpool.

Gerrard was named on the substitutes' bench again as Liverpool went to Aston Villa looking to bounce back from their defeat to Everton, but another surplus of cards, including a red one for Steve Staunton, left Liverpool wounded as they limped to a goalless draw. Gerrard featured again, this time as a 32nd-minute replacement for Vladimir Smicer when Liverpool shuffled their pack after being reduced to ten men. Playing in an unfamiliar role at left-back, he demonstrated his astonishing versatility, and made a worthy contribution to Liverpool's clean sheet on that particular afternoon.

After appearing for the England Under-21s, where he was making a telling impact, Gerrard returned to begin his suspension. He sat out Liverpool's 2–1 defeat to Southampton in the League Cup; their 1–0 victory over Chelsea at Anfield; and also their 1–1 draw with Southampton in the league. And Gerrard was not about to walk back into the team. Upon return from the ban, he was employed only as an unused substitute in Liverpool's 1–0 victory over West Ham at Anfield. Then, with Dietmar Hamann firmly embedded in the central midfield role alongside Jamie Redknapp, Gerrard was left out of the squad completely while Liverpool cantered to a 3–1 victory over Bradford. It was plainly obvious that he had his work cut out if he wanted to force his way back into Gerard Houllier's reckoning.

ALLEZ GERRARD AND HOULLIER

In an effort to stake a valid claim for a starting place in Houllier's team, Gerrard lined up for the Liverpool reserves after a late cameo in the seniors' 2–0 victory over Derby. The Reds' second string beat Sunderland reserves 4–0 at Knowsley Road in St Helens and Gerrard hit the opening goal of the rout, hitting a low shot in off the foot of the post after good work from Patrick Berger and the returning Robbie Fowler. And with Vladimir Smicer ruled out of first-team reckoning with a hamstring problem, Houllier left the game convinced that Gerrard was worthy of regaining his place in Liverpool's starting XI. And that he did, playing on the right-hand side of the Reds midfield as they travelled to the Stadium of Light to face Sunderland's newly promoted senior side. The comfortable 2–0 victory, with Berger and Owen finding the net, was Liverpool's fourth successive victory and their seventh game without defeat. The Houllier revolution was beginning to bear fruit at last.

An injury to club captain Jamie Redknapp came as a blessing in disguise for Gerrard's Liverpool career. The England midfielder's persistent knee problem saw him ruled out for three months with cartilage damage. Undeniably, with Redknapp on the sidelines, Gerrard had a chance to establish himself fully into his manager's plans.

'If somebody gets injured, I'm happy to play there. Don't forget, I'm only nineteen,' said Gerrard, reported in the *Sunday Times*. 'Jamie and Didi are seasoned internationals, and I can't argue with not playing in their positions. I just go out and give it 100 per cent and try to work as hard as I can. I get stuck in amongst it and keep my passing as good as possible. I like to score a few goals, too, but they're not coming at the moment. But by the time I'm Jamie

Redknapp's age, I hope nobody will be able to move me from the place I want.'

With Redknapp absent, Gerrard slotted into his desired central midfield position, playing behind Didi Hamann in a 1–0 away defeat to West Ham. 'A solid if unspectacular look,' said the *Observer* of Liverpool's midfield pairing.

Gerard Houllier was not a manager satisfied with the unspectacular, nor was Gerrard as a player. The studious management skills of Liverpool's French coach were clearly under deep scrutiny and the defeat at West Ham dealt the Reds a crushing blow after an excellent run of form. Houllier had promised to preserve a sense of local identity in the dressing room when he had taken the reigns a year previously and with Liverpool bereft of experience, his protégés, David Thompson, Danny Murphy and Steven Gerrard, were all officially set to make the grade in the first team alongside previous graduates, Jamie Carragher and Michael Owen. Houllier had announced that he wanted to 'keep a Liverpool heart beating' within the club – his wish would be granted.

Sheffield Wednesday at home, Sunday, 5 December 1999, is a game and a day that will be etched on Steven Gerrard's memory forever. Live on Sky Sports, Liverpool's credentials were thrust back into the public spotlight as they endeavoured to bounce back from their defeat at West Ham against Danny Wilson's side, who were bottom of the table.

Without their first-choice midfield trio of Patrick Berger, Jamie Redknapp and Vladimir Smicer, Gerrard was named in one of most youthful looking Liverpool sides for years. Of the fourteen players that Gerrard Houllier employed that afternoon, seven had come through the youth ranks at Anfield. Michael Owen, David Thompson, Dominic

ALLEZ GERRARD AND HOULLIER

Matteo and Gerrard began the match; Steve Staunton, Robbie Fowler and Jamie Carragher came off the bench. The 42,517 spectators present were treated to a dazzling display of precocious talent.

Sheffield Wednesday were first out of the blocks, as the Reds' young legs found their feet and Swedish midfielder Niclas Alexandersson's 20-yard rocket after 19 minutes served to wake Liverpool from their cots. Playtime ensued. Sami Hyypia, the reigning Premier League player of the month and new Liverpool captain, comfortably headed home a Thompson corner only two minutes after the visitors had nosed in front.

Four minutes before half-time, the home side, applying the enterprise the Kop demanded, made the lead their own. Thompson, who was later crowned Man of the Match, flashed in a cross-shot that Wednesday goalkeeper Kevin Pressman could only parry and Danny Murphy was on hand to hook home his fifth goal of the season. Liverpool's one-goal advantage looked ever fragile until a moment of celestial proportions shortly before the hour-mark – Gerrard's first senior goal for Liverpool.

With purpose and poise, the nineteen-year-old gathered the ball 40 yards from goal and burst forward. Displaying a magnetic touch, so synonymous with the finest attributes of Steve Heighway in his Anfield prime, Gerrard weaved his way around the close attention of Brazilian stalwart Emerson Thome and former England defender Des Walker before slotting a cool right-footed effort wide of Kevin Pressman and into the net. The Kop erupted in sincere admiration of such a remarkable debut goal and the player himself could hardly contain his delight. David Thompson, not to be upstaged by his friend, curled a delightful left-footed effort around Pressman to add some gloss to the scoreline and round off a wonderful afternoon for Liverpool's young stars.

Gerrard was quick to defend one of the key contributors to Liverpool's win that day. Michael Owen had been the subject of some criticism after finding the net only once in ten games, but the Kop's latest hero claimed the striker's success only continued to inspire him, even if he was a bit off the mark in his future premonitions.

'I don't think I'll ever get the publicity Michael gets, but you could not pick a better role model,' reported the *Daily Express*. 'He's always ready to help the likes of me and David Thompson and the others. He keeps saying, keep working hard, and keep trying not to let things get you down. I've known him for years and the stick he's getting now is totally undeserved. Maybe he's not scoring as he'd like, but even then he's contributing. If there are two defenders worrying about him the rest benefit. He'll prove everyone wrong.'

Gerrard was also keen to point out the impact of Gerard Houllier on his career so far. The French manager had given him a furious dressing down after the sending-off in the Merseyside derby, but had proceeded to put his teenage pupil back on the right track. 'He had a go at me over the sending-off and the subsequent suspension I picked up,' said Gerrard. 'But he grabbed me after the Sheffield Wednesday game and said I was improving but I must keep my feet on the floor and keep working hard. I feel on top of the world at the moment, but the manager changes the team all the time, so you can't get complacent. All the lads know that every time they go out they have to do well because there is somebody ready to step into their place. I have taken on board everything the gaffer told me.'

ALLEZ GERRARD AND HOULLIER

Gerrard was true to his word, and his spectacular goal against Sheffield Wednesday left him hungry for more as Liverpool headed across the Pennines to begin their assault on the FA Cup at Huddersfield Town. The First Division league leaders more than fancied their chances of causing an upset, but the Reds tossed aside a potential banana skin, courtesy of goals from Titi Camara and Dominic Matteo. Vladimir Smicer's return from injury saw Gerrard revert to right-back for the game, but he delivered a typically mature and composed performance to aid his side's progression to the next round.

Liverpool returned to league action and began the festive period with a home game against Coventry. The gamed marked the fortieth anniversary of Bill Shankly's arrival at Anfield and the Kop belted out a poignant rendition of 'You'll Never Walk Alone', saluting their heroes of yesteryear, who gathered in the centre circle prior to kick-off.

Shankly's arrival all those years ago had heralded a new dawn for Liverpool and, after just one defeat in ten games, Gerard Houllier's reign looked to be heading in the same direction – towards success and silverware. There was no doubting that Houllier was blessed with a crop of youthful talent that exuded enthusiasm and his side duly proceeded to see off Coventry with ease. With Patrick Berger back in the side, Gerrard was once again employed as a full-back, while Michael Owen ended his troublesome goal-drought, joining Titi Camara on the scoresheet as the Reds recorded a routine 2–0 victory.

Owen was motoring back into form. A cool brace in a 2–2 draw at Newcastle served to end any doubt that he was not set to become a world beater. Indeed, Kevin Keegan, the watching England manager who was presiding over the array of home talent on show at St James' Park, must have rubbed his hands together with the European Championships only six months away. Owen's Boxing Day brace underlined his imminent contribution to England's cause; so too Alan Shearer, who opened the scoring that afternoon. But even if Keegan had his preferred strike pairing sewn up for the summer, his midfield options were less certain. Jamie Redknapp's injury had cast a doubt over his prospects of making the squad for the tournament, so there seemed like no better time for Gerrard to put himself in the international frame. Playing in his preferred central midfield role alongside Hamann, he continued to thrive on the extra responsibility given to him by his manager against Newcastle. Without playing the finest game of his career, his performance left nobody – and certainly not Kevin Keegan – doubting his qualities.

Two days later, Liverpool welcomed Robbie Fowler back from injury and proceeded to demolish Wimbledon 3–1 at Anfield. Michael Owen, Partrick Berger and Fowler hit the goals, as Liverpool continued to breathe down the necks of the Premiership title contenders. Gerrard partnered Jamie Carragher in midfield in the absence of Dietmar Hamann, who was ruled out due to illness.

'To see Murphy, so eager on the right, Gerrard, leggy and inventive just inside him, and Carragher, such a force in the centre of midfield, is evidence indeed of schooling of excellence. When youths such as this can step in then, as Houllier said, it is a fine way to end a century,' said Rob Hughes in the *Times*.

Liverpool came crashing back to earth with a bump when they broke into the new millennium against Tottenham at White Hart Lane. The Reds' preparations were hardly helped by the enforced absence of Michael Owen and Robbie Fowler, both of whom were ruled out through injury. Owen had felt his troublesome hamstring against Wimbledon and Fowler's ankle had swollen up again in the same match.

So, bereft of their most prominent goalscorers, Liverpool were knocked off their pedestal by Chris Armstrong's solitary strike for Tottenham. Gerrard was moved back onto the right-hand side of midfield, an area only dominated by the fearsome wingplay of Spurs' wide man and Gerrard's old foe, David Ginola. And if Liverpool were tormented by Spurs, then they were tortured by First Division Blackburn Rovers in their FA Cup fourth-round tie at Anfield. With Rovers struggling after their relegation from the Premiership the year before, the Reds were expected to see them off comfortably. But if Liverpool needed a reminder that Gerard Houllier was some way short of having a trophy-winning squad, it came when Nathan Blake sealed a shock 1–0 victory for the Lancashire side four minutes from time. Gerrard was employed at right-back again, as he continued to be shuffled like an ace in a pack of cards. With Liverpool not participating in European competition that season, he was destined for a prolonged wait for his first taste of senior silverware. Liverpool's only option following their FA Cup exit was to step up their quest for a place in Europe.

An away trip to lowly Watford seemed like just the tonic for Houllier's school of young players to pick themselves up again – and so it proved. With Gerrard terrier-like and tenacious alongside David Thompson in central midfield, it allowed Dietmar Hamann to dictate the game and Patrick Berger to thrive off a more advanced role behind Titi Camara and the returning Michael Owen. The Czech midfielder converted a Thompson pass to score, before Thompson himself netted before half-time. Watford, who had won at Anfield in the return fixture, hit back with Richard Johnson and debutant Heider Helguson pulling them level. Vladimir Smicer, a Liverpool substitute that day, had other ideas, however, taking a perfectly weighted pass from Owen and guiding the ball home, to ensure Liverpool's first win of the new millennium. The 3–2 victory at Vicarage Road began a thirteen-match unbeaten run that propelled Liverpool to the brink of European qualification.

Michael Owen's taxing injury problems saw him ruled out until March, joining Jamie Redknapp and Robbie Fowler on the Anfield treatment table. For most of Liverpool's young stars forced to step into the breach, it was make or break time. The run-in to the end of the season saw Gerrard earn only more praise. One of his keenest admirers was an England manager preparing for a major tournament.

'I've watched Gerrard a few times now and I've seen him do an excellent job,' Kevin Keegan told the *Mail on Sunday*. 'If he continues in that vein and stays fit, I'll fetch him in. He can play on the right side or in the centre of midfield. In future, I think he could fit into the back four comfortably as well.' And Keegan was clearly a fan of Houllier's Anfield regime, as the Frenchman was preening a host of youngsters for international stardom on Merseyside. No wonder he attended so many Liverpool matches that season.

Gerrard continued to live out his childhood dreams in a red shirt. Middlesbrough's visit to Anfield in late January saw him come face to face with an old hero of his – one

ALLEZ GERRARD AND HOULLIER

Paul Gascoigne. It proved quite an experience for the wily young pretender.

'I used to try and model myself on Gazza, but it never worked,' Gerrard told the *Independent*. 'He was so exciting to watch; you never knew what to expect from him. I liked the way he could go past people and score goals... I tried to nutmeg him in the game. It never came off and he gave me a slap on the back of the head and told me to start behaving.'

Gerrard was clearly beginning to enjoy his flourishing Liverpool career and the chance of playing against his idols.

'It's a nice time for a young lad to come in at Liverpool with the team doing so well. We are in a Champions League qualifying position and we hope to stay ahead of Chelsea and Arsenal. I know how much European football means to Liverpool fans and maybe, in three or four years, we could win a European medal. I think we are still behind Manchester United and Arsenal, but we are gradually improving as a team.'

Liverpool's notable improvements came to the fore as Leeds United visited Anfield. In front of Keegan again, they put a disappointing goalless draw with Middlesbrough behind them by cantering to a commendable 3–1 victory over the title-chasing Yorkshiremen to enhance their prospects of qualifying for the Champions League. And how Gerrard, while playing his own pivotal role in the win, must have looked on in awe as fellow midfielders Dietmar Hamann and Patrick Berger unleashed long-range rockets either side of a Leeds equaliser to put Liverpool in command. Danny Murphy also crashed in a thunderbolt to leave the Kop marvelling and pondering a potentially glittering future. How right they were.

Hamann's goal against Leeds was his first goal for

STEVEN GERRARD: PORTRAIT OF A HERO

Liverpool since his move from Newcastle the previous summer. It is rarely emphasised just how much of an influence the German has had on Gerrard during his time at Anfield. The experienced international's calming influence, rational approach and sublime passing skills have long been admired, not least by Gerrard. And if the young Liverpool star needed a contemporary role model, then it was Hamann – a player who is so similar in stature and presence to him. It was no coincidence that Hamann's return to the Liverpool team that season from injury had coincided with Gerrard brushing aside any qualms about his temperament to look increasingly accomplished in the central-midfield role – the hardest position to play in a football team. Hamann, himself, was quick to laud over the precocious talents of his new midfield partner.

'There is not a better midfielder player in the Premiership at the moment and, if Steven carries on like this, he is a certainty for a place in the England team for Euro 2000... He has all the qualities to go on and become captain of his country before too long. He really has the lot. Those attributes are going to take him into the England line-up, and there is every chance that he and I are going to be against each other in the European Championship this summer when England meet Germany. The way he is going, we will have our work cut out coping with him. I envy England having young players like Steven coming through. Steven not only has a long, illustrious international career ahead of him, he will be England captain one day.'

Newspapers began to speculate over whether or not Gerrard would be included in Kevin Keegan's squad for a pre-Euro 2000 friendly against Argentina at Wembley, having performed so remarkably for Liverpool since the turn of the year.

'What's happening to me now is what I've aimed for since I first came to Liverpool's academy as an eight-year-old,' Gerrard told the *Sunday People*. 'I'm just interested in working hard and staying in Liverpool's first team. That's all I want at the moment. People are now asking the question "Are you ready for England?" My answer is that any footballer should be confident in his own ability and I say "Why shouldn't I play for the England team?" I've heard I'm going to be named if I'm fit and, if the call does come, I'll be excited. Then I'll just go and do what I've been doing for Liverpool all season. I'm relaxed about the England thing, but my mum and dad and my older brother Paul are a bit anxious.'

Gerrard was thankful for the chance he had been given by his manager, even though his swift ascent into a settled midfield role had been helped by injuries to other key players. The nineteen-year-old had built a solid working relationship with Gerard Houllier. The mutual respect the pair had for one another was obvious.

'Before the season started we went to do a promotional thing with Adidas and I went with the manager,' continued Gerrard in the *People*. 'I drove there and he drove back and, while we were in the car, he told me he was looking to play me in fifteen to twenty games this season. Against Leeds, that was my twenty-first game so I suppose I can't complain, even though my chance came because first Didi Hamann got injured then Jamie Redknapp was out.'

The spring of 2000 proved a valuable learning curve for Gerrard – it was the period that effectively earmarked his awesome potential. Following on from their excellent home win over Leeds, Liverpool travelled to Arsenal for one of their toughest assignments of the season. It was Gerrard's final chance to make an indelible mark on Kevin Keegan's notepad, four days before the England boss named his squad for the friendly against Argentina. Liverpool's transformation under Gerard Houllier remained under the microscope. Could they keep up their combative and clinical approach that had seen them lose just twice in sixteen league games?

Gerrard's effective midfield union with Hamann continued and Liverpool duly sustained their notable run of form to overcome Arsene Wenger's side at Highbury. Oliver Holt, writing in the *Times*, said:

> It was not a goal that shone out like a beacon of their transformation. It was a tackle. It came from Steven Gerrard, the teenager who is the most potent symbol of the regeneration of the Merseyside giants. It was an act of selflessness, of a devotion to a wider cause than the individual, a perfectly timed interception that prevented a certain goal. What made it especially worthy of note was that Gerrard risked everything to make the tackle that stopped Fredrik Ljungberg in his tracks. Struggling with a groin strain, he had already signalled to the bench that he wanted to come off when he threw himself into the challenge with Ljungberg that ended his run just as he was about to sweep the ball past Sander Westerveld, the Liverpool goalkeeper. That tackle, that lunge, could have ruined his chances of being picked in a full England squad for the first time on Thursday, but that did not cross Gerrard's mind.

ALLEZ GERRARD AND HOULLIER

Before that particular moment of bottle from Gerrard, he had provided a precise pass to tee up Titi Camara for Liverpool's only goal of the game – the winning goal. But where Liverpool won to move within six points of leaders Manchester United in the Premiership, they also suffered the loss of Gerrard, who had to be replaced by Vegard Heggem after just 34 minutes, having suffered a groin injury. As a result, his chances of making England's squad for the friendly with Argentina looked over.

The physiotherapists at Melwood administered their own Midas touch and gave Gerrard at least a glimmer of hope of making the game. On Thursday, 17 February 2000, Gerrard, despite his fitness concerns, was named in the England senior squad for the first time in his career. Leeds midfielder Lee Bowyer and West Ham's Frank Lampard had been overlooked in favour of the Liverpool man, and pundits quickly stepped on the bandwagon of admiration for the nineteen-year-old Reds star. Chris Kamara, the former Bradford manager and Sky television pundit, compared Gerrard to one former England midfield hero. He said:

> There is no doubt that Bryan Robson is the best central midfielder this country has produced in my lifetime. He may not have had the vision of Glenn Hoddle or the sublime skill of Paul Gascoigne, but he had everything else. Even I was scared to tackle him. He was the complete midfield machine. There has never been an English midfield leader like him, but now perhaps the new Bryan Robson is emerging on the horizon at Anfield. Steven Gerrard's incredible rise from Liverpool reserves to Kevin Keegan's England

squad is fully deserved. Gerrard's performance against Leeds recently reminded me of the way Graeme Souness used to patrol Anfield in his heyday. He is awesome in the tackle, has great vision with a subtle touch and a stamina that is frightening.

Such praise was not isolated, nor was it fabricated. Steven Gerrard had made such an astonishing impact that Kevin Keegan would have been hard pressed to leave him out. It was the versatility and freshness of Gerrard that impressed Keegan most, and no doubt Gerrard relished the chance to work with one of Liverpool's all-time greats.

'Whenever I have watched him – or whenever I have read a report on him – he has been outstanding,' said Keegan. 'His versatility excites me; you can ask him to do any number of jobs. In a squad of twenty-two, there is room for that. I also love the way he passes a ball – he can play one-twos and hit it 30 or 40 yards. He has a great future.'

Gerrard joined up with his new team-mates at England's Bisham Abbey headquarters still hoping to shake off his groin problem. Sadly, the game came too soon for him, and England earned a creditable goalless draw against Argentina at Wembley without his services.

Liverpool were forced to wait three weeks for their next outing following the excellent victory over Arsenal. Manchester United, seemingly heading for a thirteenth league title, were next in line, and the Reds would have to make do without Gerrard, Robbie Fowler, Michael Owen and Jamie Redknapp for the game. A scorching free-kick from Patrick Berger put Liverpool ahead in the Old Trafford showdown, but Ole Gunnar Solskjaer earned United a draw to quell any excitement that Liverpool were about to make

ALLEZ GERRARD AND HOULLIER

an unlikely late assault on the title. Qualifying for the Champions League had always been the No. 1 target, and Liverpool seemed set to achieve that goal. Gerard Houllier signed Emile Heskey from Leicester in an £11 million deal to bolster the Reds' striking options and the new man was an instant hit, winning a penalty minutes into his Liverpool debut – a 1–1 draw with Sunderland at Anfield. Gerrard joined Heskey back in Liverpool's starting XI, but struggled to make an impact and was replaced at half-time by Danny Murphy.

With Jamie Redknapp on the brink of a return from injury, Gerrard was certainly no longer guaranteed a place in Liverpool's starting XI. A goalless draw at home to Aston Villa saw him retain his position alongside Hamann in midfield and, accordingly, he proceeded to pull the strings and produced a number of incisive passes as Liverpool sought to break the deadlock. Redknapp did make his long-awaited comeback 12 minutes from the end, coming on to replace Gerrard. Michael Owen, himself still easing back after injury, missed a penalty in the match, effectively ending Liverpool's chances of winning the Premiership. With only ten games remaining, the pressure was on Liverpool to make their noticeable improvements under Gerard Houllier count with a place in the Champions League.

The Reds travelled to Derby in search of three crucial points to put themselves in the box seat for European qualification. Michael Owen signalled his timely return to both form and fitness with a tidy opening goal before Titi Camara complemented a concerted effort by hitting the net and completing a 2–0 victory. The Liverpool midfield again read from right to left: Thompson, Gerrard, Hamann,

Berger – it was a midfield fast becoming the envy of the Premiership, such was its cohesion and enterprise. And, by the game, Gerrard was looking more confident, more influential and more likely to crown his first full season with an England cap. With a Champions League place now within reach, Newcastle United came to Anfield looking to halt the Reds' charge. Gerrard was his orchestrating self again – providing a precision pass for Titi Camara to put Liverpool ahead early in the second half. But Alan Shearer headed an equaliser and Liverpool were left requiring new impetus. That renewed energy came in the shape of fit-again Jamie Redknapp, who came off the bench to replace Gerrard. He promptly headed Liverpool's winning goal.

Much speculation surrounded the future of Redknapp, who was desperate to prove his fitness ahead of the European Championships. The maturity and effectiveness of Steven Gerrard had forced many critics to ponder whether Redknapp even had a future at Liverpool. In hindsight, Gerrard's fine form had signalled the beginning of the end of Redknapp's Liverpool career.

He was hurt by the rumours. After the Newcastle game he said: 'I'm supposed to be on my way out of Anfield for £8 million – although it's surprising how much your fee drops when you are out injured,' Redknapp said, bemused by the speculation. 'Sometimes that can get to you. There is all this stuff being said about me, and I haven't even played a game. I am trying to get back to full fitness, and I just want to play for Liverpool and help them get into the Champions League. When I scored, it was a release for me. It was a very emotional moment because I have been through a lot trying to get back. There have been doubts, fears and dark periods. You think to yourself: "Will I ever be the same player and will I ever get my place back?" But it's going in the right direction and I finally feel I am close to the level I am capable of.'

Redknapp's doubts as to whether or not he would win his place back weren't being eased by his young understudy's increasing popularity. The luckless Anfield captain then injured an ankle in a midweek reserve game and his comeback was put on hold again. And Gerrard was at his gallant best once more as Liverpool crushed Coventry 3–0 at Highfield Road. Michael Owen was also at his lethal best, scoring a first-half double before Emile Heskey scored his first Liverpool goal to crown a fine display by Gerard Houllier's side. Gerrard was instrumental in both of Owen's goals – carving open Coventry's defence to devastating effect before being replaced by Danny Murphy with 20 minutes remaining, having worked himself into the ground. Houllier was using his managerial expertise in order to ensure that the youngster did not suffer a burnout in the infancy of his Liverpool career. After all, the French maestro had helped nurture France's finest – so why should he have been any different with his star-in-the-making at Anfield? Gerrard was thus rested completely as Liverpool moved up to second in the Premiership with a 2–0 home win over Spurs.

He was never going to be left out of the team for long, though, and, having recharged his batteries, he was back alongside Dietmar Hamann in the heart of the Liverpool midfield as the Reds marked the eleventh anniversary of the Hillsborough disaster with an away win at relegation-haunted Wimbledon. Emile Heskey's brace earned Houllier's men a 2–1 victory – they turned out to be Liverpool's last goals of the season with five games still remaining.

STEVEN GERRARD: PORTRAIT OF A HERO

After his sending-off earlier that season in the Merseyside derby, Gerrard would have been more eager than most as Liverpool locked horns with Everton at Goodison Park. Far from being overawed and hot-headed this time around though, he could only have impressed the watching Kevin Keegan with a confident and resolute display as Liverpool battled to win a point in a goalless draw. The Reds then lost their first game in fourteen outings – a 2–0 reverse at Chelsea – and, in doing so, virtually guaranteed Manchester United the league title.

In this particular game, with Jamie Redknapp back after his ankle injury, Gerard Houllier chose to replace Gerrard's sprightly young legs with the club captain after just 50 minutes. Gerrard had picked up another groin injury and his absence told, as Liverpool hosted Martin O'Neill's Leicester City at Anfield. The Foxes bite was far too much for the Reds to cope with, and their 2–0 victory sent Liverpool crashing out of the top three – and left their Champions League dream hanging by a thread. Jamie Redknapp returned to the midfield to try and prove his fitness but, in truth, the writing was already on the wall for him as Leicester tore Liverpool's midfield apart far too easily.

In reality, the only way Liverpool were going to make it into Europe's premier competition was with Gerrard in the side, to provide it with due vitality. Yet he was absent again as Liverpool saw their Champions League hopes all but evaporate with a goalless draw in their last home game of the season against Southampton.

Gerrard did return to see out Liverpool's season, away at Bradford. His return had no bearing on the outcome, as Paul Jewell's battling side ensured they would stay in

ALLEZ GERRARD AND HOULLIER

the Premiership for another season with a hard-fought 1–0 victory.

In all, Gerrard made twenty-eight appearances for Liverpool during the 1999–2000 season, scoring one goal in the process and earning a place on the shortlist for the PFA Young Player of the Year award. Liverpool finished in fourth position; some twenty-four points behind the champions Manchester United. They also finished just two points adrift of a Champions League berth. UEFA Cup qualification was all Liverpool had to show from a season of renewed optimism, direction and purpose. However, Gerard Houllier's reign was slowly but surely heading in the direction of success.

Chapter Five
Country Boy

Gerrard had to be quick in casting aside Liverpool's disappointment of not qualifying for the Champions League – he was progressing at such lightning-quick tempo that he hardly had time to draw breath. His whirlwind breakthrough season had seen him mature into the kind of versatile and robust footballer than any international manager would be glad to have on board – including Kevin Keegan.

However, despite all the fine displays for Liverpool in the 1999–2000 campaign, it was perhaps one game for Howard Wilkinson's England Under-21 side that told Keegan, once and for all, that Gerrard was ready to make the giant leap into the senior set-up for a major tournament. It came on 29 March 2000 – a European Under-21 Championship qualifying play-off with Yugoslavia in Barcelona and Gerrard's fourth and final cap for the Young Lions. Ironically, somewhat bizarrely, he was playing to try and keep himself out of Howard Wilkinson's summer squad so

STEVEN GERRARD: PORTRAIT OF A HERO

as to ensure his place in Kevin Keegan's European Championship twenty-two. The game was supposed to have been played over two legs later in the year, but war in Kosovo, and perhaps fate, determined that a neutral venue would host the play-off and England's young stars would get a late chance to impress Keegan.

David Batty, the Leeds United midfielder, looked set to be ruled out of the summer tournament due to continuing injury problems and Jamie Redknapp was also losing his battle for fitness. Gerrard was the most likely of the Under-21s' school of midfield talent to step up and help solve one of Keegan's main problems. And his dazzling performance against Yugoslavia proved that his young legs were ready. Once again, he figured as a holding midfielder in front of a three-man defence. Versatile and mobile, his tackling was both timely and decisive: his vision and passing devastatingly accurate.

Gerrard's ability was best demonstrated when, with great poise and foresight, he delivered a 63rd-minute cross-field pass for Derby's Seth Johnson who, in turn, set up Lee Hendrie to score England's third and final goal in a 3–0 victory. Frank Lampard and Middlesbrough's Andy Campbell were already on the scoresheet as England cruised into the eight-team European Under-21 Championships, but it was the bar measuring Steven Gerrard's profile that had been raised the highest. The Liverpool midfielder was left stunned by his own fine form.

'Really, England is a dream – something that at the start of the season I would never have even dared think about,' he said in the *Daily Mirror*. 'I never expected to come this far so soon. But now that I have set such high standards, I just want to keep it going. Now that I have got this close to the England side, I am desperate to get in the final twenty-two for the European Championships. It was important that I put up a good performance in Barcelona... I feel that I've done my chances no harm with my performance and I have got to improve on that. I think it all depends now on how I play for Liverpool in the final eight games.'

Kevin Keegan had undoubtedly already made up his mind. Gerrard was just so energetic and so fresh. There wasn't a better English ball-winning midfielder around at the time.

'I have probably watched Steven Gerrard more than any other player this season,' Keegan exclaimed on his return from Barcelona. 'He has impressed me every time and I cannot speak too highly of him. He is mature beyond his years, he is a great athlete and he has shown he can perform on the big stage.'

Gerrard had already enjoyed a productive spell as a young England star. He had put the disappointment of his exclusion from the England schoolboy set-up behind him by appearing for the Under-16 side where he featured in his first international tournament played in Austria. He then made his mark as captain of the England Under-18 side prior to his introduction to the Premiership with Liverpool. In March 1999, barely four months after his senior Reds debut, he was invited, along with Leeds defender Jonathan Woodgate, to train with the full England side as they prepared for a crucial European Championship qualifier with Poland. Gerrard hadn't even made an Under-21 appearance at that time – it was a measure of just how highly rated he was.

In September of that year, Gerrard made his debut for the Under-21s. It was Howard Wilkinson's first game of a second spell in charge and the opponents were Luxembourg in a European Under-21 Championship qualifier played at Reading's Madejski stadium. Wilkinson had been manager of the Under-18s the previous year, so he knew Gerrard well and the Liverpool youngster responded admirably to the challenge of his debut in front of 19,000 fans. The Young Lions had already won their group and duly recorded a seventh-successive victory, treating the crowd to a five-star show. Gerrard lined up as the midfield anchor in a 3-5-2 formation behind West Ham United's Frank Lampard and Aston Villa's Lee Hendrie. And his imposing performance was complemented when he scored the opening goal of the game in the first half. The Liverpool starlet tucked away a cool left-foot shot from the edge of the area after seeing a right-wing cross from Manchester United's Luke Chadwick deflected into his path. Lampard, Hendrie, Everton's Francis Jeffers and Wimbledon's Carl Cort all added goals in front of the watching Keegan.

Four days later, Howard Wilkinson took his side to face Poland in their final qualifying match. A 3–1 defeat prevented England from making the record books with an eighth-successive victory but, again, Gerrard demonstrated his vast potential with a domineering midfield performance. A month later, normal service was resumed as the Under-21s beat Denmark 4–1 at Bradford's Valley Parade. Gerrard, who was enjoying his Liverpool baptism, provided the spark of inspiration – he helped create England's opening goal for Leeds' Alan Smith before Lee Bowyer, Carl Cort and Liverpool team-mate David Thompson completed the rout.

Gerrard's first call-up to the senior squad in February 2000, for England's friendly with Argentina, spelt the

COUNTRY BOY

beginning of the end of his time with the Under-21s. Only injury prevented him from earning his first senior cap in that game and, following his starring role in the England Under-21s victory over Yugoslavia a month later, he was in line for another call-up as the senior side warmed up for the European Championships with games against Brazil and the Ukraine.

When Howard Wilkinson named his squad for the European Under-21 Championships, Gerrard's name was not read out. Wilkinson admitted that Kevin Keegan had specifically asked for Gerrard and fellow Under-21s Emile Heskey, Kieron Dyer and Rio Ferdinand to be left out.

'Kevin and I have discussed at length the selection of my squad and the selection of his squad,' he said. 'The fundamental thinking was that if there was anyone who might conceivably appear in Holland and Belgium, he wouldn't come into consideration for the Under-21s.'

Gerrard's delight at being confirmed in Keegan's plans was not shared by his Under-21 team-mates Frank Lampard and Gareth Barry. Lampard had captained the Under-21s throughout their successful run and Barry had previously made the senior squad – both had played at senior club level for much longer than Gerrard, but both were named in Wilkinson's squad, thus ruling them out of contention for the European Championships. Gerrard, having begun the season as a fringe player at Liverpool, was set for one of football's greatest honours – representing his country at the top level for the very first time. The Under-21s would certainly miss him – they went on to fall at the group stage of the European Under-21 tournament in Slovakia.

Kevin Keegan was eager to give Gerrard his first taste of international football on home soil. The friendlies against

STEVEN GERRARD: PORTRAIT OF A HERO

Brazil and the Ukraine gave the England head coach the ideal chance to run a final rule over his squad before naming his final twenty-two.

'Steven has done very well this season, he's been outstanding,' enthused Keegan. 'He will need to have a game before we go out there, if he's going to be in the final twenty-two, and he needs to do okay in that game.'

But rather like all his other managers, Keegan was reluctant to rush Gerrard and allowed him time to settle in. The Liverpool youngster gazed from the bench as England earned a creditable 1–1 draw with Brazil at Wembley in the first preparation match – with Michael Owen, now back to full fitness, scoring England's goal. However, Gerrard did not have to wait long to get his first taste of the hallowed Wembley arena.

Gerrard celebrated his twentieth birthday by being handed his first cap by Keegan against Ukraine. However, his England team-mates were quick to dispel any myths that his England adventure was going to be a walk in the park and aided the Liverpool man's birthday celebrations by filling his trainers with toothpaste.

Inspector Gerrard quickly compiled a list of suspects, namely his Liverpool team-mates in the squad. The press reported him saying:

> I have asked Robbie Fowler if it was him and he has sworn on his baby's life it wasn't, so it is definitely not him. They broke into my room when I was having a bath. I couldn't put my shoes on because they were so heavy! I don't suspect I will ever find out who it was. It couldn't have been the manager, could it? He gives me my first cap and then does that to me?... The greatest birthday present I

have ever been given was when the manager told me I was in against the Ukraine. I will buy myself a present when I get home. I have already got a Mercedes ordered. There is nothing I want now after being given my first England cap... apart from a new pair of trainers.

And Gerrard had the added incentive of making his England debut at the most famous stadium in the world.

'I have only been there as a fan,' he said. 'Michael Owen and I sat together as twelve-year-olds when Leeds beat Liverpool in the Charity Shield. Eric Cantona got a hat-trick. A lot has happened quickly. I only made my Liverpool debut sixteen months ago and, if someone had said then that I would play for England and go to the European Championships, I would have called them a liar.'

Gerrard and Michael Owen had come a long way with one another, both as friends and as footballers. They were now destined to play for England together and could revel in the telepathy they shared, both on and off the field, at the very highest level. Gerrard said:

> Michael is a great role model for me with the way he has handled all the success. I have spoken to him about what he has done and how he achieved it. We have come right the way through together at Liverpool and are good mates. When the gaffer told me I was going to make my England debut, I immediately spoke to Michael. He was great and just told me to do what I have been doing for Liverpool all season.

Those final moments before kick-off – the roar of the crowd and the national anthems – ceremoniously marked a new chapter in Gerrard's career. He announced himself into the England senior realm with a composed and, above all, convincing performance. Robbie Fowler, Gerrard's Liverpool colleague who had endured a torrid spell of injury trouble, opened the scoring for England, before a second-half Tony Adams strike completed a 2–0 victory.

With that, Kevin Keegan included Gerrard in his squad for Euro 2000, but the Liverpool midfielder, following his outstanding international debut, was not prepared to settle for a role as a back-up player. At a press conference he said:

> Now I'm in the final twenty-two, I just want to play a part in Euro 2000... I didn't expect it a year ago. I was expecting to maybe get into the Under-21 squad this season and maybe play for England at a later stage of my career. The atmosphere out there was tremendous. I think every young English lad wants to play for England at Wembley. The first 15 minutes was hectic and Tony Adams was helping me get through, but after that I thought I settled down. Tony was telling me where men were behind me who I couldn't see and helping to get me into the right positions, but all the other lads helped me get through.

In fact, Adams, the Arsenal stalwart, later told the *Sunday Times* of the conversation he had had with the youngster in the Wembley tunnel prior to the match. 'I told him "You know what to do, don't you?" He looked at me and said, "What?" I said, "Panic, but don't bloody pass it to me." It was just something to break the spell. He was okay after that. I told him to go out and enjoy it. It's a special moment for anybody.'

COUNTRY BOY

Kevin Keegan shared Adams' bullish attitude towards the new stars of England's crusade and was equally enthusiastic about the future of his team. The England manager exclaimed:

> We believe in ourselves and I'm sure I've picked a squad that can win us the European Championships... The match against Brazil, especially the first half, and the match against the Ukraine have gone such a long way to helping our preparation... The players adapted and I was delighted with them. There were superb performances from a lot of them... Gerrard did so well. I told him I was throwing him in at the deep end. He was trying to work the position out early on, but he sorted it out well.

Such salutation from the manager suggested that Gerrard was set to play a pivotal role in England's quest for glory. The other twenty-one players lucky enough to be travelling to the European Championships included Gerrard's Anfield pals, Michael Owen, Emile Heskey and Robbie Fowler; his former team-mates Paul Ince and Steve McManaman would also be coming. The twenty-year-old would be in rousing company.

The Three Lions still had one more warm-up game to play – on a pre-tournament trip to Malta. They won 2–1, thanks to goals from Martin Keown and Emile Heskey. Gerrard wasn't involved at all and, indeed, Kevin Keegan's team selection still had everyone guessing as to exactly what formation and personnel he intended on fielding in England's first game of Euro 2000.

STEVEN GERRARD: PORTRAIT OF A HERO

Paired with Portugal, Germany and Romania in Group A, the Three Lions would have to be at their very best if they were to make it through to the quarter-finals. They began in Eindhoven against the Portuguese, a side that was being hotly tipped for glory. Keegan chose Paul Ince to play alongside Manchester United goal-getter Paul Scholes in central midfield and the selection looked to be paying dividends as Scholes, and then Steve McManaman, put England two goals ahead inside the opening 20 minutes. But a Luis Figo-inspired Portugal hit back to win 3–2. As a result, Keegan was sent back to the drawing board.

Gerrard had not figured at all in the opening game, and Keegan had both tactical and positional problems to address as he prepared for England's second game – against arch-rivals Germany. Sadly, Gerrard's lack of experience counted against him. And experience was the mainstay of the Germans – it was something that England had to combat or they would risk early elimination. The pressure was on Keegan to deliver a team of winners in Charleroi. Paul Ince's role in midfield was subjected to deep scrutiny in the build-up to England's game and many believed that Gerrard's youthful energy was a worthy substitute for Ince's increasing immobility.

'So much of the argument comes back to Paul Ince and the role at the back of midfield,' wrote the *Guardian*'s David Lacey. 'At thirty-two, he no longer has the legs to cover ground in his old manner. The game in Eindhoven was more a battle of wits than a test of stamina, but you still wondered how he would cope against Jens Jeremies, the driving wheel of the German team, and Liverpool's Dietmar Hamann. This is why one school of opinion

COUNTRY BOY

believes that Keegan should be reinforcing his midfield with the younger, fresher Steven Gerrard, so impressive when he won his first full cap against the Ukraine, while recalling Gareth Southgate to tidy up behind Keown and Campbell in a back three.'

Sir Alex Ferguson had also joined Gerrard's army of admirers. He had no doubt that England were in need of the Liverpool man's Midas touch.

'I would fancy playing Steven Gerrard as the anchorman midfielder,' the Manchester United manager told the *Sunday Times*. 'He is only twenty, but he is physically and technically precocious. He has a good engine and displays remarkable energy on the pitch. He already reads the game quite well, can pass and is quick. He would be helped by the experience of those behind him and I feel Steven could be one of the positive surprises of the tournament. If you brought him on and gave him a job, his head would come up and he would do the right thing. People are already comparing him to Roy Keane, but I reserve my judgment on that one. I'd hate to think Liverpool have somebody as good as Keane.'

Whatever the country's top managers, or indeed the media, perceived to be England's best line-up, Keegan kept faith with Ince and replaced the injured Steve McManaman with Chelsea's Dennis Wise as England took to the field against Germany. And despite the majority believing that Keegan had to turn to youth in order to overcome the German challenge, it was his old guard that came up trumps. Alan Shearer – the captain who was playing his penultimate England game before international retirement – sweetly headed home to put his side ahead early in the second half.

STEVEN GERRARD: PORTRAIT OF A HERO

On the hour mark, while the Three Lions battled to hold on to their slender lead, Keegan felt the need to call for reinforcements. Cue Steven Gerrard. On he came for his second cap, replacing Michael Owen, as England stocked up their midfield cavalry to stifle the Germans. Keegan's men duly surmounted a barrage of pressure to hold on for their first victory over Germany in thirty-four years.

'The Liverpool starlet added fresh bite and bulldog spirit to England's midfield, with coach Keegan clearly in no mood to surrender the lead this time around,' read the *News of the World*. 'Young Gerrard refused to be intimidated by the electric atmosphere in Charleroi and even bossed his much more experienced midfield partners Paul Ince and Dennis Wise around at times.'

Gerrard had hustled and bustled around the England midfield in the half-hour he had played. He even clattered into his Liverpool team-mate Dietmar Hamann, who tentatively stepped back from the youngster's firm tackle.

'I thought I'd be booked. I was a bit late, but we're still mates and he said congratulations. He screamed like a girl and you can tell him that,' said Gerrard jokingly, after the game. This was no joke. It was the measure of a young man, valiant in everything he did.

'I was nervous when I went out,' the Liverpool star admitted in the *Independent*. 'Then Kevin Keegan asked me to get stripped. My heart started to go and I said: "What me?" I thought I might get five or ten minutes, so it was unbelievable. The gaffer asked me to come on and keep it tight. As soon as I got my first few touches and kept the ball, I settled down and felt quite comfy. I've always been confident I'll play at this level and the gaffer said I'll have a big part to play in the tournament. It was a brilliant experience, the greatest moment of my career.'

Keegan had ordered Gerrard to track Mehmet Scholl, Germany's marauding midfielder, and also to support Paul Ince.

'Steven gave us a cameo of the future of English football,' enthused the England head coach. In hindsight, and to the watching critic, it was much more than that. How sad then, for England, that Keegan could not call upon Gerrard to start the final, crucial group game against Romania due to a niggling thigh strain.

Romania were England's last group opponents and, at half-time in Charleroi, Keegan's men found themselves ahead. After falling behind early on, Alan Shearer's penalty and a Michael Owen strike had turned the game back in the Three Lions' favour. But in the second half, defensive benevolence gifted Romania an equaliser and then a desperately late challenge from Manchester United defender Phil Neville gifted England's opponents a penalty with just minutes to spare. That was it. Lacking both much-needed steel and a cutting edge, England were on the early plane home.

For the likes of Gerrard and Owen, two of just a handful of players who came away from the tournament with any credit, the future looked good. However, Kevin Keegan's England career was grinding to a halt.

Chapter Six
Triple the Glory, Minus the Injury

'Now there comes the second season, when opponents know Gerrard's strengths and he has to claim a place from a fit, enlarged Liverpool squad. Achieve that, and the next decade is his.'

ROB HUGHES, THE *SUNDAY TIMES*. 16 JULY 2000

After Euro 2000, Gerrard barely had time to pause and take stock of what was happening to him before he was back in training ahead of Liverpool's most important season in years. The 2000–01 season was also set to be a tremendously telling year for him.

Gerard Houllier had spent £20 million on new talent and the signings he had made suggested that Liverpool would finally have a sturdy backbone on which to rely on. In had come German defender Markus Babbel and Christian Ziege, from Bayern Munich and Middlesbrough respectively; Nicky Barmby, the England midfielder arrived from rivals Everton; Auxerre midfielder Bernard Diomede; Leicester goalkeeper Peggy Arphexad; and perhaps most significantly of all, as far as Gerrard was concerned, Gary McAllister the veteran midfield enforcer from Coventry.

STEVEN GERRARD: PORTRAIT OF A HERO

McAllister's arrival on a Bosman free transfer was billed as the surprise transfer of the summer but, whatever the doubt, Gerard Houllier had valid motives. Jamie Redknapp was due to go to the United States for a second operation as he battled to overcome the serious knee problem that had kept him out of Euro 2000. And Dietmar Hamann had looked distinctly out of form as Germany followed England out at the group stage of the competition. Liverpool needed midfield reinforcements and an experienced head to help Gerrard's continuing progress. McAllister, at thirty-five, was a welcome addition to the Liverpool squad, not only as an insurance policy but as a seasoned professional to boot. Gerrard later revealed:

> Robbie Fowler wears the armband, but as far as I'm concerned Gary is another skipper here. Both on the field and in the dressing room he is a massive influence on myself and every other youngster here. It's like walking onto the field on a Saturday and playing beside a coach! It's like I've got a manager on my shoulder, because he is constantly there talking to me and giving me the right advice. The man is never off my back – but it's all in a good way... I work with him every day and he is the ultimate pro as far as I'm concerned.

Where there were telling arrivals, there were also departures from the Anfield dressing room: Dominic Matteo joined Leeds; Stig Inge Bjornebye headed for Blackburn; and David Thompson, who had made a considerable impression alongside Steven Gerrard since his graduation from the Liverpool academy, switched to Coventry.

Gerrard himself signed a lucrative new contract with

TRIPLE THE GLORY, MINUS THE INJURY

Liverpool that summer, having impressed so much the season before. If anything, it allowed him the chance to stop driving his dad's Honda car into training and buy a spanking new car of his own. And the twenty-year-old was brimming with excitement over the season that lay ahead, saying:

> I know more will be expected of me this season, but I'm not really one who feels pressure. I like a challenge, and the first one will be trying to play every week for Liverpool because everyone here is such a good player. I know this will be a very big season for me – much bigger than last year – but I'm looking forward to it.
>
> I want to play against Vieira and Keane and compare myself with them. One day I will be as good and then be better. My Liverpool manager Gerard Houllier is always saying I still have a lot to learn and that I'm not the finished article. He's right – I know I can get better. It goes without saying that I didn't expect to end last season playing for England. I would have liked to have been involved a bit more, but I had one or two niggling injuries which meant I wasn't 100 per cent. The fans keep asking whether I'll be okay for the start of the season, and I hope and believe so.

After some rigorous treatment on those niggling injuries at Melwood, Gerrard was fit and raring to go. The question was – were Liverpool ready? Their pre-season run-outs only returned encouraging signs, culminating in a 5–0 victory over Italian giants Parma at Anfield. Houllier had a £50 million squad at his disposal that included a wealth of midfield talent. Nick Barmby, Gary McAllister, Patrick

STEVEN GERRARD: PORTRAIT OF A HERO

Berger, Dietmar Hamann, Vladimir Smicer, Danny Murphy and Gerrard were all vying for midfield positions in his starting XI. Only the best would prevail.

With expectations high, the Reds began the 2000–01 campaign against the side with whom they had concluded the last – Bradford City. Gerrard had earned the right to a starting place, having worked tirelessly in pre-season to prove that there were no lasting effects from Euro 2000. He partnered Hamann in central midfield, with Barmby and Smicer on the flanks. The eager Anfield spectators were forced to wait patiently for Liverpool to step into their groove, but Gerrard's 48th-minute curling effort – well saved by Bradford goalkeeper Matt Clarke – sparked life into Houllier's men. A stunning display of power and determination saw Emile Heskey score the winner for Liverpool. Gerrard, before making way for McAllister late in the second half, had delivered another dynamic performance and looked increasingly confident – especially when it came to shooting from long range. However, Houllier, incessantly answering questions about his young prodigy, was quick to emphasise the role he, as manager, had to play in Gerrard's continuing development.

> In the eighteen to twenty-four age group, that of Lampard, Carragher, Gerrard, Heskey, Owen, Barry and Joe Cole, the raw material is there to make a good national team. They can be your base. The problem is the way some of them choose to live their lives. I'm talking about what sort of professionals they want to be. It's not just my opinion; I read all the papers and there are managers everywhere saying that something has to be done.

TRIPLE THE GLORY, MINUS THE INJURY

England have got a lot of good young players, but at a certain age they need to be saying to themselves, 'Do I want to be a winner? If so, I've got to behave like one.' It depends on them, the players... Steven is a tremendous asset to the club. He's a steady Eddie, so there's no danger of all the publicity spoiling him and, if he stays fit and overcomes the various muscular injuries he gets, he'll be even better than last season.

Those close to Gerrard would have agreed. He just didn't have the character of someone who was about to throw a glittering career away with needless off-the-field antics. Nevertheless, there was still an important role to play for the likes of Houllier, who had to ensure that Gerrard never strayed from being the model young professional.

The French manager was delighted with his side's winning start to the season, but he was less than impressed with Sky television's orchestration of the fixture list: Liverpool's second match of the season, away to Arsenal, would kick off barely forty-eight hours after the end of their opening game.

Emile Heskey and Patrick Berger had both picked up injuries against Bradford and the Reds were set to start the clash at Highbury without valuable firepower. With the abundance of talent in his squad, however, the Liverpool manager had the ability to switch his team around when required. He employed a 4-5-1 formation against Arsenal and took the bold move in resting Gerrard completely, keeping both him and Michael Owen on the bench. The England pair were badly missed. With Berger facing a couple of months on the sidelines, in came McAllister and

STEVEN GERRARD: PORTRAIT OF A HERO

Jamie Carragher to the cauldron of fire that greeted them at Highbury. Arsenal eventually won the match 2–0, thanks to goals from Lauren and Thierry Henry, but referee Graham Poll had the final say in a fractious night's football. He sent off McAllister and, somewhat harshly, Dietmar Hamann – both for over-elaborate tackling – and then dismissed Arsenal's Patrick Vieira for a nasty two-footed lunge. Liverpool also acquired four bookings in the match: that meant an automatic £25,000 fine.

Gerrard, who was in line for a rapid recall to the Liverpool side with suspensions pending, was named in Kevin Keegan's England squad later that week for a friendly with France. He was joined by the other young starlets who were earmarked to turn England's fortunes around – Kieron Dyer, Rio Ferdinand and Gareth Barry.

In the meantime, Liverpool's coach-load of internationals travelled to Southampton for a critical test of their credentials with the season still in its infancy. Gerrard was named in the starting XI and the Reds strolled into a three-goal advantage thanks to two goals from Michael Owen either side of a Sami Hyypia header. However, defensive frailties were woefully exposed as Southampton, with barely 30 minutes to spare, hit back to level the score. Liverpool's only solace came from Owen's sparkling return to form, and also from the fact that not one player saw a card, on either side, all afternoon.

Gerrard had looked inhibited in his central-midfield role against the Saints. His bothersome groin had hampered his efforts: it was preventing him from playing two games a week. Gerard Houllier urged caution as the star jetted off to join Kevin Keegan's squad in Paris for England's friendly against France.

'Steven has a sore groin at the moment. He can't repeat

games at the moment and that is why he was on the bench at Arsenal,' Houllier explained to the *Daily Mirror*. 'Kevin knows the position with Steve, but he will report and it is up to the England camp to decide whether or not he should play.' Keegan took heed of the situation and agreed that it would be wrong to force Gerrard to play.

'Provided he is fully fit, I would like to involve Steven in this one, but he missed part of pre-season, and I'll have to have a look at him in training,' said the England manager in the *Sunday Times*. 'I've talked to Gerard Houllier and to the Liverpool physio, Dave Galley, and it seems he's still growing and hasn't got all his strength yet. We'll see how he is. I won't do anything to jeopardise his long-term future.'

Gerrard's groin problem was also giving him cause for concern.

'My fitness is a lot better than it was during the summer,' he explained. 'I've been given a stretching routine to do before and after matches, but I have to accept that I may have to miss a few games this season when they come close together. I haven't got one particular injury as such. It's a case of the shape of my back causing trouble in various leg muscles and around my groin. The exercises I've been given are to improve my back, which in turn will help with the muscular thing. I hope the stretching will enable me to play more games than I did last season, when I missed a few, maybe because I wasn't strong enough.'

The Liverpool star was also keen to emphasise the impact that the frequency of games had on young bodies, comparing his problems to those that Michael Owen had suffered. 'I think a lot of us have the same sort of trouble playing so many games in such a short space of time, but I expect a lot of the problems. I'm hoping they will clear up over the next couple of years. Meanwhile, I've got to deal with it as best I can.'

Gerrard also admitted that he had missed the Arsenal game, not through injury, but through stiffness incurred from the game against Bradford two days earlier. 'I wasn't really injured, and I could probably have played,' he continued. 'But if I had, I might have suffered for a couple of weeks afterwards, so it was agreed that I'd miss that one. I felt that the three players who were sent off were all a bit unlucky, so perhaps it was a good one for me to miss. I might have gone the same way myself.'

Many pundits, fans alike, had suggested that Liverpool were worthy title contenders that season, but Gerrard was keen to dispel such hype.

'I think it's a year or two too early for us to win the league. Maybe it will happen, but a realistic target is to finish in the top three... After Manchester United and Arsenal, I think you'll have ourselves, Leeds and Chelsea fighting for third place.'

And then there was the conundrum of exactly what position Gerrard wanted to play in. He still only had one senior goal to his name.

'I feel comfy either holding, in front of the back four, or advanced, just behind the strikers,' he said in the *Sunday Times*. 'I'm happy as long as I'm in the middle. I prefer centre midfield to anywhere else. If you play the more advanced role you've got to score a few goals, and that's definitely one part of my game where I'm lacking. I know I've got to improve there. I think when I play with Didi [Hamann], I'll do the advanced job, but if he is injured or suspended and I play with Gary [McAllister], I'll hold and he'll be the one further forward.'

TRIPLE THE GLORY, MINUS THE INJURY

As far as England were concerned, Gerrard was being hotly tipped to take over from Paul Ince as England's midfield general. 'Incey isn't getting any younger,' Gerrard said. 'But he's still a great player and he's going to fight on for as long as he can. I've got to keep trying to produce the form for Liverpool that has got me this far and hope that that's enough to hold down an England place for years to come. When you get a taste of international football, you get such a buzz that you just want more, and to be a permanent part of the set-up. France are the best team in the world, with the best players in the world. Of course I want to have a go against them, but if I don't, I don't. I'm still only young and I want to be part of it for the next ten years.'

Gerrard's dream of facing France – and earning his third England cap – was ultimately thwarted by his unrelenting injury. The stricken star was forced to head back to Merseyside for treatment. A disappointed Kevin Keegan said in the *Daily Mirror*:

Steven has got a groin problem and it's pretty much ongoing. You train some days and think 'let's start getting into a real formation involving him' and the next day he's got a slight problem. It is very disappointing. He offers something a bit different to most other players, not least because of the fact that he's unknown. We saw that in the half hour against Germany, which was very, very impressive. It's disappointing he hasn't got the chance to build on that in a fantastic arena [the Stade de France] on Saturday, because I would have played him. I think it is something that Steve's had to live with now for about a year. If he's not fit to play for his club regularly and to train every day, then that is worrying. They have nursed him through a bit this season and he still has a problem. Please God that they will sort it out.

And Keegan was not the only one saying his prayers in the hope that Gerrard would regain full fitness. Without him, there would be no silverware for Liverpool.

England, for whom silverware couldn't have been further from thought, improved on their recent performances to earn a commendable 1–1 draw with France. Michael Owen was England's goalscorer in Paris, easing any thought that Alan Shearer's absence would jeopardise England's future. Owen was back to his lethal best: that would be confirmed in Liverpool's next match – at home to Aston Villa.

Normal service was resumed, you could say, as Gerrard returned to the Reds' starting XI and Owen proceeded to fire a shattering first-half hat-trick to sink Villa. There was no doubting that the two players, having orchestrated this 3–1 win, were set to play a monumental role in Liverpool's season. They were the hub of a side that was about to inflict its potent magic both on English football and on the European stage.

Just three days later, Manchester City met the same fate as Aston Villa at Anfield, albeit with slightly more resilience. It was another test of fitness for Gerrard and, in respect of his infirmity, he was spared a bruising central-midfield role, instead switching to the left-hand side of midfield.

An in-form and on-fire Michael Owen scored his seventh

TRIPLE THE GLORY, MINUS THE INJURY

goal in four games – with England's World Cup qualifier with Germany on the horizon – to put Liverpool on their way before Dietmar Hamann stole the midfield limelight with a 25-yard thunderbolt. City hit back to level the score before Hamann struck again to complete a rare brace and to ensure Liverpool another home win. Gerrard, feeling the pain of his groin once more, was withdrawn with 20 minutes to spare, allowing German full-back Christian Ziege a debut appearance.

And Gerrard was absent for Liverpool's long-awaited return to European competition in Romania. Nick Barmby was the Reds' goal-scoring hero as they defeated Rapid Bucharest in the UEFA Cup first-round first-leg tie. Little did they know it then, but it heralded the beginning of a magnificent march to glory.

Gerrard had undertaken a week of rest and recuperation before he donned his boots – his scoring boots on this occasion – when Liverpool made a Sunday visit to bottom-of-the-table West Ham. It took the twenty-year-old just 12 minutes of the Upton Park encounter to score the second Liverpool goal of his career. The strike typified Gerrard's astuteness. Nick Barmby stole the ball from opposing midfielder Steve Lomas, darted forward and set Danny Murphy away down the left-hand side. His superb switch-back cross eluded a static West Ham defence and Gerrard, having scampered forward with intent, stretched to smash the ball home clinically from eight yards. His joy was tempered in the second half, however, as Paolo Di Canio levelled the score from the penalty spot and the Liverpool starlet was forced off with a reoccurrence of an injury problem that was fast becoming a terrible burden.

Gerrard was left on the bench for Liverpool's next game

and his absence told as Sunderland, the visitors to Anfield, took an early lead through Kevin Phillips. However, Michael Owen, Liverpool's 'other' youthful gem was enjoying a new lease of injury-free, goal-scoring life, and he ensured that Liverpool took a point from the game with a firm header. Gerrard did replace Dietmar Hamann midway through the second half, but couldn't inspire the Reds to victory. Above all else in the half hour or so that he had on the field, Gerrard showed a keener, more confident eye for goal. Obviously buoyed by his exploits of the previous week, he forced Sunderland goalkeeper Thomas Sorensen into action before side-footing inches wide of the post.

Robbie Fowler, another of Liverpool's crocked stars, returned to action as the Reds limped into the second round of the UEFA Cup at home to Rapid Bucharest. Gerrard, playing on the right side of midfield, was one of the few Liverpool players to take any credit from a dour goalless draw, with Fowler a regular beneficiary of some precision crossing from the young England star.

A fiery encounter with Chelsea saw Liverpool succumb to their first defeat of the season at Stamford Bridge. Gerrard locked horns with his England colleague Dennis Wise as Chelsea capitalised on an error-strewn Liverpool defence to win 3-0 to give their new manager Claudio Ranieri his first win in charge. Wise and Gerrard contributed to the fractious atmosphere, exchanging crunching tackles all afternoon before the Chelsea captain snapped. Wise kicked out at Gerrard after one particularly robust tackle had provoked the Liverpool star into retaliation. Both players were booked and then Gerrard's uncharacteristically wayward pass allowed Eidur

TRIPLE THE GLORY, MINUS THE INJURY

Gudjohnsen the freedom to score Chelsea's third goal. Despite both the error and the booking, Gerrard looked like Liverpool's most accomplished performer once again. Importantly for him, he had come through a bruising 90 minutes unscathed and was able to report for international duty fully fit:

'He is a great player and we had a good old battle on Sunday,' said Gerrard after his duel with Wise. 'As the younger of the two, I had to stand up for myself and not let him get the better of me. In every game I play, I try to match the people I come up against both physically and skilfully.'

Gerrard was soon reunited with Wise as the England squad gathered for their World Cup qualifier with Germany – the Three Lions final game at the old Wembley Stadium. The Liverpool star had not featured in England's previous friendly against France and was eager to get his third cap having seemingly shaken off his injury problems. It was the first time that Gerrard had been 100 per cent fit for some time, having battled with injury through the summer. He said to the *Daily Mirror*:

> In the summer, there was a time when I was getting trouble every time I went out to play or train. It was problem after problem. I was thinking in the back of my mind – am I going to get injured today? It keeps coming from my back. It makes other parts of my body niggle – my groin and my hamstrings. They are not serious injuries and they go off after a couple of days, but they force me to miss training sessions and big games... It was a big disappointment to miss [the game against] France. I had already missed Argentina

and Brazil this year, but you do have to play big games back-to-back in a short space of time. That is going to be the case right through the season, so I have to come to terms with myself that I am going to miss some of them.

Another reoccurrence of his groin injury while training at Bisham Abbey ended Gerrard's hopes of playing against Germany. With injury problems dominating England's preparations, the Liverpool midfielder had been billed as a certain starter for the match. In his absence, Gareth Southgate, the Aston Villa captain, was chosen ahead of Paul Ince and Dennis Wise to partner Paul Scholes in central midfield and England produced a lacklustre performance.

A long-range Dietmar Hamann free-kick which evaded the flailing arms of David Seaman was enough to deliver a critical blow to Kevin Keegan's reign. The beleaguered manager quit almost immediately after the match, claiming that his role had become untenable. It was a bitterly disappointing end for the manager who had given Gerrard his first opportunity at senior international level.

Howard Wilkinson took up a caretaker role for England's second qualifying game in Finland four days later and an injury-hit side, minus Gerrard, David Beckham and captain Tony Adams, among others, could only see out a goalless draw in Helsinki. The national side were in turmoil and were desperately in need of new spark and invention.

Liverpool also needed to install some pride into their ranks and where better for them to do so than at Pride Park. The Reds returned to action with a resounding 4–0 win over Derby, with Emile Heskey grabbing a hat-trick and Patrick Berger adding a trademark thumper. Gerrard

TRIPLE THE GLORY, MINUS THE INJURY

had to sit out the game while he continued to receive treatment for his ailments. However, it was never going to be a prolonged absence and, after some rigorous rehabilitation, the twenty-year-old was restored to Liverpool's starting XI as they entertained Leicester at Anfield. With Jamie Carragher and Stephane Henchoz left out by Gerard Houllier, Gerrard slotted in at right-back and created the only goal of the game with a searching long pass for former Leicester favourite Heskey to turn into the net. Aside from that, Gerrard showed his true worth with a steadfast performance that allowed Leicester winger Darren Eadie little chance to shine.

Liverpool squeezed past stubborn Czech Republic outfit Slovan Liberec in their UEFA Cup second-round first-leg clash at Anfield, thanks to a late goal from Heskey, who was fast living up to his £11 million price tag. Gerrard was rested along with defender Sami Hyypia with one eye firmly on Liverpool's next game – the first Merseyside derby of the season.

Nick Barmby was the centre of attention as red met blue at Anfield. Branded as Judas by angry Everton fans, the England man gave an almost poetic answer by scoring Liverpool's opening goal. Heskey emphasised his lethal form with a booming second goal before a Patrick Berger penalty rendered Kevin Campbell's late goal meaningless. With veteran Gary McAllister showing resurgent form alongside Dietmar Hamann in central midfield, Gerrard was again employed as a right-back – this time to mark Everton's Israeli tormentor, Idan Tal. Once more, he was imperious in thwarting the Toffees' winger with some clinical tackling and expert marking. Gerrard and Heskey were rightfully singled out for their starring role in the derby victory, which put Liverpool in an enviable position in the Premiership.

'Everyone is buzzing in our dressing room because we've not beaten Everton very often in recent years. And Emile is on fire and proving the critics wrong,' said Gerrard. 'Now it's important we stay in the top three and, although my favourite position is in midfield, I'm quite happy to play at the back when the boss selects me there.'

Another glory trail began the following Wednesday as Chelsea visited Anfield for the League Cup initiation. With Gerrard rested, Danny Murphy and Robbie Fowler sent Liverpool through after another tempestuous affair between the two sides. Heskey saw red before Fowler struck his first goal of the season in extra-time to put the Reds into the fourth round.

With Gerrard's absence for the Chelsea cup-tie blamed on his groin trouble, it came as no surprise when he was only named as a substitute for Liverpool's trip to Leeds three days later. The game petered into disaster for the Reds, who were two goals ahead after just 17 minutes – thanks to headers from Sami Hyypia and Christian Ziege. Rampant Leeds fought back to level the score, thanks to two goals from Mark Viduka, before the Reds nosed in front again as Vladamir Smicer pounced. But then Gerard Houllier rattled the Liverpool cage by hauling off Gary McAllister and Danny Murphy, replacing them with Gerrard and Robbie Fowler. It was the change of shape, not personnel, that disrupted the Reds' efforts. Viduka was Leeds' star man – completing a devastating hat-trick before winning the game for the home side with a decisive fourth goal. Gerrard was booked for his efforts as Liverpool showed their inconsistency.

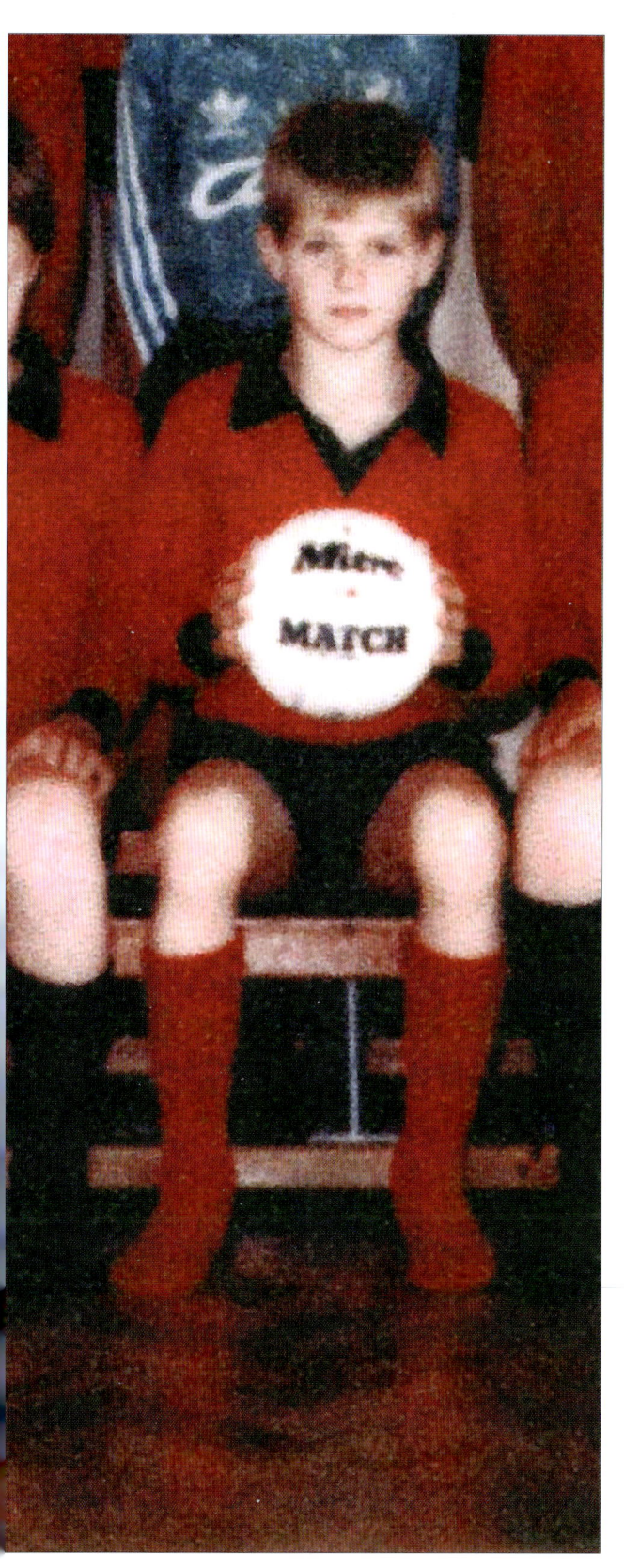

Steven Gerrard in 1990, aged 10. Like many football-mad youngsters he proudly wore a replica England shirt. His youthful talent, however, had already marked him out as a special lad.

Above: Instrumental in championing Gerrard's cause was Steve Heighway, former player and School of Excellence coach at Liverpool FC.

Right: Already displaying his future trademark qualities, a domineering midfield performance marked Gerrard's second game in the England U21 side, against Poland in September 1999.

Above: Steven Gerrard and Denmark's Claus Jensen battle for the ball during an England U21 friendly in October 1999.

Below: The day after his 20th birthday, Gerrard lines up before his senior England debut vs Ukraine in May 2000.

Above: England vs Ukraine. Gerrard showed confidence and the ability to run with the ball on his senior debut.

Below: Gerrard and defensive stalwart Tony Adams sit out training during Euro 2000 in Belgium. Adams proved a steadying influence on the young Gerrard in the early days of the Merseysider's international career.

At the end of the 2000/01 season, Gerrard deservedly received the prestigious Professional Football Association Young Player of the Year Award.

Gerrard unleashes a blistering drive to score England's second goal (and his first international strike) in the memorable 5-1 World Cup qualifier victory over Germany in Munich, September 2001.

Above: Thousands of Liverpool supporters turned out in Liverpool city centre, May 2001, to welcome the team after their treble-winning season. The Reds won the Worthington Cup, the FA Cup and the UEFA Champions League in one season.

Left: Gerrard celebrates scoring his first goal under the reign of inspirational Liverpool manager Gerard Houllier, vs Levski Sofia in the UEFA Cup third round, February 2004.

Gerrard has always been careful to preserve his mobility. Here he stretches during England team training at the end of August 2004.

TRIPLE THE GLORY, MINUS THE INJURY

In need of solidarity and control, Liverpool had Gerrard back in the centre of midfield for the second-round second-leg tie against Slovan Liberec. Peter Taylor, England's interim manager, had named Gerrard in a strong Three Lions squad for a friendly with Italy in Turin, and Gerrard was out to prove his fitness once and for all. Liverpool certainly needed his services when they fell behind to an early goal. As was required, Gerrard inspired a Reds' comeback, as goals from Nick Barmby, Emile Heskey and Michael Owen sent Liverpool tumbling through. The twenty-year-old was unlucky not to score himself with a couple of long-range efforts as he continued to take a firm grasp of European football – something he was still relatively alien to.

Three days after their trip to the Czech Republic, Liverpool returned to Anfield to face Coventry. Peter Taylor was present to witness an exemplary display by the Reds' medley of English talent.

It was an old Scottish flame that set the home side on their way, however, as Gary McAllister crashed home a goal against his former club. And the veteran's superbly administered free-kick set up Gerrard for the third goal of his senior career. Jumping higher than Coventry's Mustapha Hadji, he delightfully nodded home McAllister's cross at the near post to put Liverpool 2–0 up. David Thompson, on his first return to Anfield, gave Liverpool food for thought with a stunning 30-yard effort, before two clinical efforts by Emile Heskey completed an emphatic victory. Gerrard had partnered McAllister in central midfield for the first time and the combination had worked superbly. The youngster was substituted 12 minutes from the end in order to save his unceasing legs and he left the pitch to a deserved ovation from the Anfield faithful.

Sven-Goran Eriksson had been confirmed as England's future head coach and the Swede was present to see his new charges take on Italy in Turin. Despite Peter Taylor naming a youthful England side for the game, Gerrard's name was not on the team sheet – his international injury jinx had struck again. This time it was a hamstring problem that kept him out of a narrow 1–0 defeat in a game that showed so many encouraging signs for England fans, mainly due to the refreshing injection of youth. The future looked brighter for England, but for Gerrard, who was yet to embrace his third cap, his international future remained unclear.

Liverpool's exhausting season continued with an away game at Tottenham. Although Gerrard had been nursed back into action just after the hour mark, as the Reds were 2–1 down and short of inspiration, he could not provide the required ammunition, and Liverpool fell to defeat in the capital and slipped to fourth in the league table. The Reds had to buck up – and fast. A UEFA Cup third-round tie away to Olympiakos was next – a game dubbed as Liverpool's most arduous European assignment in years. Gerrard was passed fit and lined up alongside Dietmar Hamann in midfield. Nick Barmby opened the scoring for the Reds before the Greeks levelled early in the second half. Riled and alert, Liverpool hit back as Gerrard gleefully powered home a bullet header from Barmby's pinpoint corner. His first-ever European goal was not enough for victory, though, as Olympiakos set up an intriguing second leg with an injury-time equaliser. Liverpool's quest for glory was proving no easy ride, and their away hoodoo continued

TRIPLE THE GLORY, MINUS THE INJURY

four days later with a 2–1 defeat to Newcastle. Worryingly, Gerrard failed to complete 90 minutes again, after another assiduous display. At least there was Gary McAllister to share the mantle of such an important midfield role. He was proving an astute acquisition by Houllier, not least because of his role in shadowing Gerrard's responsibilities.

And where there was Jekyll in the Liverpool team of the time, there was also Hyde: evident in the 8–0 thumping of Stoke City in the League Cup. Gerrard missed that romp, but he was back for the Reds' home game with Charlton having had a full week's recuperation. The rest proved effective as he completed a vibrant 90 minutes, supplying a fine right-wing cross for Markus Babbel to head home his first Liverpool goal on the way to a 3–0 victory.

If Liverpool had let themselves down in the first leg of their UEFA Cup clash by conceding a last-minute equaliser, they more than made up for it when Olympiakos visited Anfield for the crucial second leg. Tord Grip, England's new assistant manager, was in attendance to see the wealth of English talent on show in the Liverpool ranks – and they didn't disappoint. Even with Michael Owen and Robbie Fowler on the bench, Emile Heskey, Liverpool's top scorer and man of the moment, was on hand to suggest that all of England's finer striking options were employed at Anfield. The powerful striker joined fellow England star Nick Barmby on the scoresheet while Gerard Houllier's side enhanced their trophy-winning credentials with a stunning performance. If Grip had been impressed by Heskey, then he would have been doubly overawed by Gerrard's gripping midfield display. Only a remarkable save from a stunning left-foot volley denied the twenty-year-old the goal that his performance richly deserved.

STEVEN GERRARD: PORTRAIT OF A HERO

Back in the Premiership, Ipswich stunned Liverpool with a 1–0 robbery at Anfield as the Reds fell awkwardly foul of Gerard Houllier's rotation policy. Gerrard, somewhat understandably following his heroics three days earlier, was left as an unused substitute, but Emile Heskey was also named on the bench, much to the surprise of the Liverpool fans. New signing Igor Biscan received his baptism as a second-half replacement, but neither he, nor Heskey, could turn around an adverse Anfield display.

If that game was tough, then the visit of Fulham provided Liverpool with a further test of resolve in a League Cup quarter-final clash. The Cottagers, who were top of the First Division under Jean Tigana at the time, were more than a match for Liverpool. However, they could not overcome Gerrard's almighty Man of the Match influence. And how the Reds needed him. The dynamic midfielder was in his pomp once again to ensure that Liverpool, already the favourites to win the competition, overcame a particularly high hurdle. Emile Heskey was unable to take advantage of a couple of incisive passes from Gerrard, before the Reds exploded into life in extra-time. Michael Owen, on his twenty-first birthday, contrived to break the deadlock, before Vladimir Smicer and Nick Barmby put an extra gloss on the scoreline to see Liverpool advance to the semi-final.

Having limped off with cramp minutes from the end of that cup-tie, Gerrard was considered a doubt for Liverpool's trip to face Manchester United. However, he recovered in time and partnered new boy Igor Biscan in midfield as Danny Murphy's memorable free-kick handed the Reds a shock win in Gerard Houllier's 100th game in charge.

If Gerrard had been outstanding at Old Trafford against

TRIPLE THE GLORY, MINUS THE INJURY

Roy Keane, then he was world class when Arsenal came to Anfield with Patrick Vieira – another of the players he looked up to. What a game, what a performance! If any game signified the true, if tardy, resurgence of Liverpool Football Club under Gerard Houllier, then this was it.

Having won at Old Trafford for the first time in ten years, confidence was sky high and title-winning dreams were very much alive. Gerrard personified such hope and, if he hadn't been already, was crowned King of Liverpool's midfield with a stunning goal – his fifth senior strike. Vieira, Arsenal's midfield guru, was simply outclassed and could only look on in amazement following his poor defensive header, as his young adversary intelligently allowed the ball to drop and, without hesitation, lashed a right-foot bullet past David Seaman into the far corner of the net: such opportunism was to become a mainstay of Gerrard's game. After Michael Owen had hit Liverpool's second, a typically full-bodied ball-winning tackle from Liverpool's hero of the hour led to Nick Barmby making it 3–0. Gerrard was taken off to a euphoric ovation from the Kop, before Robbie Fowler made it 4–0 and sealed the wrapping paper on what had been a blissful Christmas present for the Liverpool fans. 'We are not going to win the league ... our target is the top three. But if we keep performing like this, who knows?' said an excited Gerrard after the game.

That optimism was fraught by another uncertain result on Boxing Day when Liverpool lost 1–0 to Middlesbrough on Teesside. The Reds were in need of a rest after a strenuous spate of matches, and an unexpected favour from Mother Nature afforded Gerrard and company a chance to recharge their batteries when their scheduled festive clash with Bradford at Valley Parade was postponed due to snow.

STEVEN GERRARD: PORTRAIT OF A HERO

Fully refuelled, Gerrard broke in 2001 with another sparkling display – arguably his best yet for Liverpool. Southampton came to Anfield on New Year's Day looking to reap another disconcerting result on Liverpool's expectant support. However, in Gerrard, the Kop had a matchwinner to rely on. He proved his class with a one-man show against the Saints. Having stung the gloves of Paul Jones with an early rasper, he was at it again in the 12th minute, taking a square pass from Vladimir Smicer before unleashing an unstoppable right-footed drive from fully 35 yards into the top-left corner of Jones' goal. 'It could be the goal of the season,' said an admiring Gerard Houllier after the game.

The goal was so good that the rest of the Liverpool side seemed to wallow in its wake. Southampton forced an equaliser, before a late Markus Babbel header earned the Reds all three points. 'We were up against a confident side and we knew it would be difficult. It was the type of game that we would have lost a year ago and I'm delighted to have won it,' said Houllier. The truth was that they would have lost it had they not been able to call upon Gerrard.

Liverpool began their FA Cup campaign with a relatively routine 3–0 victory over Rotherham at Anfield, a game in which Gerrard was spared only as a second-half substitute ahead of a League Cup semi-final first leg away at Crystal Palace. The game at Selhurst Park, despite Gerrard's efforts, proved a torrid one for Liverpool. The Reds faced an uphill second-leg struggle by losing 2–1 to the First Division side.

A critical match away at Aston Villa in the Premiership gave Houllier's men a chance to bounce back from their League Cup nightmare. The game at Villa Park only yielded yet more persuasive evidence that Gerrard was Liverpool's

TRIPLE THE GLORY, MINUS THE INJURY

answer to a decade of trophyless monotony. New signing Jari Litmanen made his debut, but his class was eclipsed by another sterling display from the twenty-year-old. Sandwiched in between a terrific double by Danny Murphy came another Gerrard rocket. This time the shot was delivered from much closer range – from the edge of the box – but, nevertheless, Gerrard's sixth goal of the season had the same devastating effect and a 3–0 win revived Liverpool's title ambitions.

'It was another magnificent goal,' enthused Houllier to the *News of the World*. 'Believe me, Stevie is going to be a player. I think he could be another Vieira or Keane.' His prophecy was altogether true but, for many, Gerrard was already a player on a par with both Keane and Vieira. It remained to be seen whether Sven-Goran Eriksson – on the verge of naming his first-ever England squad – thought the same. Houllier wanted the new national coach to exercise caution with his young star.

'England will exercise the same caution with Gerrard as I do – otherwise I will do it myself,' he said. 'I know what my players can and can't do. Steven is only twenty and he cannot repeat games just like that. You have to be careful with him. I will have contact with Mr Eriksson about this. Steven can improve and do better, but you push them and they come on the international scene and don't produce if you push them too hard.'

Liverpool, by now, were second only to Manchester United in the Premiership goal-scoring charts. Sadly, they had to settle for a disappointing draw with Middlesbrough at Anfield before setting about making their first major cup final under Houllier – in the second leg of their semi-final tie with Crystal Palace. With the objective set at turning round the 2-1 aggregate deficit, Liverpool emphatically achieved it. Although Gerrard, playing again at right-back, suffered a second-half injury, the Reds cantered to a 5-0 victory and a place in the Worthington Cup final.

Another hamstring injury meant another enforced absence for Gerrard. He missed Liverpool's 2-0 away win at Leeds in the FA Cup fourth round before returning to play in the unorthodox – even by his versatile standards – position of left-back in a 1-1 draw with Manchester City at Maine Road. With injury problems gripping the Liverpool squad, many critics started to ask: just where would Liverpool be without Steven Gerrard? It is a question that lingered for a long time.

The virtuoso performer was back in midfield when Liverpool crushed West Ham 3-0 at Anfield at the beginning of February. Another gifted performance and another industrious and charismatic display was all the watching Sven-Goran Eriksson needed to see of Gerrard. Robbie Fowler, also hoping to make it into Eriksson's notebook, scored twice to complement Vladimir Smicer's superb strike.

Gerrard's hopes of making Eriksson's squad for a friendly against Spain were cast into doubt when he limped out of Liverpool's 1-1 draw with Sunderland at the Stadium of Light. And worse heartache was to follow when he was forced to remain at home for treatment while Liverpool flew to Italy for a UEFA Cup fourth-round first-leg clash with Roma. The groin injury that had dogged him almost relentlessly had returned with a vengeance. The Reds were able to combat his absence somewhat with the return to action of Michael Owen,

TRIPLE THE GLORY, MINUS THE INJURY

who scored two momentous goals as Liverpool beat Roma, the Italian giants, 2–0 in the Olympic Stadium. Liverpool then progressed to the quarter-finals of the FA Cup with a 4–2 defeat of Manchester City at Anfield, again without Gerrard, but the Kop's dream of lifting an unprecedented Treble of trophies, at least, was still very much alive.

That tantalising prospect nearly fell flat when Roma visited Anfield for the UEFA Cup fourth-round second leg – a game where Gerrard's prolonged absence finally told. The Italians sneaked a 1–0 win on the night and got mightily close to forcing a below-par Liverpool into extra-time. Nonetheless, the Reds had earned a place in the quarter-finals of the UEFA Cup. In front of them, though, was the Worthington Cup final.

Kenny Dalglish, the legendary former Liverpool player and manager, gave the *Daily Mirror* his assessment of the Reds' re-emergence as a force in English football before their biggest game of the season so far:

> There are happier times to look forward to, more than the club has had in the ten years since I have been away. That is the culmination of several factors: they are being rewarded for their investment in producing their own players; they are benefiting from the generosity of chairman David Moores; and they have a manager bringing in quality players in key areas.
>
> I do think it helps that they have a sprinkling of local lads in the squad and, for that, Steve Heighway deserves to be given credit. Through his department have come Owen, Fowler, Jamie Carragher and Steve

STEVEN GERRARD: PORTRAIT OF A HERO

Gerrard, who is going to be one of the best players in the country, if he isn't already.

Dalglish was right in every sense. In Gerrard, the Liverpool fans had an affable and hearty Scouser that they could associate with. He was a major catalyst of Liverpool's impending glory.

The first happy day of many occurred on 25 February 2001: the day the Reds lifted the Worthington Cup in Cardiff's Millennium Stadium.

Gerrard had been cast as a serious doubt for the showpiece but, after some near-non-stop treatment at Melwood, he was passed fit for a return to action in his first-ever cup final. He was put on the right side of midfield as Houllier sought to get the best out of his team's creativity against their opponents, First Division Birmingham City.

Gerrard's emergence from his injury nightmare provided the inspiration Liverpool needed – even if he didn't last for the full duration of the contest. Robbie Fowler put the Reds ahead with a stunning volley, before a penalty deep in second-half stoppage time from Darren Purse sent the game into extra-time. Well before that, Gerrard had hobbled off – suffering another relapse of his groin problem; it was a moment that signalled a decline in Liverpool's hold on the match. Too many games too young, was the simple diagnosis.

At least Liverpool had the ever-ready Gary McAllister in reserve to take the youngster's place. Despite his agony, Gerrard returned to the podium at the end of the match to pick up his first winners' medal after Liverpool won in a dramatic penalty shoot-out. The celebrations gave Gerrard

TRIPLE THE GLORY, MINUS THE INJURY

the first chance to revel in his – and Liverpool's – painstaking rise to success under Gerard Houllier. They weren't finished either. A 'flash in the pan' Gerrard, nor Liverpool, were not.

Houllier had urged Sven-Goran Eriksson to be vigilant of Gerrard's fitness, claiming that the twenty-year-old could not stand up to two games a week. For the sake of Liverpool's gruelling March schedule, Gerrard missed England's friendly with Spain at Villa Park as the national team christened Eriksson's reign with a resounding 3–0 win thanks, no less, to goals from Liverpool's Nick Barmby and Emile Heskey.

Having recovered sufficiently, Gerrard was back in Liverpool's midfield when they met Leicester at Filbert Street in the Premiership. Entering their most important period in years, Liverpool lost 2–0 to the struggling Foxes with Gerrard failing to provide his side with any spark alongside his mentor Gary McAllister. Interestingly, Gerrard completed a total of seventy-two passes in that match – more than any other Premiership player over that weekend – an excellent evaluation of his exceptional passing ability. Despite that contribution, Liverpool's title-winning aspirations were all but extinguished and question marks now hung over their Champions League qualification as well.

Porto were Liverpool's quarter-final opponents in the UEFA Cup, a trophy that still remained a distinctly realistic target. The Reds first travelled to Portugal and came away with a creditable goalless draw after a resolute display. Far from being a backs-to-the-wall affair, however, Liverpool may well have won in the Estadio das Antas had another

STEVEN GERRARD: PORTRAIT OF A HERO

astounding Gerrard display been rewarded when his fierce 30-yard strike only found the sturdy gloves of Porto's Sergei Ovchinnikov. The result set up another cherished European night at Anfield and the Reds had made themselves firm favourites to progress as well.

'Stevie played against Leicester on Saturday and here; if he can make Tranmere on Sunday it will be tremendous,' said Gerard Houllier, having seen Gerrard come through two 90-minute games in the space of four days. 'Those who worry about his injury problems tend to forget that he is still growing; he has grown an inch in the last three months.'

Indeed, Gerrard had added three inches to his height and a stone to his weight in just twelve months – a growth spurt that had stunned him:

'When I was fifteen I was the same size as Michael Owen, but he is a midget next to me now,' he beamed to the gathered media at a press conference. 'The rapid growth has given me posture problems and my muscles get tired, but it is getting better... It is impossible to put a date on when it will be perfect, but I am playing more games this season than I did last time.'

And Gerrard wasn't just growing physically; his glowing reputation was also growing at a phenomenal rate. Porto's former Aston Villa defender Fernando Nelson said fittingly – simply – after playing against him: 'Gerrard makes Liverpool tick.'

The FA Cup quarter-final tie at Tranmere yielded yet more honour for Gerrard – his first goal in the world's most famous knock-out competition. With his side leading 2–1 after goals from Michael Owen and Danny Murphy, Gerrard rose to meet a 52nd-minute Gary McAllister corner and powered a header into the net. Liverpool eventually

TRIPLE THE GLORY, MINUS THE INJURY

overcame their stubborn Merseyside neighbours to win 4–2. Gerrard completed 90 minutes once more, receiving a booking but atoning for it with his goal – his seventh of the season.

Just three days later, Liverpool made it into the semi-finals of the UEFA Cup by seeing off Porto at Anfield. Michael Owen and Danny Murphy scored on a night of spine-tingling excitement on Merseyside but, again, it was Gerrard who rose to take the responsibility of firing Liverpool forward on his own young shoulders. Playing his fifth full game in a row, he teed up both goals with crosses of devastating accuracy: his all-round imposing presence and perseverance caused Porto no end of problems during the game. Sven-Goran Eriksson was in the crowd to watch; the qualities of Gerrard would have been enough to fill the Swede's notepad ten times over, as Liverpool marched into their third semi-final in as many months.

The country's most exciting young player was given a well-earned rest on the bench for Liverpool's home Premiership encounter with Derby. After the hullabaloo of recent games, the Reds stuttered. Typically, Gerrard's 55th-minute introduction injected vitality into their play, but he could not prevent Liverpool from only coming away with a disappointing 1–1 draw. Crucially though, for Gerrard at least, he was fit and ready for England's World Cup qualifying matches against Finland and Albania – and also Liverpool's alluring UEFA Cup semi-final tie with Spanish giants Barcelona.

Gerrard was duly excited about playing a full game for England for the first time, having battled with injury all season long. He had been visiting an orthopaedic specialist

STEVEN GERRARD: PORTRAIT OF A HERO

in France to try and combat his injury worries. The treatment had done him good.

> I am fine. There is no injury problem. I am fit and available and ready to play for England if I am selected... I desperately want to play.
>
> Missing out all the time was getting me down – especially when you have been told you would have played. I have missed out on possibly five or six caps and watched other lads come in. But I have played four full games for Liverpool in twelve days recently. I was not able to do that last season, but I always knew it would sort out... I still feel only 70–80 per cent fit because I am still missing the odd training session here and there. When I am training on a regular basis I know my performances will get better.... I have played thirty-six times this season and we still have around fifteen games to play. If at the end of the season I have played in nearly fifty games that would be good amount. Not many other players have played in more.
>
> Hopefully I can get through the next couple of days of training and be fit for selection for the weekend. I would rather be patient and not play than go out at less than 100 per cent and not do myself justice. I don't want the manager to see me play badly and then decide he doesn't fancy me on the evidence of a game I wasn't fit enough to play in.

Gerard Houllier's paternal instincts were apparent when he reiterated to the *Observer* his concerns over Gerrard's development.

The boy is still growing and he is not ready to repeat

TRIPLE THE GLORY, MINUS THE INJURY

games at that level. International football is a step up from club games, and two games in five days would be too much. I am perfectly happy for him to be involved against Finland if Mr Eriksson wants him, especially as the game is at Liverpool. But going straight out to Albania would be too much of a rush, especially as it is the travelling that gives Stevie a problem. Mr Eriksson knows the situation, and in any case he would realise it for himself. He has grown this much this season. You've got to give him time and not be impatient with him. If he gains confidence with his club, it will be good for the country, too.

Tord Grip, the England assistant manager, respected the wishes of Liverpool's manager: 'We know he can't play too many games in a row,' said Grip. 'If his club say he can't play in both these games we have to accept that. This will not always be the case, as Gerrard's strength is improving all the time... My main thoughts are for his future. I want to protect him and don't want to ruin his career. I was only going to play him if the situation was urgent.'

However, Gerrard's seventeen starts in his last twenty games suggested that he was a little more agile than most appeared to think. However, on the other side of England's brace of World Cup qualifying matches lay Liverpool's biggest league game of the season – a home game with rivals Manchester United. Houllier's fears were, perhaps, understandable. Gerrard flew to France in the week leading up to England's game with Finland to see the French specialist who was helping him overcome the problems that had plagued him from his early teens.

'I will be carrying on seeing this bloke for some time,'

STEVEN GERRARD: PORTRAIT OF A HERO

said Gerrard in the *Daily Telegraph*. 'The specialist hasn't mentioned complete rest to me because I don't think Gerard Houllier would let him mention that because he wants me to play for Liverpool. If I play a full game against Finland, I will know myself whether I will be fit to play against Albania. I have to be honest with everyone. If I pulled a muscle against Albania, I could miss six weeks for Liverpool and you know the amount of important games we have coming up.'

Despite the misgivings about his condition, Gerrard passed a late fitness test to line up for England at Anfield – a fitting venue for him to shrug off all doubt and earn his third England cap while Eriksson took charge of his new-look side for the first time in a competitive game.

'All the best ... have a nightmare on Saturday,' had been Gerrard's cheeky final words to Finnish Liverpool teammate Sami Hyypia before the match. However mischievous that was, Gerrard was more of a nuisance on the field. His lion-like display for the Three Lions was only upstaged by an awesome individual performance by David Beckham. England fell behind to an early own goal by Gary Neville, but Michael Owen equalised before Beckham, the new England skipper, won the game with a trademark curling effort. Gerrard did well to marshal England's midfield with estimable authority alongside Paul Scholes. And with Scholes licensed to go forward, Gerrard was left with the responsibility of frustrating his Anfield colleague Jari Litmanen, Finland's key player and, in doing so, completed 90 minutes in an England shirt for the very first time.

Gerrard admitted to a press conference that he felt jaded after the game and felt it best to pull out of England's second qualifier in five days away to Albania.

TRIPLE THE GLORY, MINUS THE INJURY

To get through my first 90 minutes at Anfield and help England to three points was a magnificent feeling. But to be honest, when I woke up yesterday I didn't really think I was going to play. I was still feeling a bit sore and a little bit stiff. I worked with the physios and I pulled through the 90 minutes. But straight after the game I was feeling stiff and exhausted. I put the right foods and liquids into me to see how I felt today and it's disappointing. If I thought that I would have had half a chance of making it for Albania, I would have travelled and given it a go, but it was not the case.

Sven-Goran Eriksson shared the midfielder's deep disappointment. 'It's a pity when you miss players you count on, but that's life,' said the England head coach. 'In this moment, the most important thing for Liverpool and England is that Gerrard soon gets rid of his problems so that he can play normally. We need him like Liverpool need him. I realise Steven normally requires an extra day's recovery after a match and needs specialist treatment. He is an enormous talent. I am told that his injury situation is improving and sooner or later he will solve that problem.'

Eriksson called upon Nicky Butt to take Gerrard's place in Albania, and England came away with an unconvincing 3–1 victory.

A week's rest gave Gerrard the chance to recuperate for Liverpool's much-publicised clash with Manchester United. Keen to stir things up ahead of the potentially explosive clash, the newspapers drew blood from both sides of the M6. Gerrard was particularly looking forward to his meeting with Roy Keane. He said at a press conference:

STEVEN GERRARD: PORTRAIT OF A HERO

I admire Keane and Arsenal's Patrick Vieira because that's how I want my game to be. I've got closer to them this season and hopefully next season I'll be as good, if not better. You've got to set your standards high. I knew at the end of last season that I needed to score more goals to be rated as highly as Keane and Vieira, because I only scored once last season. I set myself a target at the beginning of this season to score ten goals. A class midfielder these days needs to score ten and I've scored six so far, so I'm on target. When I first broke into the team I'd be scared to have a shot, but now I'm smacking them and a few are flying in. I've put a few in the Kop as well, mind.

Gerrard's perceptible improvements in all aspects of his game were earning praise of the highest order from across the football spectrum.

'Gerrard reminds me of Bryan Robson,' Sir Bobby Robson, the former England manager told the *Times*. 'He possesses the four Cs in abundance: courage, consistency, confidence and class.'

All four of those attributes oozed from Gerrard as Manchester United fell before his warrior-like leadership at Anfield. His luminescent talent set Liverpool on their way to an illustrious victory when he scored arguably the finest goal of the 2000–01 Premiership season. Fully 32 yards from goal after being set up by Robbie Fowler, he unleashed a 67mph thunderbolt that rocketed past United's Fabien Barthez in the blink of an eye.

'I think it was my best goal for Liverpool so far,' stated Gerrard later. 'Wow,' said the Kop – collectively. More was to come. The roving midfielder returned the favour by

TRIPLE THE GLORY, MINUS THE INJURY

supplying a deft pass for Fowler to notch and send Anfield wild. With that, Liverpool had completed a sensational double over their arch-rivals – a feat not achieved by them for twenty-two years. Anfield, quite rightly, lauded the contribution of a twenty-year-old who, only three days earlier, had been branded a crock. Far from being that, Gerrard had proved, if he hadn't already, that he was a colossus in mind, body and soul. Mind: to overcome the doubt that had enveloped his injury lay-offs; body: to possess the extraordinary physical ability that made him a cut above the rest; and soul: to have the ability to almost single-handedly revive and personify the heart that had been ripped away from Anfield during the 1990s. Liverpool versus Manchester United, as with so many games that season, will live long in the memory of all who revelled in its grandeur.

If that was a big game, then Barcelona away in a UEFA Cup semi-final was monstrous. The Reds flew to Spain with one primary objective: to defend and earn a mouth-watering second-leg tie at Anfield. For Gerrard, it was a chance to shine in one of the finest football stadiums in the world – and how he graced the Nou Camp arena with his iridescent youthful brilliance. Many pundits, in the build-up to the UEFA Cup semi-final, saw this game as Gerrard's acid test – an opportunity to find out just how good he really was.

Before the game, Barcelona had singled out Gerrard as a potential primary tormentor.

'I thought Liverpool looked very good against Manchester United at the weekend and I was particularly impressed by Steven Gerrard,' defender Michael Reiziger warned. 'He looks like he has everything he needs to make a great midfielder and at such a young age. Judging by the quality of that goal he scored, I think he's the one we need to stop.' Barcelona did, at least, prevent 'Stevie G' from scoring on a balmy night in Spain, but a goalless draw nudged Liverpool a little closer to European glory.

Robbie Fowler, Liverpool's goal-hungry front man, gave his own eulogy of Gerrard's ability after seeing him play so well at the Nou Camp. In the *Daily Star*, the Liverpool captain said:

> Stevie has been getting all the plaudits lately, and rightly so. But for me the best thing about him is that he is only young and that means he can only get better. That is a frightening thought. I remember that when I was growing up, people were saying that you don't reach your peak until you're twenty-seven. If that's the case, then Stevie is going to be a Superman!... There isn't a weakness in his game. In fact, I rate him so highly in his temperament as much as his technique that I'm sure he's a future captain of England.

Gerard Houllier had to take his players off the European pedestal swiftly as Liverpool's marathon season continued at Villa Park in an FA Cup semi-final against Second Division troopers Wycombe Wanderers. Gerrard, somewhat understandably, was rested, although he did appear as a second-half substitute to set up a goal for Emile Heskey, as the Reds made the final with a 2–1 victory.

Liverpool's mounting fixture congestion gave Houllier reason to be unsettled. How could he leave his most influential stars, in particular Gerrard, out as Liverpool

TRIPLE THE GLORY, MINUS THE INJURY

entered their most important spell in near on a decade? The answer was simple – he couldn't.

Barely forty-eight hours after the FA Cup semi-final, the Reds were at Portman Road for a crucial Premiership encounter with Ipswich. And their tired legs could only muster a 1–1 draw; Gerrard, at his best, teed up Heskey for Liverpool's solitary goal. The Reds' Champions League qualification hopes were then left hanging in the balance three days later when Leeds came to Anfield. Rio Ferdinand and then Lee Bowyer – capitalising on an uncharacteristic error by Gerrard – had Liverpool on the rocks and 2–0 down. But riled and resurgent, Houllier's men hit back and Gerrard kept his composure to pull a goal back for Liverpool, meeting a Michael Owen cross and smashing the ball home. Joy then turned to despair for the twenty-year-old. Having been booked for a feisty challenge on Leeds' Alan Smith in the opening half, Gerrard was already walking a tightrope in a wholly fractious encounter. So referee Alan Wiley had no choice but to brandish a second booking after a late, retributive tackle on David Batty. Gerrard's second career dismissal ended Liverpool's challenge in the match. They had to recover quickly – Goodison Park was the next port of call.

Liverpool's demanding Easter schedule had taken its toll on Gerrard and, having played three games in five days, he was excused more bodily punishment in the Merseyside derby. Following their defeat to Leeds, Gerard Houllier's side had slipped to sixth in the Premiership table and simply had to beat Everton to revive their Champions League qualification hopes. Gerrard's exclusion seemingly made that task a whole lot harder.

'Steven's physical condition is getting better and he is

progressing all the time, but you have to be careful with him,' explained Houllier in the *Daily Mail*. 'We still have to take it day by day. There is a question mark over him after every training session. Next season, I think he will be much better and then he will just get stronger in the following season... Because of his quality, there is a temptation to take the extra mile with him. But I try to keep out of that situation, because at times I pay for it with Steven.'

Gerrard was not even in the squad as Igor Biscan stepped into his midfield role alongside Gary McAllister against Everton. And if the acquisition of McAllister needed any justification, then Liverpool had to look no further than the thirty-six-year-old's 94th-minute free-kick that earned the Reds a stunning 3–2 victory and put their league form back on track.

The monumental matter of Liverpool's twenty-third cup-tie of the season – the second leg of the UEFA Cup semi-final against Barcelona – exacted Gerrard's return.

'This is a new generation of Liverpool players. It is now down to them to make a name for themselves,' said Gerard Houllier upon handing Gerrard a recall. 'Thanks to the achievements of generations of players in the past – through the 1960s, '70s and '80s – this club is about winning trophies and reaching finals. We know this generation is a developing and progressing team and they want to make a name for themselves and reach a European final.'

Gerrard passed a late fitness test and played an integral role on the right side of midfield as Liverpool made their first European final in sixteen years. His industry led to the Reds' decisive goal after he cleverly won a corner on the right-hand side. Gary McAllister's flag-kick delivery was

TRIPLE THE GLORY, MINUS THE INJURY

handled by Barcelona's Patrick Kluivert and the Scottish veteran-turned-hero slammed the resulting penalty into the net for his second essential goal in the space of four days. Liverpool were through to the UEFA Cup final and an extraordinary Treble lay in reach.

The primary objective, for Houllier at least, remained to qualify for the Champions League. The Reds hardly had time to take stock of their achievements in Europe before Tottenham came to Anfield. Man of the moment McAllister, clearly donning some of Gerrard's mantle, scored yet again as Liverpool won 3–1 in front of a partisan home crowd. Gerrard rammed a now-trademark long-range effort against the Tottenham bar, eager to make his mark ahead of his one-match suspension.

McAllister's guile was needed with Gerrard banned for Liverpool's away game at Coventry City. Another goal by the imperious former Scotland international earned him the Player of the Month award for April as his side edged closer to the much-coveted Champions League spot.

The single-game suspension afforded Gerrard a welcome rest as he faced up to arguably the biggest month of his life so far. Liverpool began May 2001 with an away match at Bradford, the scene of their Champions League demise at the end of the previous season. But in McAllister and Gerrard, the reliable and steadfast midfield duo, Liverpool had more mettle than most. A full and authoritative 90 minutes from the twenty-year-old and another blistering goal from the thirty-six-year-old – not to mention a strike from Michael Owen – handed the Reds a 2–0 win at Valley Parade.

If Owen had contributed in that game, then a hat-trick in Liverpool's next game – at home to Newcastle –

confirmed him as the best striker in English football and put Liverpool on the brink of the Champions League. And Owen was in his customary goal-scoring mood again when Chelsea visited Anfield for Liverpool's sixtieth game of the season. The England hit man scored twice, but Jimmy Floyd Hasselbaink capitalised on Liverpool's lethargy to hit a brace himself and ensure the Reds' Champions League hopes would rest on their final-day trip to Charlton Athletic. Gerrard was named Man of the Match again – a good omen for what was to come.

Before the trip to the Valley, Liverpool had the small matter of two major cup finals to contend with. Gerrard had proved his fitness, his importance and his ability – it was time for him to step up to a new level and to play in his first-ever FA Cup final. The Reds prepared to face Arsenal at the Millennium Stadium with the belief that a decade of anonymity was nearing its timely end. Of course, the emergence of Gerrard had played a substantial role in propelling Liverpool forward that season – it seemed only right that his sparkling contribution be the spearhead of the Reds' bid for glory. Couple Gerrard's awesome talent with the goal-scoring magic of Michael Owen and Liverpool's true overwhelming power was instantly recognisable – as Arsenal discovered in Cardiff.

Liverpool's principal midfield man came up against the same Patrick Vieira he had overawed earlier in the season. If Gerard Houllier's men were going to win the FA Cup, then the outcome of a duel between two of the country's most influential midfield players would have to read Gerrard as the winner once again. Gerrard himself admitted to having a 'horrible fear' of being left out of a game he had dreamt about playing in since he was a child. The UEFA Cup final

TRIPLE THE GLORY, MINUS THE INJURY

against Spanish outfit Alaves was only four days after the FA Cup final and having been spared the weight of two games in the space of a week earlier in the season because of his ongoing injury problems, he feared that his talents would be wrapped in cotton wool again in order for him to be 100 per cent fit for the trip to Dortmund.

Gerard Houllier was a shrewd man, however, and knew only too well the importance of having Gerrard in his midfield against one of the Premiership's best sides – and best players. But far from Liverpool being a one-man operation, there was also an engaging team spirit – always a sturdy foundation for success. Gerrard said in the *Daily Telegraph*:

> Everyone sticks together; everyone helps each other when things aren't going well. Liverpool got their big name from what they won in the past and it's up to me and the other players to carry that on. The fans have been starved of success over the last ten years. It's our job to bring trophies back to Anfield... I'm desperate to have three medals by the end of the season. You don't get remembered for being runners-up. You get remembered for being a winner. I'm more interested in winning trophies than new contracts and wage increases.

Gerrard had built an outstanding rapport with the Liverpool fans, and knew only too well their importance in guiding Liverpool towards success. He wanted to win for them, more than anybody else.

'The bond between supporters and players remains strong,' continued Gerrard. 'I go to supporters' meetings;

being a local lad, I can't get any closer to the fans. They're near enough on my back, particularly when the tickets came out for the final.'

Around 35,000 Liverpool fans descended on Cardiff for the Reds' first FA Cup final since 1996 and they were treated to a classic.

Gerrard rarely broke forward in the game, pegged back by Arsenal's armoury of attacking talent. Instead, he stifled the Gunners with some combative tackling, excellent link-up play and, of course, his non-stop energy. Critics suggested, however, that Vieira was the better of the midfield generals over 90 minutes. After the game, the Liverpool man commented:

> I learned what a great player Patrick Vieira is – a lot better than me. I went out determined to run the game, win the midfield battle and show everyone the progress I have made this season. But Vieira wouldn't let me do it. He's such a great player that I just couldn't get on top of him. He dropped deep for the first half and ran the show. He picked up the tempo after the break, moved forward and ran the show again. There are so many things about him I admire. He's fit, he dictates the pace, he's strong, he moves with the ball, he gets back to cover, he tackles. He has everything. There is no other player who is such a role model... Yes, he gave me a bit of a lesson in the cup final but, at the end of it all, I was still the one with the medal.

Despite the best efforts of Vieira, it was Gerrard's Liverpool that lifted the famous English trophy. They did fall behind in the Welsh capital, as Arsenal's Freddie Ljungberg stole in

TRIPLE THE GLORY, MINUS THE INJURY

to score with just 19 minutes remaining, but where Arsenal had a wealth of foreign talent in their ranks, Liverpool had two young English individuals with the ability to turn a game on its head. One of them was Gerrard, the other – Michael Owen. And Owen it was who upstaged all others to swing the handles of the FA Cup back towards Anfield. First, he clinically volleyed home after a Gary McAllister free-kick had caused mayhem in the box and then, with just two minutes remaining, he stunned the watching millions by latching onto Patrick Berger's long clearance, accelerating past Lee Dixon and finding the far corner of David Seaman's goal with a quite magnificent left-footed effort. Gerrard was one of the first to congratulate his best friend on the brace that won the pair their first-ever FA Cup-winners' medal.

'Tell me ma, me ma, to put the champagne on ice, we're going to Cardiff twice,' beamed the Liverpool fans, in reflection of their two trips to the principality that season. It was a spellbinding climax to a domestic season that had seen Liverpool roll back the years to days of old, where trophy-winning was the norm. The Reds had become only the second English team to win the League Cup and FA Cup in the same season. With two items of gleaming silverware added to the famous Anfield trophy room, Gerrard and his team-mates now turned their attention to the UEFA Cup final.

Liverpool travelled to Germany under strict orders not to over-indulge in celebration. In fact, they had celebrated on the Saturday evening after the final with fruit juice and fizzy water at their Vale of Glamorgan training base. Jennifer Ellison, Gerrard's soon-to-be-confirmed girlfriend, accompanied the other player's wives and girlfriends.

STEVEN GERRARD: PORTRAIT OF A HERO

The UEFA Cup final posed unpredictable opposition to Liverpool in the form of little-known Spanish giant-killers Alaves, who had made a big impact in the competition. And Gerrard, having struggled to weave his magic against the might of Patrick Vieria in Cardiff, now faced a very different proposition in Alaves' influential Yugoslav midfielder Ivan Tomic – on loan to the Basque side from Roma.

'I had never really heard of Alaves before the last couple of months,' said Gerrard. 'It's over these couple of months that I took note. It's going to be a very hard game. It's a massive competition and they would not have achieved it without a lot of hard work.'

Alaves coach Jose Manuel Esnal had earmarked Gerrard as the biggest threat to his team. 'He's got big problems if he's only worried about me because we have got some great players,' continued the midfielder. 'We will give them the same respect that we gave Barcelona and Roma.'

Gerrard, who had been crowned PFA Young Player of the Year before the FA Cup final, was adamant his side could win their twenty-fifth cup-tie of the season and complete the Treble.

'If we show the same character as we showed on Saturday in Cardiff, then we will win the UEFA Cup as well,' he said. 'The FA Cup final was special, the highlight of my career, but I hope things will get even better on Wednesday, and then on Saturday against Charlton. Arsenal are a great side and because they are ahead of us in the league they are probably a better team than us, but we beat them on the day and that's all that matters. It still hasn't sunk in yet, I have not really had the time to think. We had a celebration on Saturday night, without alcohol, and we won't start the party until after the Charlton

TRIPLE THE GLORY, MINUS THE INJURY

match... I know we are favourites to win in Dortmund because of the club's European history, but we know Alaves are a very good side.'

Out of all the many games Liverpool had played that season, the penultimate proved the most utterly enthralling contest of them all. The Reds were on their game, but so were Alaves. Gary McAllister was drafted into the side, giving the Reds extra midfield bite. That meant Gerrard was moved out onto the right of midfield, where he had flourished so often.

Gerard Houllier's team selection appeared justified when Liverpool raced into a two-goal lead inside of 16 minutes in the Westfalenstadion. McAllister set up Markus Babbel to head in the first goal after just four minutes and then Gerrard, with a formidable surging run, took a clever pass from Michael Owen and buried the ball past Alaves' stricken custodian Martin Herrera. The twenty-year-old's tenth Liverpool goal of the season, his second in European competition, gave the Reds a firm cushion to rest on.

However, Alaves had other ideas, and Ivan Alonso, moments after coming on as a substitute, headed past Sander Westerveld with 27 minutes on the clock. McAllister's penalty, after Owen had been fouled, reaffirmed Liverpool's advantage prior to half-time, but Javi Moreno, Alaves' main marksman, hit a quick-fire double early in the second half to draw the Spaniards sensationally level. Liverpool's enterprising qualities were tested to the limit again, but an old hero was on hand to put them back in the box seat. Robbie Fowler, who had been left out of the starting line-ups for both the UEFA and FA Cup finals, leapt off the bench to score with a splendid left-foot drive from the edge of the area in the

73rd minute to the wondrous delight of the 20,000 travelling Reds' fans.

Fowler's goal epitomised Liverpool's fighting spirit, but whatever Gerard Houllier's side did that night, Alaves matched, and Jordi Cruyff's late header sent an already-remarkable contest into extra-time, with the score level at 4–4.

Liverpool gained the upper hand in additional time, by way of a red card issued to Alaves' Cosmin Contra four minutes from the end. And the pulsating match would not have been complete without a last-gasp winning goal. Fate and fortune ensured that it would be Liverpool who took home the honours: McAllister's curling free-kick from wide left was inadvertently flicked on by Delfi Geli and the ball ended up in the back of the net. An own goal it was, and this time there was no way back for the courageous Spaniards – Liverpool were Treble winners having won their first European trophy in seventeen years.

With the score 3–3, Gerard Houllier had withdrawn centre-back Stephane Henchoz, replacing him with Vladimir Smicer and moving Markus Babbel into the centre of defence. That meant Gerrard moved back to right full-back and, in turn, it gave Liverpool the defensive solidarity they needed to halt Alaves' enigmatic attack. It was the tactical switch that won the game.

The Liverpool players were greeted to a rapturous reception when they returned home to English soil but, for them, celebrating the completion of such a remarkable achievement remained, for the time being, on hold: there was still one more critical match left – arguably the biggest of them all.

TRIPLE THE GLORY, MINUS THE INJURY

If Liverpool didn't qualify for the Champions League, then their season, at least in terms of solid progression, would have been deemed a failure. A massive game awaited them at The Valley on the final day of the season – Charlton away. Liverpool's sixty-third and last game of the campaign would be no simple task and what a wonderful crowning climax it proved to be.

Extra-time in Dortmund had done enough to send legs dizzy and emotions drained. The likes of Gary McAllister and Gerrard, who had toiled tirelessly, not just in that game, but for the entire season, had to deliver one final time. The tiredness showed in South-East London but, in truth, the Reds were probably only conserving their energy for the second-half storm that swept them into the Champions League.

Gerard Houllier, claiming his players were 'playing for immortality', reinstated Robbie Fowler into his line-up and it was he who galvanised the Reds. A superbly crafted volley and a low drive after neat interplay between Gerrard and Michael Owen put Liverpool in the driving seat in the second period. Sandwiched in between Fowler's brace was a 20-yard screamer from Danny Murphy as the Reds raced ahead. Gerrard was booked for a petulant rant at an assistant referee, before Owen rounded off an incredible year by making it 4–0 before the end as cries of 'Three cups and the Champions League' emanated from the jubilant Liverpool fans who had seen their side beat Leeds to third place in the Premiership.

Gerrard and his fellow heroes returned to Merseyside for the biggest celebration Liverpool had seen in years. The open-top bus that paraded them around the streets of the city barely had room for the three trophies and all the people that had contributed to an unimaginable achievement. At the front of the the bus, manager Gerard Houllier held aloft the UEFA Cup, Robbie Fowler waved the FA Cup and a beaming and proud Gerrard flaunted the League Cup.

'This season has not been a victory for eleven or fourteen players. It is for the entire group,' exclaimed Houllier. 'When you have the skill, and on top of that the will, you'll achieve. We have come through because of the belief the players have in themselves and the trust they have in each other.'

Liverpool had astounded even their own hardy supporters, so too had a twenty-year-old who had overcome injury to put himself in the echelon of Europe's best midfield players. In total Gerrard started twenty-nine league games in the 2000–01 season, making four appearances as a substitute, scoring seven Premiership goals and spending a total of 2,529 minutes on the pitch. He picked up just four bookings in those games, and saw red on one occasion. In cup competition, he hit three goals in contribution to Liverpool's Treble triumph. A total of eleven goals and near on fifty club appearances was an amazing input from a player labelled a liability because of his injury problems.

With the champagne corks still popping, Liverpool's contingent of England stars headed off on international duty for a friendly against Mexico. The Three Lions had to be prepared; a crucial World Cup qualifier with Greece was to follow closely behind. Sven-Goran Eriksson needed the game against Mexico to find the right formula for his team. He had a wealth of talent to choose from: a pool that included the sunshine talents of Gerrard, a player eager to

TRIPLE THE GLORY, MINUS THE INJURY

make his international mark after an incredible season at club level.

'I want to make a name for myself on the international stage. It's been extremely frustrating to miss out on so many England games over the last year,' Gerrard had exclaimed. He now had his chance to rubber-stamp his position at the heart of England's midfield and to transfer some of his abiding magic from the club stage onto the international one.

Mexico were torn apart by England at Derby's Pride Park. And Gerrard, five days ahead of his twenty-first birthday, was at the pinnacle of their activity: combining with midfield cohort Paul Scholes to set up a goal for the Manchester United star; and then crossing for Robbie Fowler to score England's second. Gerrard came agonisingly close to firing home his first England goal before wholesale half-time changes saw him replaced by Liverpool team-mate Jamie Carragher. David Beckham and Teddy Sheringham scored a dazzling free-kick apiece to round off a fabulous 4–0 victory.

Gerrard's fitness had been the main talking point before the game because he had missed training sessions. But, fit as a butcher's dog, he took his place in an England midfield that read, from right to left: Beckham, Gerrard, Scholes, Heskey. In Scholes, the experienced midfield goal-getter, Gerrard had a perfect partner and, if the pair were to stay free of injury, Eriksson had a ready-made midfield combo to take on the world.

Gerrard admitted that the marathon season he had endured was helped by his frequent visits to France, a vigorous diet regime and some strenuous exercises undertaken to help cure his back problem. He wanted to

STEVEN GERRARD: PORTRAIT OF A HERO

shake off doubts over his long-term fitness once and for all, and had certainly signalled his fine health in the game against Mexico. At the press conference after the match, the Liverpool man said:

> I had been reading all week that I was injured and stuff like that. But I have to go to France once a month for treatment. It means that I can't train the day after. That's what happened last week. I trained on the morning of the game and I came through the 45 minutes with no problems. I will be fit for the Greece game. The osteopath I visit in Paris manipulates my body. He is changing the shape of my back over a period of time. It's all to do with the way I have grown quickly over a short space of time and my back was in a bad position. I will have to carry on seeing him, maybe for another couple of years.
>
> There's no more McDonalds or Burger Kings. It's pasta, rice and potatoes and it's a case of laying off alcohol. The osteopath has told me that all this will pay off.

The man who had been responsible for helping Gerrard overcome the problems he had abided since childhood was Dr Philippe Boixel. The Liverpool hero visited the French guru every three weeks in the French town of Laval for some painstaking manipulation of his troublesome back. The medical expert, personal trainer to some of the best players on the planet, told the *Sunday People* in an exclusive interview that his client was winning his fight against the problem.

TRIPLE THE GLORY, MINUS THE INJURY

All great players should consider their bodies to be like Formula One racing cars. People like Michael Schumacher drive them, but the men who spend most of their time working on them are the mechanics. Steven Gerrard is a great talent, but he can only express himself fully when he is free of pain. The problem has arisen from injuries he suffered early in his career. It could have been something as simple as a twisted ankle to start with. What has happened is that, as a reaction to injuries of that kind, he has developed what we call a bad posture. The position of his body is not as it should be. It goes back some years. That, in itself, brings fatigue on more quickly and, when the muscles are tired, they are more prone to damage. It's only by constant manipulation and monitoring of the spine that Steven can improve.

Boixel had worked for the French national team when Gerard Houllier had been the team's technical director. Many of the world's biggest clubs sought his services to find the cure for ailments that were hampering their top stars. Zinedine Zidane, the French maestro, was one such player who undertook a personal fitness examination every month with Boixel and former England captain Tony Adams had also had treatment from him.

The treatment Gerrard had been administered, judging by the extensive mileage he had clocked up that season compared to the previous one, was proving its worth. Thanks to Bioxel, England's World Cup qualifier with Greece in Athens saw the England midfielder complete back-to-back international appearances for the first time in his career.

Gerrard was resigned to celebrating his twenty-first

birthday at England's training camp in the Spanish resort of La Manga. Despite being pictured toasting the occasion opening a magnum of champagne, he was not allowed to consume any of the contents with the Three Lions' crucial trip to the Greek capital only days away. Sven-Goran Eriksson, however, did allow the players a couple of beers to wash down Gerrard's birthday cake. Memories of the 'toothpaste' prank administered by a fellow squad member a year earlier, however, had the birthday boy on hotel-room red alert.

'Sven let us all have a couple of beers and we got stuck into the birthday cake,' Gerrard told reporters in La Manga. 'There have been no practical jokes yet, but I'm expecting some. That's why this key is not leaving my sight – they can't get into my room.'

Where there was no doubting the jovial team spirit in the England squad, the doubt surrounding Gerrard's fitness had also been somewhat alleviated. 'If I really want to make an impression, I have to be 100 per cent every time I go into a game,' he continued. 'I also have to learn to be a lot more composed on the ball. Sven said he wanted me to get stuck in from the off against Mexico, so I took him at his word. I went at them with all guns blazing. The Mexican No. 6 seemed to be having a go at David Beckham, so I went over to lend a hand. I had another one of them lined up as well, only for the ref to blow his whistle!'

Such a combative attitude was music to the ears of Eriksson; Greece were no easy team to face, especially away from home. The England head coach had been mightily impressed by Gerrard's affiliation with Paul Scholes in midfield.

'Gerrard and Scholes are technically both good on the

TRIPLE THE GLORY, MINUS THE INJURY

ball,' he said in the *Sunday Mirror*. 'They are both good passers, hard workers and can shoot well. They can do everything; they are very modern midfielders. They complement each other perfectly. It's not like one can attack and the other can defend. I've never had this kind of situation in the past where my teams have boasted two excellent midfielders who are equally good at getting forward and tracking back. I've known about Gerrard for a while, but the great thing is, if he goes up the right or left flank, I now know Scholes can cover for him. I didn't know so much about Steven before I took the job. I had seen him on television a couple of times, but I didn't know just how good he is. I just hope he can stay fit.'

David Beckham, the England captain, enthused: 'Stevie is the best young player in England. He's a great talent. He has proved that in the games he has played for us. No one is stopping him. He's such a powerful runner for a young lad.'

And Beckham, Scholes and Gerrard combined to nullify Greece's midfield in Athens as England made further progress towards qualifying for the 2002 World Cup. A 2–0 victory, owing to a goal from Paul Scholes and a typically divine David Beckham free-kick, put the Eriksson era in full motion. Gerrard's raking passes, tough tackling and all-round maturity exemplified the Three Lions' thoroughly professional performance. At the post-match conference, Gerrard said:

> We have a very young team and a lot of us are still learning about international football. This is a very exciting time for the whole country. The rest of the world has been watching our games. They know we

have improved a lot and are going to get even better. And I think that will scare a few teams off. I don't think we are far away from winning things with this team. Maybe this World Cup might be a bit too soon, but if we keep improving and developing, I don't see why we can't go and win it in 2006.

England's next World Cup qualifier would be against Germany in Munich – on paper, the most arduous of all their group games. With Greece brushed aside, Gerrard and company could, at last, fall back and reflect on a gruelling, yet rewarding, year.

Chapter Seven
Heartbreak High

Barely four weeks after England's game with Greece, Liverpool were back in pre-season training ahead of their long-awaited jaunt back into the Champions League. Jamie Redknapp had returned from injury after missing out on the whole of the Reds' Treble-winning campaign, and he was joined by some new faces on Melwood's manicured training pitches. Norwegian wide man John Arne Riise had been drafted in from Monaco and he was soon to be followed by Chris Kirkland, the young Coventry goalkeeper, and also the Polish custodian Jerzy Dudek. Christian Zeige was the only major name to exit Anfield, as Gerard Houllier sought the same kindred spirit in his squad that had reaped so much reward the year before. Redknapp's return to action proved a timely blessing; only one week into the preparations, Gerrard, who had put pen to paper on a new contract committing himself to Anfield until 2005, was nursing another injury – this time to his ankle. He picked it up while he was at Liverpool's training camp in Switzerland and the early prognosis suggested that the England star would be out of action for a prolonged period.

'It is a big blow,' said a despondent Gerard Houllier to assembled press. 'We have a heavy programme in August, but it looks as though he will be absent for a minimum of six weeks. It was a complete accident. He was controlling the ball with his left foot when he went over and injured his right ankle. He will have a scan when we get back, but we already know he will be out for a while. He was fit and we were all looking forward to carrying on our preparations for the new season.'

Without Gerrard, Liverpool gained more silverware by winning the Charity Shield with a 2–1 victory over Manchester United in Cardiff and then saw off West Ham in similar fashion as they began their assault on the Premiership on the opening day of the season at Anfield. Gerrard was also forced to sit out England's 2–0 defeat to Holland in a friendly at White Hart Lane – a scoreline perhaps indicative of his vital importance at international level.

Gerrard eventually returned to action as a 72nd-minute substitute for Jamie Redknapp in the second leg of Liverpool's Champions League qualifier against FC Haka at Anfield. Gerard Houllier's side were already leading 5–0 after the first leg in Finland so a 4–1 victory at Anfield more than confirmed Liverpool's place in the group stages of Europe's most prestigious competition.

If there was any doubting Liverpool's potential in the Champions League, then it was firmly laid to rest in the European Super Cup final in Monaco. Bayern Munich, the reigning champions of Europe, were the opponents, but it was the UEFA Cup holders who reigned in the Stade Louis II. Gerrard returned to make his first start of the new season and his very presence boosted the Liverpool midfield. It took him only 22 minutes to break down a Bayern attack and conjure a fabulously weighted pass to enable Michael Owen to tee up John Arne Riise for the Reds' opening goal. Such unceasing telepathy between the two England men boded well for the forthcoming showdown with Germany. Gerrard, lacking none of his usual wealth of attributes, lasted 65 minutes before being replaced by Igor Biscan. Bayern subsequently reduced a 3–0 deficit by two goals, but Liverpool held on to win their fifth trophy in six amazing months.

Three days later, Gerrard completed his first full 90 minutes of the season in Liverpool's 2–1 defeat to Bolton at the Reebok Stadium. England head coach Sven-Goran Eriksson had wanted the match postponed due to its close proximity to his side's World Cup qualifier with Germany. 'All Steven needs is matches,' argued Gerard Houllier. 'I realise the England situation and will take it into account, but if he can play, he will play.'

Having proved his fitness, Gerrard was raring for an England return for their blockbuster encounter with the Germans. He had sat frustrated the last time the two teams had met when his Liverpool team-mate Dietmar Hamann's solitary strike brought down the curtain on Kevin Keegan's spell as England manager. In reflection of that day less than a year earlier, Gerrard said:

> I sat in the stands and watched at Wembley and it was devastating – a bad day for the country. It would be nice to get one over on Germany because Didi rubbed

it in a little bit when they won at Wembley. He got Man of the Match as well that day, so fair play to him, he played very well. But hopefully we can get a bit of revenge and then do the same to him. We're a lot stronger than we were at Wembley and the team is playing a lot better. We're all up for the game and if everyone is fit it shouldn't be a problem.

Gerrard had been employed as a right-sided midfielder in Liverpool's defeat to Bolton, and doubts over David Beckham's fitness suggested he was about to play in the same role for England in Munich. Gerrard continued:

Gerard Houllier puts me on the right wing because there is more running involved and it helps me get fitter quicker. That was definitely the case against Bolton. I needed a casket after 60 minutes. I still go to France to see a medical specialist. But I've not been for ten days and my trips are becoming less and less frequent as he is so pleased with the progress I'm making... Patrick Vieira showed me just how much I need to improve during last season's FA Cup final. I want to match the quality that Vieira and Roy Keane produce every week. I've got a 100 per cent record for England and I hope that continues.

If Gerrard was going to make it six caps and six wins, then he would have to be on his best form to suppress Germany's midfield riches. If Beckham was to play, then it would be Gerrard in the holding role, charged with tracking Sebastien Diesler, the ace in Germany's midfield pack.

'Whoever plays in the holding role will have

responsibility to keep an eye on him as he drops deep to find space,' Gerrard explained, referring to his studious observation of the German star. 'We must stop him as he's a dangerous player. If I get picked to play that role, that will be a big responsibility… If there are a few players in the team who don't perform, Germany will capitalise on that – and beat us.'

1 September 2001: Munich's Olympic Stadium buzzed in anticipation as England took to the field with Germany. Never in their wildest dreams could an England follower have envisaged what was about to happen. Any forecast that this game was going to be anything less than difficult was seemingly blown out of the window when Carsten Jancker prodded Germany ahead inside five minutes. Far from being overawed by the early sucker punch, the Three Lions roared back in style. Sven-Goran Eriksson, in his nine or so months in charge, had instilled a sense of unity in his side and it was the Liverpool contingent that united to electrify a stunning England fightback.

Michael Owen levelled with a typical poacher's goal as England got down to the serious business of seeing off Germany. With their tails up, Eriksson's side nudged towards half-time baying for the lead. Two minutes and 31 seconds into stoppage time at the end of the first half, Jens Nowotny, the German centre-back, scythed down David Beckham on England's right side. The captain's initial free-kick delivery was headed away by Dietmar Hamann but, upon retrieving the ball, he got a second chance to cross on his left foot. Rio Ferdinand leapt up on the edge of the penalty area to guide Beckham's centre into the path of Gerrard, who was lurking like a predator 30 yards from goal and seemed to have read exactly what the Leeds United defender was going to do. From that moment on, it was all Gerrard. He deftly controlled the ball on his chest and, with the most adept technical ability, arrowed a low shot via a crowd of players into the bottom right corner of Oliver Kahn's goal. The German goalkeeper had no chance in reading the sheer pace and swerve on the shot and England's latest hero sprinted away in celebration to be mobbed by his jubilant team-mates and applauded by a beaming Eriksson. Gerrard's first-ever England goal, a moment of sheer genius, had England 2–1 ahead at half-time in Munich.

'Rio Ferdinand deserves a lot of credit for the goal,' said Gerrard later. 'As the ball came over I asked him to set it. He set it up perfectly for me to chest down and hit it into the bottom corner. It was a great time to score, to give the lads a boost at half-time. We came out and played a lot better in the second half.'

Owen made it 3–1 shortly after half-time and, suddenly, memories of Geoff Hurst's hat-trick against Germany in the World Cup final of 1966 came to the fore. On 66 minutes, even comparisons to that epic final were well and truly invoked when Owen completed his remarkable treble. And who better than his best friend and long-time club companion to supply the pass that afforded him the chance. This was no ordinary assist from Gerrard – it vividly illustrated exactly what he brought to England's cause. As Michael Ballack strode forward inside his own half, Gerrard closed him down with purpose, anticipating the German midfielder's next move sufficiently enough to steal the ball away, spot Owen's run and play an incisive and nimble pass into the path of the striker who finished

HEARTBREAK HIGH

with assurance to send the whole of England into ecstasy. Without wanting to miss out on the merry dance led by those who plied their trade on Merseyside, Emile Heskey joined in the scoring fun with England's fifth goal. Germany had been quite remarkably humbled.

'It hasn't really sunk in yet. I'll probably have to read the papers in the morning to believe it!' Gerrard said to the *News of the World* in reflection of the night he scored his debut England goal. 'I said we could be better man for man than Germany and we proved that was right tonight. They were on their own soil and we knew they were confident, but we were a lot stronger than the last time we played them at Wembley. There is nothing we can't achieve if we play like this now. I wondered what it would feel like to score against Germany. When it happened, I felt like running into the crowd. I was so elated. The atmosphere in the changing room after was fantastic. The manager was quiet, but I think inside he was dying to let himself go.'

Gerrard had been spared the final 13 minutes in Munich, in order to save his tired legs from harm for the game against Albania, which was next on England's World Cup qualifying agenda. St James' Park, Newcastle, provided the setting for them to build on their win against Germany and edge closer to the World Cup finals. The Three Lions' Liverpool posse orchestrated proceedings again, as Owen bagged another and Robbie Fowler, a forgotten man to many, added another as England ran out 2–0 winners. Gerrard's combative edge earned him his first-ever booking in an England shirt when he tripped Albania's Arian Bellaj. He was, however, named Man of the Match, but England's adventure in Munich had clearly had its effect on busy legs. By playing back-to-back matches for England in the space of five days, Gerrard had reached a personal milestone in his battle with injury.

The euphoria of England's astonishing victory in Munich lasted barely a week for Gerrard; his return to action with Liverpool was less than inspiring. Aston Villa travelled to Anfield seeking to inflict a second-successive Premiership defeat on the stuttering Treble-winners. That looked likely from the moment Dion Dublin punished some errant defending to put Villa ahead with a thumping header past debutant goalkeeper Jerzy Dudek. Gary McAllister's inswinging corner invited Gerrard to nod in an untidy equaliser just seconds into the second half, but Villa, more robust than their opponents, were back in front soon after thanks to Lee Hendrie. Gerrard, who had been Liverpool's most dynamic player again, despite being employed on the right-wing, let out his frustration with a late, knee-high lunge on George Boateng after 74 minutes. Referee Andy D'Urso immediately brandished a red card for the crunching tackle, signalling the end of Liverpool's challenge in the match and also a three-match suspension for the guilty party. Villa's Darius Vassell scored to make it 3–1 and compound Liverpool's dismay.

'It was a reckless tackle by Steven,' conceded Gerard Houlier in reaction to the third dismissal of Gerrard's career. 'It's something he has to learn from. Frustration got the better of him. We need him on the pitch, but don't just blame him; the whole team was off-colour.'

A 1–1 draw with Portuguese champions Boavista followed, as Liverpool began their Champions League challenge. Gerrard was restored to a central midfield berth and his engineering crafted a stunning equalising goal for Michael Owen, but it did little to lift the gloom of the

HEARTBREAK HIGH

previous weekend. What Liverpool needed was a Merseyside derby to reinvigorate their senses and to kick-start their season.

Everton welcomed Liverpool to Goodison Park with a goal from Kevin Campbell after just five minutes, but blue joy in the 165th meeting between the two sides was short-lived – Gerrard had a score to settle. After just 12 minutes, the twenty-one-year-old, outstanding throughout, pounced on a defensive clearance by David Unsworth, shuffled away from Gary Naysmith, and then crashed a rising drive into the Everton net. The ecstatic midfielder reeled away in celebration, having scored his first-ever goal in a Merseyside derby, cupping his ear and sticking out his tongue in jest. It was a sweet moment for the lifelong Liverpool fan. A Michael Owen penalty and a superb John Arne Riise goal – his first for the Reds – capped a splendid afternoon for Gerard Houllier's side. The 3–1 victory signalled a welcome return to league form for both Liverpool and Gerrard, who had been so apologetic after his sending-off the week before, made up for that misdemeanour with a Man of the Match showing while throwing a classic goal into the bargain.

An old England legend appeared for Everton that day. Paul Gascoigne, the player who Gerrard had watched as a eagle-eyed ten-year-old during the 1990 World Cup, was one of the first to congratulate the lively new ornament on England's mantelpiece. In reflection of the twenty-one-year-old's characteristics, Gascoigne said in the *Independent*:

> He's bigger than I thought. He's got a great frame and scored a superb goal. He's like Michael Owen at the moment, oozing confidence. I'm proud

because he's English and so am I. It's good to see him giving his all for his country. I said to him: 'Enjoy every moment you get with England and do the right things that will make you play in every game,' which is what I still want to do myself. He's just twenty-one and things seem to be happening for him the way that they did for me. He is different class. I didn't make mistakes so Steven doesn't need to learn anything from me. Everything worked out for me. By twenty-three I was in the World Cup and by twenty-five I had a move to Italy. It was the injuries for me, and he has had some problems in that respect but, like me, he's determined to get back from them. I think we have the same background and mentality: football, football, football.

For all the similarities between 'Gazza' and 'Stevie G', Liverpool's hero still had to eradicate an unhealthy tag of ill discipline. His sending-off against Aston Villa had cast an untimely shadow over his irrepressible form on the pitch. With a suspension looming, Gerrard's favourite food of football was going to be off the menu for a short spell, but he still had time to contribute another commanding performance on Liverpool's return to the scene of their UEFA Cup triumph. Borussia Dortmund were considered the toughest of the Reds' opponents in the first group stage, but with the steel of Gerrard in their ranks, a creditable point was gained after a 0–0 draw in the Westfalenstadion.

Igor Biscan stepped into the void left by Gerrard's suspension as Liverpool beat Spurs 1–0 at Anfield thanks to

HEARTBREAK HIGH

a goal from Jari Litmanen. And the sprightly Finn was in goal-scoring mood again as Gerard Houllier's side registered their first Champions League win, a 1–0 triumph at home to Dynamo Kiev. Gerrard returned to Liverpool's midfield and it was his deflected free-kick which rattled a post and allowed Litmanen the opportunity to crash home his second goal of the week.

Gerard Houllier then had to make do without Gerrard and the injured duo of Michael Owen and Dietmar Hamann, but his side still managed to beat Newcastle 2–0 away from home before an international break that saw England qualify for the 2002 World Cup finals.

Greece, an unpredictable European side at the best of times, came to Old Trafford intent on blotting Sven-Goran Eriksson's copybook. The Greeks twice took the lead, either side of an equaliser from Teddy Sheringham, against a lacklustre England. How the home side needed its heroes to deliver. Step forward Gerrard to rally the fallen troops, and then David Beckham to curl home a fabulous free-kick at the game's death, levelling the contest and booking England's plane to Japan.

Before the game, Gerrard had made the headlines after an alleged late-night drinking binge while out with his then-girlfriend Jennifer Ellison in Southport. He admitted after the game at Old Trafford that the criticism he received that week made him realise exactly what he had to lose. He said:

Everything that has happened to me might act as a jolt. To be honest, I didn't really think I had done anything wrong. I went out for a meal with my girlfriend and friends and I wasn't drunk or anything like that. I would say the timing wasn't the best, but I don't think I was guilty of anything more than being a bit naive. These are the things that happen when you are a young player and you have to learn from them. I intend to do that, because the last few days haven't been nice. Until this week, I didn't realise how people will deliberately go out of their way to make trouble for you... People have talked about me in the same category as David Beckham and Michael Owen, which is nice – and I wouldn't have it any other way, because they are the best players in the country, so I have to start behaving like them.

The only player misbehaving at Anfield as Liverpool began their defence of the Worthington Cup was Grimsby's Phil Jevons. A lifelong Liverpool fan, dumped by the club as a youngster, he hit a superb 35-yard goal to send the Reds out of the competition. The misery of that night was compounded in very different circumstances when Liverpool hosted Leeds. Gerard Houllier, an astute manager, gentleman and mentor to his players, was taken to hospital after suffering chest pains at half-time. Phil Thompson oversaw Gerrard's return to Premiership action in Liverpool's 1–1 draw but, for once at least, football was not at the forefront of Anfield minds.

Thompson, charged with guiding Liverpool onwards in the absence of Houllier, who needed surgery for a hole in his heart, took the Reds to the Ukraine to face Dynamo Kiev in the Champions League. And who better than Gerrard, a player nurtured so admirably by Houllier, to rouse Liverpool into sending the perfect 'Get Well Soon' message back home. Playing alongside an in-form Danny

HEARTBREAK HIGH

Murphy, Gerrard supplied the cross from which his midfield partner scored, and then, after Kiev had levelled, won the game with his first-ever goal in Europe's premier competition. Patrick Berger sent in a cross from the left, Smicer nudged the ball on and Gerrard used his strength to beat off close attention and smash a low, deflected shot into the net with his weaker left foot. The England star sprinted to the bench in celebration, emphasising the true meaning of a goal that meant so much more than just Liverpool's first three points in the Champions League.

'Everyone was down in the mouth before the game,' admitted Gerrard. 'It's been a bad few days for us, but we'll dedicate that performance to the gaffer. Hopefully now he'll be on the up and will recover 100 per cent. It was a great team performance and a tremendous three points. Phil Thompson said before the game that if our defending was perfect, we'd win. And apart from their goal, it was. Danny finished his goal well and I'm delighted to get the winner. But the whole squad stuck together and it's down to all of them. It's not about individuals.'

Gerrard's desire to give Houllier yet more cheer was hampered by a sore hamstring that ended his involvement at half-time in Liverpool's 4–1 victory at Leicester – a game which saw Robbie Fowler bag a hat-trick and Jamie Redknapp make his first Premiership start in a year and a half. Gerrard was also left at home for treatment as Liverpool drew 1–1 with Boavista in Portugal the following Wednesday. He returned to set up a goal for Redknapp as Liverpool continued their good form with a 2–0 away victory at Charlton in front of a watching Sven-Goran Eriksson.

Four days later, Liverpool honoured Gerard Houllier in

the best possible way when they qualified for the second stage of the Champions League by beating Borussia Dortmund 2–0. Gerrard was forced off in the game after an lunge by Dortmund's Dede but, with his brawny frame now able to recover from any slight knock like never before, he was fully fit to face Manchester United at Anfield with Liverpool's title-winning credentials set to be examined under the microscope. A 3–1 victory over United, enough to stir the senses of even the most pessimistic of Liverpool followers, epitomised the sheer potential of the Reds' players, both individually and collectively.

Gerrard was sorely missed as England mustered a 1–1 draw with Sweden in a friendly – he was omitted as he was still suffering with a hamstring problem picked up during the game against Manchester United. He quickly recovered and that scorching ability to visualise and administer the perfect goal-inducing pass was demonstrated when he set up a Michael Owen headed goal in Liverpool's 1–1 draw at Blackburn Rovers.

Back-to-back 1–0 victories over Sunderland and Derby, plus a 2–0 victory against Middlesbrough, put them on top of the Premiership pile, but then an indifferent run of form prior to Christmas, a spell that included a 4–0 defeat at Chelsea and a home reverse to Arsenal, severely dented the Reds' title aspirations. Merseyside also said a fond farewell to Sander Westerveld and, most poignantly, to Robbie Fowler, who joined Leeds for £11 million. Former Arsenal striker Nicolas Anelka joined the ranks as the Reds brought the curtain down on a momentous year.

On New Year's Day 2002, Phil Thompson, still minding the side in Gerard Houllier's absence, named the Liverpool side for their home game with Bolton. Gerrard, who had

HEARTBREAK HIGH

endured an inconsistent run of form, was recalled having been on the bench for the Reds' previous game – a 1–1 draw at West Ham. The England star, with only three goals to his name in a Liverpool shirt so far that season, repaid Thompson's judgement with a typically determined performance and a goal. Michael Owen's neat pass teed him up and one divine touch saw him glide past a clutch of Bolton defenders, before he clipped the ball into the net with apparent ease. However, another former Liverpool academy pupil spoiled the Reds' day; Kevin Nolan equalised for Sam Allardyce's side late in the game.

Liverpool then put their wayward league form to one side to begin their defence of the FA Cup. Gerrard provided the pass that allowed Nicolas Anelka to score his first goal for the club in a 3–0 defeat of Birmingham in the third round. The Reds were not replicating such rampant scorelines in the Premiership, however, and a 2–0 defeat at Southampton illuminated such form. Gerrard, evergreen in Liverpool's troubled side, produced another defence-splitting pass for John Arne Riise to score in a 1–1 draw at Arsenal, before his problematic hamstring forced him off after just half an hour of a 1–1 draw with Southampton.

Gerrard recovered to produce his best performance of the season away to Manchester United. With Roy Keane such a menacing and overriding influence in United's midfield, Gerrard's inclusion was paramount to Liverpool's gameplan. And, more than a match for Keane, it was the Liverpool hero who imposed himself on the contest with all the power and expertise that envelops his game. He was booked after just 47 seconds of the match for a foul on Ryan Giggs, but later cut United down to size in style with a cleverly lofted pass for Danny Murphy to latch onto and lob Liverpool's stunning winner.

An encounter with Arsenal – a game that saw three players, including Liverpool's Jamie Carragher, sent off – then ended the Reds' challenge in the FA Cup. That 1–0 defeat did not hamper a return to league form, however, and despite Gerrard's absence with a neck injury, Liverpool beat Leicester 1–0 at Anfield to firmly revive their title hopes. A 4–0 victory over Leeds and a 6–0 hammering of Ipswich enhanced such hopes to an even greater degree as Gerrard and his colleagues continued their inspired form.

Gerrard received his ninth international cap as England began the countdown to the World Cup with a 1–1 draw with Holland in the Amsterdam Arena.

However, a groin injury, picked up in Liverpool's goalless draw at home to Galatasaray in the Champions League, ruled Gerrard out of an important spell in Liverpool's season as they continued their assault on the Premiership title. He spent three weeks on the sidelines and returned to France to see the French specialist in the hope of overcoming his latest injury setback.

He eventually returned to training at Melwood ahead of Liverpool's crucial Champions League second-phase match against Barcelona at the Nou Camp. With Michael Owen ruled out, Gerrard's fitness was vital for the trip to Spain. He passed a fitness test to start the match and played a key role in a 0–0 draw against the Catalan giants, although he did reassure all Reds' fans that he was human, with a couple of glaring misses that cost Liverpool all three points. Liverpool would have to beat Roma at Anfield in their final second-phase match to progress to the quarter-finals.

HEARTBREAK HIGH

Because of that forthcoming match, Gerrard was only used sparingly as a late substitute in Liverpool's 2–1 victory at Middlesbrough. Their task to beat Roma was made all the more unenviable by the absence of Michael Owen but, nevertheless, inspired by a return to Anfield for Gerard Houllier, who gazed from the stands, Liverpool prevailed. A rousing night – one of those Anfield occasions that are enough to make any football fan's neck hairs stand on end – saw Gerrard and his fellow warriors make their manager proud. 'Allez, allez Gerard Houllier,' was the chant that bellowed from the Kop. Inspired, Jari Litmanen converted an early penalty, Gerrard tackled abruptly and decisively all night long and Emile Heskey, Roma's chief tormentor in the game, eventually headed Liverpool's second. Roma had no answer – the Reds had made it through.

The joy of that remarkable night was short-lived for Gerrard. He was forced to limp out of Liverpool's crucial home Premiership match with Chelsea after just 28 minutes. The injury meant that he also had to withdraw from the England squad preparing for a friendly with Italy at Elland Road. The twenty-one-year-old cut a forlorn figure as he left the field in a game that Liverpool won 1–0 to move back to the top of the Premiership. Having only just recovered from three weeks on the sidelines, another injury set-back already placed question marks over his involvement in the World Cup, which was now only a couple of months away.

Phil Thompson, who was still in charge of Liverpool team affairs, speculated on Gerrard's impending absence.

'Steven felt some discomfort in his groin again,' said Thompson. 'He will be having a scan and we should have a clearer picture. It's looking like he could be out for between ten days and a fortnight.' And ten days is exactly the amount of time that Gerrard spent recuperating, missing only England's 2–1 defeat to Italy and Liverpool's 2–0 victory over Charlton.

The Champions League remained an appetising prospect, and Gerrard returned for Liverpool's quarter-final first leg at home to Bayer Leverkusen. By virtue of a goal from defender Sami Hyypia and a typically dynamic performance from Gerrard, Liverpool beat the Germans 1–0. Sadly for the Reds, a 4–2 defeat in the return leg a week later curtailed their Champions League dream.

With Gerard Houllier now back in command of his Liverpool side having recovered from his illness, the Reds put their European misery behind them with a 1–0 victory over Sunderland at the Stadium of Light – yet another game that emphasised how Gerrard had made the ball his disciple. One characteristically effective pass, a quite stunning 70-yard incision demanded better from Michael Owen, but Sunderland's downfall was settled when the pair combined again in the second half. Gerrard slipped another ball through to Owen, who elegantly chipped the ball past Thomas Sorensen.

'It was a great ball,' said Owen, in reflection of Gerrard's magnificent assist. 'He's great at those types of passes, and when I saw the 'keeper, there was not a lot else I could do.'

The pair were both selected for England's friendly with Paraguay at Anfield – with Owen set to captain the Three Lions in the absence of David Beckham. And Gerrard, playing on the right flank, supplied another precision ball for Owen to head home England's first goal. The twenty-one-year-old, England's catalyst and Man of the Match, did much to suggest that he was setting a standard for which he would always adhere to in an England shirt. For both country and club, Gerrard's prospects looked extremely good.

Michael Owen, in an equally rich vein of form, was at the double when Liverpool defeated Derby 2–0 at Anfield to complete their seventh-consecutive win in the Premiership. However, almost inevitably, Gerrard's absence from the Reds' away game at Tottenham spelt the end for their title-winning aspirations. The kingpin of Liverpool's team was crossed off the teamsheet, suffering again from a sore groin. Sven-Goran Eriksson, at White Hart Lane to run the rule over a player who he believed could make all the difference in the World Cup, could only watch on ashen-faced as Spurs ran out 1–0 victors thanks to Gustavo Poyet's goal.

Gerrard returned to action as Liverpool beat Blackburn Rovers 4–3 on a balmy midweek Anfield evening. Sven-Goran Eriksson was in attendance again, watching Gerrard come through 90 thrilling, bruising minutes unscathed. A day later, the twenty-one-year-old was named in Eriksson's twenty-three-man squad for the World Cup in Japan.

Liverpool's final game of the season, at home to Ipswich, the team who had been on the end of a 6–0 hiding from the Reds earlier in the season, was set as a celebration of Liverpool's progress – a win would ensure that they finished in their highest-ever position since the inauguration of the Premiership. Gary McAllister, such an integral part of the Reds' rise and, of course, the growth in stature of Gerrard, bade a fond farewell following his final outing before taking charge of Coventry City and Gerard Houllier also waved a message of thanks to the fans on an emotional lap of honour.

STEVEN GERRARD: PORTRAIT OF A HERO

The French manager had endured a tumultuous season on a personal level, but his fighting spirit, as ever, had rubbed off on the players and, even if they had missed out on the title to Arsenal, they had done their manager proud. 'Stevie G', as he was now affectionately nicknamed by Liverpool's adoring fans, had epitomised such fortitude. At the post-match conference, Houllier said:

> When you take into account the trials and tribulations of this club, losing Babbel, Berger and Barmby and then my illness, plus the fact that I had to change a goalkeeper, I think that in such adversity our performances have been remarkable. And we managed to finish second with eighty points; it's excellent, it's the same amount of points that won the title for Manchester United last term... we had to overcome so much and the fact that we were still in a position to compete for the title up to a few days from the end of the season was to our great credit.

Gerrard's undoubted contribution to that feat was, so painfully, about to end in ultimate heartbreak.

Gerrard lasted for only 33 minutes of Liverpool's 5–0 victory over Ipswich that cemented them in second place behind the champions, Arsenal. He limped down the tunnel in obvious discomfort, immediately raising serious doubts over his condition for the trip to Japan. England were due to fly out to Dubai for a pre-tournament get-together, but Liverpool's physio, Mark Waller, a man who knew about the behaviour of Gerrard's muscles more than most, remained optimistic that the midfielder would still be able to go.

HEARTBREAK HIGH

'Steven felt some tightness at the top of his right thigh rather than in the groin itself. At this stage, I think he will be all right for Dubai,' said Waller.

Gerard Houllier did not share such optimism. When asked if Gerrard would go to the World Cup, he answered: 'I wish it for him, but I am sure his mind is more on next season than the World Cup. I will give Sven my advice if he wants it, but they should be able to sort out Steven's problem in Dubai. It's the same injury as before. The players are no longer mine now, they are Sven's; it's up to him what he does. We were mindful of the players going to the World Cup. We told them to tell us if they felt anything, any twinges, and we would get them straight off. That's what we did, because there was no way that we would be taking any risks.'

Houllier admitted that did not want to rest any players, such was the importance of the game against Ipswich, but he refused to admit that Gerrard's inclusion was too much of a risk. 'Had we not had anything to play for, I would probably have played a different team and would have rested some players, with Stevie most likely not involved,' he continued. 'But the fact that we had to put out our best side meant he had to play and he wanted to play. He pulled out after 33 minutes, but if he'd gone with England he would have had to pull out after the first game, and you can imagine the consequences of that. It would have been a real setback. This way at least Sven can plan without him and we know we can sort the problem out so he can start the season sharp in July.'

Houllier also suggested that Gerrard's injury may act as a blessing in disguise. An operation on Stephane Henchoz's similar injury had cured the defender's reoccurring problem and the Liverpool manager believed that the same could be done for his crocked midfield star. He continued:

> Surgery could clear it up once and for all. Usually when you have a groin problem sorted, it's sorted for life. Stephane Henchoz had an even bigger problem when he came here and he's not looked back. Steve will have two months before the players come back for pre-season to rest it, but that is why, if he needs it, we need to do it very, very quickly – this week.

Steven would have preferred to go to the World Cup; he is sick about what has happened, but he is more concerned about his career and his participation with Liverpool.

The news of Gerrard's injury lay-off left England's head coach crestfallen: 'If Steven doesn't need an operation we will have to know how big the chances are that he won't break down after 30 minutes and be out for a couple of weeks,' said Eriksson, clearly fearing the worst for his midfield talisman. 'It would be a gamble to take him. Liverpool have been worried since February... I spoke to Steven and he's very down. The best thing now is that he sees the surgeon... I don't know how much it damages our chances.'

Eriksson and England waited with bated breath while Gerrard travelled to Belgium to meet muscular specialist Dr Mark Martens to learn his fate. One scan was all the doctor needed to tell the Liverpool hero, on the eve of his twenty-second birthday, that his World Cup dream was over. Immediate surgery was required, as was suspected.

'In the short term it is a big blow, but I realise I would

HEARTBREAK HIGH

have been unable to do myself or the team justice in Japan,' admitted Gerrard. 'The rehabilitation period for this type of operation is six weeks, so my target now is to be fit for the start of next season. I'm confident surgery will cure the problem, so I shall be available for other big tournaments in the future.'

With that, a player who had never experienced defeat in an England shirt was forced to stay at home, toast the beginning of the twenty-third year of his life, and watch England on television as they reached out for glory in Japan. He was pictured sporting a pair of England shorts while on holiday in Dubai with his girlfriend of the time, Jennifer Ellison, while keeping in regular contact with the squad.

'I became a fan when I realised I wasn't going to the World Cup,' Gerrard later told the *News of the World*. 'I knew I had to support the lads. I watched the Argentina game in a bar with Phil Thompson. I kicked every ball and made every tackle. It was so frustrating. I hate watching football when I'm injured, but they are games that you can't miss and it was so nice to see the lads beat Argentina.'

After beating Argentina 1–0 in the group stage, the Three Lions motored to the quarter-finals before being cruelly knocked from their pedestal by Brazil. Ironically, it was Gerrard's replacement in midfield, Nicky Butt, who received the majority of plaudits during the competition. Sven-Goran Eriksson's reign was alive and kicking – it would not be long before Gerrard was back kicking and screaming for a place in the Swede's revolution.

Chapter Eight
Tough at the Kop

The torture of having to miss the World Cup was made less painful for Gerrard in the knowledge that his groin injury would be cured once and for all. And, having gone under the surgeon's knife at the earliest possible opportunity, he was able to recuperate sufficiently to be able to take part in pre-season training at Melwood on 10 July. On his return, the midfielder broke his silence to reveal to the *News of the World* that he could have played in the World Cup.

> I could have definitely decided to have the surgery after the World Cup. I could still have gone and played, but I wasn't confident that I could play in the three games in such a short space of time. I wasn't confident that I could do the job I wanted to do... I know I could have been very selfish – and, I tell you, I wanted to go so badly – but I had to think about

Liverpool and England. I had to be honest; I knew it would have been the wrong decision. I had built myself up so much for this World Cup. To think I wasn't going was a massive blow.

Even when I came off in Liverpool's last game, I still thought I would go to the World Cup. But I knew in the back of my mind that the problem was happening regularly and that it was getting worse and worse. The club told England that I was going to see a surgeon on the Monday and he told them I needed surgery. He advised me to have it done as soon as possible. I asked him when and he said: 'Wednesday.' And so that was it; in two days I had the operation. That was when it hit me. When I walked out after seeing the surgeon, that's when I knew I definitely wasn't going to the World Cup.

Gerrard had received a special commendation from Brazilian legend Pele, who claimed that the Liverpool star was the best player not to be taking part in the World Cup. 'It was nice to read the things Pele said about me, but it would have been better if he had come out and talked about Nicky Butt's performances, because I thought he was magnificent,' said Gerrard, modestly. 'He came in and did my job very well. It would have been better to praise him, not talk about me.'

Gerrard made his playing comeback with a 45-minute run-out in Liverpool's first warm-up game against Le Havre and admitted that it was a relief to be able to play again: 'Thanks to missing the World Cup, I'm steaming for a game of football again.'

Liverpool had been busy in the transfer market as they

sought to build on their progress over the previous two seasons. Gerard Houllier acquired the services of Milan Baros, the Czech striker, and El Hadji Diouf and Salif Diao, who had impressed while playing for Senegal in the World Cup. A batch of young European starlets were also invited to join the Reds as they set about winning more silverware. Jamie Redknapp departed for Spurs, having seen his first-team chances diminish in Gerrard's shadow. Nick Barmby and Jari Litmanen also left Gerard Houllier's team.

Gerrard renewed acquaintances with Patrick Vieira as Liverpool began the new season in Cardiff against Arsenal in the renamed Community Shield. The Liverpool midfielder announced his return to action by letting out a little pent-up frustration after his injury absence.

'Reckless, dangerous and deserving of a red card,' claimed Arsenal manager Arsene Wenger in reference to a tackle by Gerrard on Vieira as early as the sixth minute. Such was Gerrard's tenacity in the challenge that the yellow card he received seemed like a let-off and he could well have seen red after clattering Thierry Henry to the floor moments later. Arsenal won the game 1–0 thanks to a goal from their new signing Gilberto Silva.

Gerrard, at least, if he hadn't been able to rescue the Reds in Cardiff, had proved his fitness with a vigorous road test of his groin.

'Steven hadn't played a full game before today, but I'm looking forward to having the real Steven Gerrard back before long,' said Gerard Houllier. 'Maybe we'll have to give him a rest now and then. I believe his problems are behind him now, and that is good news for us because he is so influential.'

Fit and raring to go, Liverpool opened the new

STEVEN GERRARD: PORTRAIT OF A HERO

Premiership season with a 1–0 victory at Aston Villa. Gerrard was back to his effervescent best: contributing a Man of the Match performance and winning a penalty that Michael Owen missed, before John Arne Riise scored the game's only goal.

The *Birmingham Post*'s match report, written by Hyder Jawad, read, endearingly: 'The mere sight of Gerrard is enough to make supporters of the opposition want to call the police.' That was after the England midfielder had shown England exactly what they had been robbed of in the World Cup. Gerrard had managed Liverpool's midfield with awesome guile and intelligence, both in a defensive capacity and in attack – Villa had no answer. In hindsight, this was the real 'Stevie G' – there were no more inhibitions about his fitness – he had finally been released from the chastising chains of injury. Now he could unleash himself on the Premiership like never before, and Liverpool would be the sole beneficiaries.

Liverpool continued their positive start to the season and Gerrard gained the opportunity to pull on an England shirt again, at least for 45 minutes, in the Three Lions' 1–1 draw in a friendly against Portugal at Villa Park. Days later, his good form was rewarded with his first goal of the new season.

Gerrard had not enjoyed the greatest of luck in front of goal the previous year, having found the net on just three occasions in the Premiership. He sought a change in such fortune, and he got it as Liverpool hosted Birmingham in their fifth league game of the season. Already a goal ahead thanks to Danny Murphy, Gerrard scampered onto a pass from El Hadji Diouf at the beginning of the second half; he shot straight at Birmingham's goalkeeper Nico Vaesen, but the ball squeezed into the net. The Reds may have squandered their two-goal lead to draw 2–2, but they were back to winning ways at Bolton, with Gerrard setting up new signing Milan Baros with a delicious right-wing cross during a 3–2 victory at the Reebok Stadium.

That result ignited a run of seven successive league victories for Gerrard Houllier's men – a run where Gerrard was irrepressible. He clocked up 150 appearances for Liverpool as they strolled past West Brom, Manchester City and then Chelsea, with ease: a 1–0 victory over the London side affirmed the Reds' title challenge.

Having healed the wounds of missing out on the World Cup, Gerrard remained adamant that he could become an even better player following his performance against Chelsea. He said, in the *Daily Star*:

I've been steady this season – I've still got a couple of gears to move up to. I was poor against Chelsea last Sunday. Hopefully, I can put that behind me. It was just one of those games, because I've been quite consistent this season. Against Chelsea, though, I was blowing hot and cold. My passing wasn't right. I'm my own worst critic, but I was trying too hard to get Michael [Owen] through. Part of my game is to get assists if I'm not on the scoresheet myself.

Gerrard had been the guiding light in Michael Owen's hour of need. The England striker had endured some unfair criticism in the midst of a goal drought, but that emphatically came to an end when he hit a hat-trick at Manchester City.

STEVEN GERRARD: PORTRAIT OF A HERO

'Michael needed a goal recently and I was trying to help him,' said Gerrard. 'He eventually scored a hat-trick at Manchester City and I got him two assists.'

The two assists were characteristic of the relationship the two England players shared on the field – a near-telepathic one – and it could only be a good sign for the future of both England and Liverpool.

Gerrard was typically diligent as he returned to competitive action for England in their opening Euro 2004 qualifier away to Slovakia. Back alongside Paul Scholes in the centre of midfield, he received a yellow card for his efforts, but helped Sven-Goran Eriksson's side to a 2–1 victory, nonetheless. 'Now, I want to get back to playing for England on a regular basis,' said Gerrard. 'I've played every game this season for Liverpool and I'm 100 per cent happy with the state of my fitness.'

He was at the pinnacle of England's attack four days later, with Macedonia the opponents at Southampton's St Mary's Stadium. The supposed European minnows proved more than a match for the Three Lions, though, taking the lead twice either side of a goal from David Beckham. Gerrard admitted responsibility, after giving the ball away for Macedonia's second goal, but he recovered to net his second international goal to make the score 2–2. In the 35th minute, he coolly chested down a clearance following a David Beckham corner and volleyed the ball without hesitation mercilessly inside the goalkeeper's right-hand post. His joy of scoring that goal was short-lived, however – he overstretched for a ball in the second half and left the field on a stretcher close to tears, raising fears that the injury demons had returned to haunt him yet again.

Medical staff at Melwood revealed that Gerrard had

suffered only a minor injury to his hip; one that would rule him out of action for no more than a week.

'It's not too bad; I think it is just bruising on the hip; it's certainly not as bad as we first thought,' said Gerrard, reassuringly. 'I got the knock in a challenge before the incident when I went down. I think I got a knee or a kick on the hip, and when I went down later, I just couldn't go on. We'll just have to wait and see how it is now.'

Gerrard's set-back was a major blow for Liverpool. Their Champions League campaign had not begun well and, as well as missing a 1–0 win at Leeds in the Premiership, the twenty-two-year-old star had to sit out the Reds' crucial European encounter with Spartak Moscow. Forced to remain at home, Gerrard was pictured looking pensive while out shopping in Manchester with his new girlfriend, Alex Curran. Liverpool, meanwhile, overcame his absence to win 2–1 in Russia.

After ten days' recuperation, he returned to action on the right side of midfield in Liverpool's home game with Tottenham. His performance, as Liverpool won 2–1 to remain in a lofty position at the top of the Premiership, wilted somewhat, and he was replaced in the second half by Vladimir Smicer. Four days later, Gerrard offered little of his normally ruthless form once again, while Liverpool were dealt a critical Champions League blow when they lost 1–0 at home to Valencia.

The midfielder's dip in form was a worry for all concerned; no longer was he a permanent fixture on the field as Gerard Houllier got tough. Gerrard admitted that the injury he had suffered playing for England hadn't helped.

'I thought I started the season off well,' he said. 'I was pleased with how I did, but the injury with England has set me back. I missed ten days' training and only did a couple of sessions before the Tottenham game. It has been a bit up and down recently.

'I think I took a lot from the Valencia game personally. You have to use games like that as a chance to learn. Then it will stand you in good stead. I thought Valencia were brilliant and when they were not in possession they worked so hard to stop us playing it was untrue. I think that is the lesson I learnt.'

Gerrard was dropped from Liverpool's starting XI for a home game with West Ham, a game that the Reds won 2-0, but he was back in the side as Liverpool began their League Cup campaign with a 3-1 home win against Southampton. The Reds' first league defeat of the season followed – a 1-0 defeat at Middlesbrough – and it was the start of a miserable week for Gerrard Houllier's side.

Gerrard endured one of the worst nights of his professional career when Liverpool met FC Basel in their final match in the Champions League first group phase. They had to win the match to qualify for the second phase, but found themselves 3-0 down after just 29 minutes in Switzerland. Gerrard, having been disadvantaged by some tactical benevolence, was substituted at half-time and was replaced by Salif Diao. Liverpool managed to pull the score back to 3-3 to threaten an unlikely comeback, but the crucial winning goal proved illusive and the Reds were dumped out of the Champions League with only a place in the UEFA Cup as consolation.

Houllier was forced to count the cost of the demoralising exit and in a press conference singled out Gerrard for criticism with a very public show of disappointment.

TOUGH AT THE KOP

He's having a terrible time. I have stuck by him, but he just wasn't good enough against Basel. He's been going through a difficult period; he's got problems with confidence and has been down after his England displays. After his injuries, he has not got back to his best.

He has had a couple of games to show his worth, but it hasn't worked out his way. I'm impatient and I don't like to wait... Players need managers when they are going through a difficult period. He cannot say I have not been supportive. Stevie can't say he's tired, because he didn't go to the World Cup. We've helped him as much as we could. He got injured for England, then the team won very efficiently without him in Spartak Moscow and Leeds, but then we brought him back... we are missing the good Steven Gerrard at the moment.

Worse was to come for the under-fire twenty-two-year-old. With criticism emanating from all directions, Houllier continued his shock tactics in trying to instil a resurgence of form by dropping Gerrard completely from Liverpool's home league game with Sunderland. A goalless draw against the lowly Wearsiders did little to lift the gloom over Anfield. Gerrard could only watch on from the bench as the Reds wasted countless chances and began a run of results that would shock even the most hardened of Kopites.

Michael Owen, who had tolerated similar condemnation and lack of form earlier in the season, rallied in support of his downbeat friend.

I'm sure if you asked him, Stevie would say he'd much prefer to be a great player taking a bit of stick than an

> average player who no one ever notices or comments on. The reason he's getting so much attention is because his standards are so high.... I've told him that he will do something in one of the next games, like a great pass or a brilliant shot, and that everything will come back. He'll go on from there and everyone will forget what's happening now. I know from experience when things aren't going well, you think of nothing else but your form all night and day. But I don't think anyone would be daft enough to write off Steven Gerrard. It's just a matter of time before he is back to his best.

Publically, Sven-Goran Eriksson also made Gerrard aware of his support.

> Was I surprised by Gerard Houllier's comments? Well, maybe yes, because normally Houllier is a very diplomatic man from what I can understand. So, maybe, yes, I was surprised. But I am sure as well that he is a very intelligent man so, before doing it, I'm sure he has thought a lot about it. I guess he tried to achieve something important by doing it.
>
> When you are judging Steven Gerrard, you are always expecting great, great things. That's a problem for those big players and if they are not always among the best on the pitch then people are surprised... I don't want to interfere between Houllier and Steven Gerrard, absolutely not... I am not worried, because I know that Steven Gerrard will play good football again, extremely good football.

TOUGH AT THE KOP

Gerard Houllier marked a noticeable improvement in training, and Gerrard returned as a half-time substitute in the Reds' game away to Fulham, but he could not arrest another slide as Liverpool lost 3–2 at Loftus Road. 'His work-rate, his success rate in tackles, runs and passing has been much higher in training recently,' admitted Houllier. 'There were a few things he knew he had to improve on, but he's only twenty-two; you have to be indulgent with some players. Like us, he went through a bad patch, but he's fine. I'm pleased with him and the good Steven Gerrard is back. We missed him and we are happy that he is back.'

Gerrard ended his exile from the Liverpool side in their UEFA Cup third-round tie away to Vitesse Arnhem. Obviously refreshed and clear of the cobwebs that had held him back, Gerrard helped create the only goal of the game, combining with Milan Baros to set up Michael Owen.

'Steve has climbed the first step on his return – and that can be the most difficult,' enthused Gerard Houllier, having seen his prize asset make his mark again. 'But there is another flight of stairs ahead. This was his best performance since he was on England duty nearly two months ago. I told him that if he kept working and his attitude was right, it would all come back naturally. There was no need to force it, and gradually he is coming back to his best. Steven trusts me and maybe my comments woke him up a bit.'

Gerrard had clearly taken heed of his manager's paternal, father-like comments. Back to his best in Arnhem, a further test lay in wait as Manchester United visited Anfield. A brace of errors from Jerzy Dudek afforded United, and two-goal Diego Forlan, a 2–1 victory, to expose Liverpool's dreadful form further.

Gerrard was then given the honour of captaining the side for the first time in his career as the Reds sought solace from their defeat in the League Cup against Ipswich. They could only muster a 1–1 draw in the fourth round at Anfield and the resultant penalty shoot-out saw Gerrard taking part in the first such lottery of his professional career, score Liverpool's first as they scraped through 5–4 on spot-kicks.

That result failed to signal an upturn in league fortunes, however, and Liverpool lost games to Charlton and then to Sunderland either side of seeing off Vitesse in the UEFA Cup. The League Cup was already looking like Liverpool's best possible chance of domestic silverware and a trip to Aston Villa in the fifth round of the competition would signal one of their most interesting matches of the season. And Gerrard proved, at least, the theory that form is temporary, whereas class is permanent.

Due to a ticketing problem, kick-off at Villa Park was delayed until 9pm and Liverpool and Gerrard caught their opponents taking an after-the-watershed nap. Brimming with confidence and zest, Gerrard helped the Reds as they recovered from going behind to race into a 3–1 lead. He himself hit the third goal – neatly tucking the ball home after an expert cross from Milan Baros – to notch up his second goal of the season. Villa fought back to level the scores but, desperately late in the game, Gerrard came to Liverpool's rescue. He beat Villa's J'Lloyd Samuel with a sumptuous burst of pace and cut the ball back coolly for Danny Murphy to pick his spot and hit the winner.

'Stevie showed we need players like that,' the *Liverpool Echo* reported from a relieved Gerard Houllier after the game, clearly delighted that the twenty-two-year-old had

TOUGH AT THE KOP

responded positively to his criticism. 'Against Villa last night he was absolutely brilliant. He had a shaky first part of the game, but once we were in the game he showed some quality. Stevie epitomised the spirit of the team. He was captain against Ipswich and his performance and energy transmitted to every player at the club.'

Assistant manager Phil Thompson shared his manager's upbeat mood in acclaiming Gerrard's return to form. 'The lad is back to his best... All the other players respond to him and when he's in full flow he can be quite frightening,' he said in the *Observer*.

Gerrard was frightening in a different way in the first Merseyside derby of the season at Anfield. Having had copious amounts of bad press and having been castigated by his manager, all Gerrard needed to do to incite further problems was to jump into a tackle with little consideration for an opponent. That's exactly what he did – providing the biggest talking point after a fractious, goalless battle with Everton.

'I want to apologise for the tackle,' said Gerrard, after he had launched into a challenge on Gary Naysmith. 'I have gone in with two feet and my studs showing, but I did try and pull back. I would never go out to hurt an opponent deliberately. I apologised to Naysmith on the pitch and when we shook hands afterwards. He has accepted the apology. We will have to see if there is action from the FA... I am glad for him that I haven't hurt him and he has been able to carry on.'

Extraordinarily, Gerrard's X-rated tackle that left Naysmith writhing on the floor in agony, was not deemed a red-card offence – not even bookable – by referee Graham Poll. Despite the heartfelt apology, the midfielder faced up to the prospect of FA action after the most ignominious act of his short career – a tackle that had undoubtedly tarnished his gleaming reputation.

He was forced to wait until after Christmas to learn his fate, with a fine and a three-match suspension the most likely punishment. Gerrard duly received stark warning in regard to his on-the-field conduct from many of his fellow professionals. Former Liverpool defender Neil Ruddock, a player who donned a 'hardman' image throughout his career, warned Gerrard not to let the incident overshadow his glittering career. The former Liverpool man told the press:

> There is absolutely no need for Gerrard to play the hard nut, as he is one of the most naturally talented players I have come across. If he carries on like that, it could not only harm his club career but also his prospects at international level. One of the hardest things professional footballers have to learn is self-control.
>
> Any kind of weakness is ruthlessly exploited – opposing players will wind you up, hoping they can get a reaction that earns a booking or a red card. Some managers will tell you to get under an opponent's skin because 'he is a volcano waiting to happen'.
>
> Even when he was fourteen, you could see that Steven had that extra special quality. Agents were ringing me up every day asking me how good he was and I'd tell them the truth – absolutely brilliant.

Liverpool's predicament refused to get any easier. A 1–1 draw at home to Blackburn Rovers on Boxing Day extended their games-without-a-win record to eight in the Premiership – equalling a record set in 1953. That

TOUGH AT THE KOP

dishonour was extended in their final game of 2002 – a 1–1 draw with Arsenal.

Gerrard was still standing out as Liverpool's finest asset, yet he was glad to bring the curtain down on the most turbulent twelve months of his career. The uproar over his tackle in the Merseyside derby, missing the World Cup, plus a well-publicised dip in form, not to mention his injury problems, will always mean that 2002 will be a year that Gerrard will never look back on with the fondest of memories. At a press conference he admitted:

> There have been highs in 2002, but I will be happy to see the back of the low times and, hopefully, 2003 will be a good one. I don't want to look back on it and say it has been a complete disaster, because I have had good times. But it has been up and down and I have had the worst experience of my career this year. Those are the things that make you stronger, though. I don't think anybody's career has all been about the high points. It is just important that you learn from them.
>
> In the last four or five games I think my form has been a lot better. I am happier and am enjoying playing again. When you are playing badly and things aren't going well, your attitude changes and you are not yourself. You are miserable. That had to stop... My confidence was the lowest it has ever been and I needed to get out of it as quickly as possible. Those are the times when you need the staff here at Liverpool behind you, and your family and friends.

In the *Express*, Gerrard also praised his manager for giving him the impetus to overcome his poor form with a public rebuke. 'I think the stuff the manager said was the turning point,' he said. 'I had had a lot of meetings with him where he gave me a pat on the back and tried to give me a helping hand and it never worked, because I still wasn't doing it. So it got to the point where I needed a rocket.'

That rocket remained where it hurt as Gerrard began the New Year in a Liverpool side not showing any signs of reversing their awful run of results. A 1–0 defeat at Newcastle was only cushioned by a 1–0 victory over Manchester City in the third round of the FA Cup.

Gerrard did little to alleviate his 'bad boy' reputation when he was booked for a careless tackle on Newcastle's Olivier Bernard at St James' Park and, as expected, the twenty-two-year-old England star was charged with violent conduct by the FA for, as it was now regarded, 'that' tackle on Gary Naysmith in the Merseyside derby. With Dietmar Hamann out injured, Liverpool had more than one reason not to want Gerrard to serve a suspension. The club requested a personal hearing and the midfielder also enlisted the help of the Professional Footballers' Association in search of leniency. The hearing was called for 3 February, which gave Gerrard the chance to help Liverpool back to Cardiff for the League Cup final. The Reds overturned a 2–1 first-leg deficit against Sheffield United in the semi-final – winning 2–0 at Anfield – to set up a mouth-watering showpiece against Manchester United.

Gerrard was slowly rediscovering his old form with a series of impeccable displays. Before Liverpool's League Cup dual with Sheffield United, he had orchestrated the Reds' first Premiership victory in twelve games – a 1–0 victory at Southampton. Whatever the suspension looming over him, it was clear that his services would be severely missed.

TOUGH AT THE KOP

The unifying bond between Gerrard and the Liverpool coaching staff, and the gratitude that the midfielder had for them having nurtured him through a difficult career learning curve, was illustrated when Liverpool travelled to West Ham on the eve of the FA hearing. With his team already a goal ahead thanks to Milan Baros, Gerrard capitalised on a weak punch by former Liverpool goalkeeper David James to drive home his third goal of the season. His celebrations took him into the lap of the Liverpool dug-out, where he received the adulation he deserved for putting his Christmas misery behind him. Emile Heskey also scored at Upton Park, and the 3–0 away victory afforded the red half of Merseyside at least a glimmer of a smile.

Bolton's Reebok Stadium was the venue for Gerrard's belated FA hearing. As feared, after three hours of deliberation, the twenty-two-year-old was found guilty of violent conduct and handed an immediate three-match ban, which would also include an England friendly match against Australia. Unusually, Gerrard was not issued with a fine by the three-man panel that delivered the verdict but, nevertheless, Gerard Houllier, who had accompanied his young star to the hearing, was left incensed.

'I am very disappointed,' the Liverpool manager fumed. 'If I had the slightest hint that he was guilty, I wouldn't have come here to defend him. It was a mistimed tackle. There was no malicious intent. It was a collision. That's all. It was an accident and these things happen in football. It wasn't malicious and even David Moyes admitted that. He has been playing well, so this is a blow to us, but we won't let this sort of thing destroy us.'

Houllier was also left angered after FA officials asked him

to allow Gerrard's ban to be delayed to ensure that the midfielder would miss the League Cup final, but meaning that he could play in England's friendly against the Aussies. FA rules meant that Gerrard could not be considered for international selection while in the midst of a domestic suspension – hence their request. The Frenchman, naturally, refused.

Regardless of Houllier's dismay, the consensus remained that Gerrard would, at the very least, emerge as a better footballer and put his disciplinary problems behind him. Fortunately for the twenty-two-year-old, Liverpool's goalless draw with Crystal Palace at Selhurst Park in the FA Cup fourth round meant that he would be available to play in the Worthington Cup final. Having feared that he would have to miss the Cardiff climax, he sat out Liverpool's FA Cup replay against the First Division side instead and his non-appearance told: although the Reds were dumped out after losing 2–0 at Anfield.

Gerrard also sat out Liverpool's draw at Middlesbrough and a 2–1 defeat away to Birmingham, but did feature in both legs as Liverpool beat Auxerre 3–0 on aggregate to reach the quarter-finals of the UEFA Cup. And with fortunes on the up for Gerard Houllier's side, despite their premature exit from the FA Cup, there seemed like no better time for them to grapple with Manchester United for a piece of silverware that they were no strangers to.

Back from his domestic banishment, Gerrard, Liverpool's re-born all-action hero, locked horns with Roy Keane. Dynamic, sprightly and industrious, Gerrard rocked United with a performance that exuded class. He scored Liverpool's opening goal, seven minutes before half-time, taking a John Arne Riise pass in his stride before – from a

TOUGH AT THE KOP

slightly acute angle – he unleashed a 25-yard effort at Fabien Bathez's goal. The ball deflected off David Beckham's boot to deceive the French stopper, but the shot's sheer pace took it into the net. Gerrard could have added to his Cardiff tally had Barthez not been on his guard on more than one occasion. However, United's resistance proved futile as Michael Owen burst through to make it 2–0 in the second half and send the Worthington Cup back to Anfield.

The post-match celebrations displayed a mixture of unbridled joy and relief from Gerard Houllier's men, who had overcome a terrible few months of bad press and poor results. Gerrard, himself tormented by such woes, celebrated as if the weight of the world had been lifted from his shoulders, spraying champagne around furiously and bellowing the words to 'You'll Never Walk Alone' in tandem with the Liverpool fans. Never in his career, despite past glories, had a result tasted sweeter. At last, the twenty-two-year-old, upon having helped his side to beat arch-rivals Manchester United so convincingly, could now look to the future and lay to rest the demons of discipline and the injury that had cruelly interrupted his career.

With the League Cup encased in Liverpool's busy trophy cabinet, the remaining priority rested with the UEFA Cup, where the Reds were all set to face Celtic in a Battle of Britain extravaganza. A 2–0 Premiership victory at home to Bolton warmed Anfield gloves ahead of the showdown that began at Celtic Park. It was already widespread knowledge that if Gerrard played well, so did Liverpool, and that theory was exemplified again as the young hero guided his side to a precious 1–1 draw north of the border to hand the Reds a marginal advantage in the tie; Emile Heskey thumped home Liverpool's crucial away goal.

Back in the Premiership, tides were also turning as Gerrard turned on his customary style and flair. Under the gaze of Sven-Goran Eriksson, Liverpool recovered from going a goal behind to Tottenham to win by virtue of another Gerrard wonder show – a special one at that. He provided the cross that allowed Michael Owen to gobble up an equaliser; scampered into the box with his energetic aplomb to clip in another cross for Emile Heskey to nod home; and then latched onto a Danny Murphy pass and dispatched a stunning 20-yard shot past Kasey Keller to register his fifth goal of the season. Spurs pulled a goal back to make it 3–2, but it was scant response to Gerrard's marvellous heroics.

That excellent display drained the midfielder's apparently limitless fuel tank somewhat, and he was at odds with his form as Liverpool surrendered their place in the UEFA Cup, beaten 2–0 at home by Celtic in the second leg of the Battle of Britain.

All that remained for Liverpool was to ensure a return to the Champions League the following season. It was a tall order for Gerard Houllier's side, given the disparaging run of form that had dogged them at the turn of the year. However, with Gerrard finding a rich vein of form, in theory nothing was beyond them, and their laudable midfield star was on the scoresheet again against Leeds United at Anfield. With Liverpool 2–1 up and heading for a vital win, Gerrard volleyed home with extraordinary technique and precision after some neat enterprise from Michael Owen. Following the wonder strike, he was rightfully named Barclaycard Player of the Month for March.

TOUGH AT THE KOP

Sven-Goran Eriksson had been mightily impressed by Gerrard's return to prominence and included him in his squad for two European Championship qualifiers against Liechtenstein and Turkey. Gerrard was keen to put his good form to the test at international level, as he felt as though he was still to display his rampant Liverpool demeanour in an England shirt, despite being undefeated as a Three Lions star. As he joined up with the England squad in St Gallen, Gerrard said:

> Now it is time for me to stamp my authority on England. I have an unbeaten record for my country, but there have been a number of games when I have not played at my best. I feel so much more confident now, and it is great to hear the England manager say that, together with Paul Scholes and David Beckham, I am one of his main midfielders. But now I know I have to perform, because I was not at my best for the Slovakia and Macedonia games.
>
> It was difficult to put my finger on one thing as to why I was playing badly. Partly I was trying too hard and maybe not working hard enough in training. I just concentrated on getting my passing right again and going back to basics and, in the last six weeks, I feel that it has been working.

Gerrard also admitted that his role for England differed greatly from his Liverpool duties. 'I have to make sure that I change my game and allow Paul Scholes to do the creative work,' he explained. 'It is my job to screen the back four. That is different to how I play with Liverpool, because there I have Didi Hamann to do all my defensive work. We have to make sure that, with England, the midfielders have the right level of understanding.'

Gerrard had already displayed a distinct level of understanding partnering Paul Scholes in midfield – a tried-and-tested combination that Eriksson undoubtedly trusted. The pair were back alongside each other against Liechtenstein as England stuttered to a 2–0 victory. Gerrard, after being rested for the final 25 minutes of that game, was then deployed in an unfamiliar role on the left as England completed an important week with an excellent 2–0 defeat of Turkey at Sunderland's Stadium of Light.

On Gerrard's return to action in the Premiership after two fine international outings, he had to endure one of the heaviest defeats of his young career. Manchester United gained revenge for their Worthington Cup final defeat by crushing Liverpool 4–0 at Old Trafford. The twenty-two-year-old may have been booked for a foul on David Beckham, but he still looked like Liverpool's only glimmer of light. Sami Hyypia, the Liverpool captain, was sent off for a professional foul after only four minutes of the game, meaning that he would miss the Reds' upcoming clash with Everton.

Following a relatively routine 2–0 victory over Fulham at Anfield, Gerard Houllier handed Gerrard the ultimate honour – the chance to captain Liverpool in the 168th Merseyside derby. The young star responded with a performance that suited such a role; inspiring the Reds to a hard-fought 2–1 victory. Goals from Michael Owen and Danny Murphy gave Liverpool's Champions League hopes a timely boost.

Two days later – on Easter Monday – Charlton visited Anfield hoping to halt the Reds' charge towards European qualification. Gerrard, having handed the captaincy role back to Sami Hyypia, proved that he did not need to don a black and white armband to convey his leadership qualities. The Reds had to win – it was their biggest league game of the season.

In hours of need, most teams look to their best and most gifted players for inspiration. Some cower with such responsibility; others revel in it. Gerrard has always been one to revel in responsibility. With 90 minutes on the clock and all hope lost that this game was going to finish in any other scoreline than its current 1–1, the gallant hero, with determination etched on his face, bustled away from the challenges of Luke Young and John Robinson close to the left touch-line and crashed a shot goalwards. Dean Keily, the Charlton goalkeeper, could only despair as the shot evaded his grasp and nestled in the net. The whole of Anfield erupted.

'For me, personally, that goal was up there in importance with the one I scored in the Worthington Cup final,' said Gerrrard in the Liverpool *Daily Post*. 'It wasn't one of the best I've ever scored, because the 'keeper should have done better, but significance-wise it's up there. I don't care whether I score spectacular goals or just tap-ins, as long as we get three points. After I'd got past the two defenders I didn't even look up. I was always going to hit it and, if the 'keeper then spilled the shot, Michael might have had a tap-in anyway.'

Gerard Houllier was delighted with the midfielder's wily contribution over the Easter weekend.

'Stevie was the captain at Goodison Park when he was an inspiration in the derby win over Everton,' exclaimed the Liverpool manager. 'And I think he performed against

STEVEN GERRARD: PORTRAIT OF A HERO

Charlton in a way that shows he can be a leader in the future for this club.'

It didn't take a genius to realise that Gerrard was on the verge of being handed the Liverpool captaincy on a full-time basis – a marvellous reward for the way he had shunned poor form and disciplinary problems to rouse Liverpool's season.

The Reds, breathing down the necks of Newcastle and Chelsea in the chase for the all-important fourth place in the Premiership, crushed already-relegated West Brom 6–0 at the Hawthorns. With only two games remaining, the result put them in pole position to qualify for the Champions League.

However, Liverpool then found Peter Schmeichel and Nicolas Anelka – dumped by the Merseysiders the previous summer – in irresistible form for Manchester City. Kevin Keegan's side caused an upset by winning 2–1 in Liverpool's final home game of the season. Schmeichel, the veteran former Manchester United goalkeeper, rolled back the years to pull off a series of stunning saves – one from a goal-bound Gerrard free-kick. And Anelka did the business for City at the other end, scoring twice to leave Liverpool with the unenviable task of having to beat Chelsea at Stamford Bridge on the final day of the season.

Champions League qualification had been Liverpool's primary target all season long. Chelsea occupied fourth position, holding the advantage over the Reds, who had to win in the capital to join Europe's elite league. It wasn't to be – Claudio Ranieri's side recovered from a Sami Hyypia goal to win 2–1 and claim the coveted position, worth a cool £20 million. Ironically, with a Champions League place now secured, it would lead to Roman Abramovich's buyout of the London club later that summer. It was a result that, quite literally, changed the face of English football.

Gerrard, desperately frustrated, ended the season with another discredit to his name. Already in referee Alan Wiley's book late in the game for a foul on Gianfranco Zola, he received his marching orders – the fourth sending-off of his career – after knocking down Graeme Le Saux. Fifth place and a berth in the UEFA Cup was not what Liverpool had hoped for. It was more of a step back than a step forward and it was also a disconcerting end to Gerrard's domestic season; having looked to be on the verge of earning the Anfield captaincy, that prospect looked tainted. Gerard Houllier, however, quickly defended his midfield star.

'I wish I had a couple more players like him,' he said in conference, frustrated at having seen Gerrard play with the fight demanded; something not demonstrated by the rest of his players. 'He was our driving force in midfield. I think what he did came out of pure frustration, but all teams need somebody like him, like Roy Keane, like Patrick Vieira, and sometimes those players get into confrontation and get sent off. Steven is a forceful English midfielder.'

In total, Gerrard made fifty-four appearances in a Liverpool shirt that season spending 4,671 minutes on the pitch taking him to the brink of 200 club appearances. He was booked four times; incurred one red card and managed to score a total of seven goals in that time, having knuckled down following the tough lesson administered by Houllier prior to Christmas.

Gerrard signed off from Liverpool duty to earn his sixteenth England cap in a rather mundane 2–1 friendly victory over South Africa in Durban. Sven-Goran Eriksson's team then returned home to play Serbia and Montenegro at Leicester's new Walker's Stadium. With captain David Beckham absent from the game with a wrist injury, the onus was on Gerrard and the rest of England's midfield to match his inspiration. The Liverpool star, having celebrated his twenty-third birthday, proceeded to extend an already-remarkable record of having not experienced defeat at international level, contributing England's opening goal in a 2-1 victory. He started on the right of Eriksson's infamous diamond formation and quickly stamped his authority on the contest; spotting runs, conjuring stunning passes and duly hitting the net after 35 minutes. Combining neatly with Frank Lampard and Michael Owen en route, Gerrard burst into the penalty area to smash a first-time shot into the goal from eight yards, following Owen's precision pull back. The Liverpool maestro was afforded a rest in the second half as Eriksson experimented with a host of substitutions.

The curtain dropped on the season in Middlesbrough when England faced Slovakia, hoping to continue their charge towards Euro 2004 qualification. Gerrard's outstanding display against Serbia and Montenegro had prompted due praise from his manager.

'Since I came to this country, Steven Gerrard has always been a great player,' Eriksson had enthused. 'He could play for sure in any team in the world. He's a complete player. The difference between when I came and now is that he seems to be a very happy young man. He smiles and talks much more than he did two years ago. That's a merit to him and the club he plays for.'

Gerrard also earned commendation for taking England's new wonder kid under his wing. Fellow Scouser Wayne

Rooney had entered the Three Lions set-up at the tender age of seventeen and the Liverpool star was making sure he was enjoying the new experience.

'With him being from the same area, I know what Wayne's about and I just make sure that he feels comfortable around the lads. In fact, he is looking after me!' said Gerrard. 'It is difficult coming into a big squad when you are only seventeen and you spend a lot of time in your room. I have been there myself and it is difficult, so it is nice to get out and have a game of pool and spend a bit of time with each other.'

The all-round team spirit in the England squad was, in itself, providing great hope for the future. Gerrard was desperate to overcome the nightmare of missing out on the 2002 World Cup by ensuring England a place at Euro 2004. They remained on course by beating Slovakia 2–1. Michael Owen hit both goals, the second of which was made in Liverpool. Gerrard, following a switch back into central midfield from wide right, sent in a perfect cross from the left for Owen to crisply head home. The goal left nobody doubting the special understanding that the two Merseyside products share. It was not the first time the pair had been so lethal as a combo and neither was it to be the last.

Chapter Nine
Captain's Honour

The summer of 2003 brought the first rumours of a move away from Anfield in a multi-million-pound, agent-infested transfer for Gerrard. He only had two years remaining on his contract and the speculation forced Liverpool to release a statement denying that he was for sale with Chelsea the media's destination of choice.

'He's happy at Liverpool and doesn't want to play for anyone else,' Gerard Houllier reassured fans. 'Steven is progressing all the time and this is the club for him. Steven is a player who is central to my long-term plans. The Liverpool board share my view on Steven's future, so there's no chance of him going anywhere. I said at the end of last season I'm sure he will sign another contract. His future is here and the good thing is he wants to be at Liverpool.'

Houllier, the man who had brought the glory days back to Anfield, began the 2003–04 season as a man under pressure – no wonder he was desperate to hold on to his most influential player. Fifth place and a berth in the UEFA Cup was deemed not good enough by Liverpool standards. The Reds needed to improve significantly and the manager deemed it wise to invest in new talent to try and arrest a steady decline. He secured multi-million-pound deals to bring in Leeds United winger Harry Kewell and Fulham full-back Steve Finnan and the pair joined up with their new team-mates on Liverpool's pre-season training camp in Switzerland.

Pre-season wasn't the best for Gerrard. As well as having to cope with all the supposition surrounding his future, he was sent off again. Liverpool took part in the Amsterdam tournament; a pre-season mix of Europe's finest, played out in the magnificent home of Ajax. In their final game, a particularly volatile encounter against Galatasaray of Turkey, Dutch referee Rene Timmink brandished two red cards – one for Gerrard and one for young striker Neil Mellor.

Gerrard had upset Galatasaray's Turkish international contingent in England's European Championships qualifier earlier in the year by celebrating provocatively at the game's conclusion – he even received a black eye after a skirmish in the tunnel. So Hakan Unsal and Hakan Sukur, both former Premiership players with Blackburn Rovers, took it upon themselves to incite the Liverpool midfielder into being sent from the field. Gerrard was initially booked for his part in an ugly brawl and then saw red for dissent, barely 20 minutes after coming on as a substitute.

'From the moment I sent the first player off, Gerrard started talking to me. I warned him twice and, after the third time, I had no choice,' said the referee after the game. 'I can't repeat what he said. It is not something you would

CAPTAIN'S HONOUR

say to a ref or another person. If we had to tolerate this, then I would stop refereeing. It surprised me the players were so quickly irritated, and that includes the Turkish players. The atmosphere on the pitch was very bad.'

Gerard Houllier was unhappy with the conduct of Galatasaray's players, but warned Gerrard that he would have to stand up to such provocation, especially in the light that he would more than likely be lining up for England in Turkey a month or so later.

'I will speak to him about what has happened,' said the Frenchman, preparing for a very important new season. 'He knows it was not right but, at the same time, it's a man's game... There was a lot of provocation going on and I don't want him to change. I want him to keep his cool because there will always be provocation because of his reputation. But I don't want to take the competitive element out of him. The boy is very disappointed. I think Hakan Sukur was out of order – he pinched him from behind and then, of course, Stevie reacted and there were immediately six or seven players around him. He was wrong to react and he knows that, but I know Stevie well enough to know it is definitely not a problem for the future.'

Luckily for Liverpool, Gerrard's misdemeanour in Amsterdam did not sustain a suspension to add to the one-match ban he was set to serve for the red card he had received at Chelsea on the final day of the previous season. The England star echoed his manager's sentiments on the eve of the new season in the knowledge that he had to curb his temper.

'Now the season's here I'm devastated about missing the opening game,' he said. 'The Chelsea thing was down to frustration at missing out on the Champions League. I'd built myself up before the game thinking that we had a real chance and when we went a goal up I thought that would be the case. My disciplinary record last year was not too bad, but hopefully I can avoid that sort of thing at Chelsea happening again.'

Despite the pledge to clean up his game, Gerrard was not prepared to change the combative, enthusiastic style that had endeared him to so many fans.

'I have built my whole game around tackling. You just have to channel that in the right direction. Be hard but fair. I have a lot of developing still to do. I'm still learning and have a lot to prove. You don't reach your peak until you are twenty-eight so I have some way to go.' And the midfielder, on the verge of signing a new contract with Liverpool, remained ever-optimistic about their prospects for the new season.

'This is where I want to be and where I want to stay and I'll definitely be driving myself over the coming months to ensure that we get back into the Champions League,' he said. 'I've experienced life in that competition for two years and that's where I feel this club belongs. I believe our prospects are brighter this season... the Premiership is a very tough league to win and, if we fall short, the target then becomes the Champions League.'

Gerrard's first competitive action of the season was not with Liverpool, but with England. He earned his nineteenth international cap playing on the left side of Sven-Goran Eriksson's diamond in a 3–1 friendly victory over Croatia at Portman Road. On his return to Premiership action, Gerrard caused more friction with some typically robust tackling when Liverpool bounced back from an opening-day defeat to Chelsea with a goalless

CAPTAIN'S HONOUR

draw at Aston Villa. Such eye-catching, fervent displays continued, as the Reds drew at home to Tottenham before crushing Everton 3–0 at Goodison Park.

Gerrard's temperament was under constant scrutiny, particularly from his respective managers and that inspection of character was extremely apparent in the Merseyside derby. Sadly for Gerrard's doubters, he was far too intelligent and mature not to have learned any valuable lessons. Having played a tellingly principal role in Liverpool's first victory of the season, against Everton, Gerrard went on to say:

> It's a test for all the local boys because for us it's the biggest game of the season. Obviously, Manchester United, Arsenal, Chelsea and whoever are big games, too. But to play against Everton, who are a stone's throw away, is fantastic, especially being a local lad who has watched so many derbies on the telly. It's really hard not to get carried away at certain times, because everyone knows the tackles fly in here, there and everywhere.
>
> A top-class midfielder doesn't get sent off for something silly or for getting carried away, which is something I've done in the past, and also recently.

In many people's eyes, Gerrard already was a top-class midfielder – an inspiration to both club and country. Having picked up an ankle injury in Liverpool's game against Tottenham, he had played through the pain barrier at Goodison Park and the aggravation caused him to miss England's 2–1 win away to Macedonia in their European Championship qualifier. After some meticulous care and attention at Melwood, Gerrard won his twentieth England cap in the Three Lions' 2–0 victory over Liechtenstein at Old Trafford – a game in which he set up both goals: for Michael Owen and then Wayne Rooney.

There were no ill-effects from his ankle problem, enabling him to be instrumental in Liverpool's victories over Blackburn and Leicester, before he was given a rest for the Reds' UEFA Cup first-round first-leg tie away to Olimpija Ljubljana of Slovenia. The break was supposed to help Gerrard overcome a slight knee injury, but it didn't last long. An injury to Danny Murphy early in the game meant that Gerard Houllier had to call upon his trusty warrior to help his side to a 1–1 draw on the night Michael Owen broke Ian Rush's goal-scoring record for Liverpool in European competition.

'I wanted to rest Steven because he has emerged as an important player for us, and for his country. The role he performs is one of the most crucial in the team,' Houllier explained to the *Mirror* after the game. 'He has some very important games coming up and I wanted him fresh for them. Steven's role is vital to us and to his country, and he has to work hard there. If you look at all the big teams, the defensive midfielder is vital to the team.'

There was no doubting Houllier's growing admiration for Gerrard. He had already said, during the summer, that the twenty-three-year-old had 'leadership qualities' and the Liverpool manager was now praising such talents on a regular basis.

'Yes, he has to do the defensive work, breaking up play, but he is also a creative influence, because he can start attacks,' continued Houllier. 'I can't see where Steven will get his rest now. The games are important, they are big

After nearly four years of England service, Gerrard was handed the captain's armband by England head coach Sven-Goran Eriksson for the March 2004 friendly against Sweden. Gerrard's characteristically powerful performance could not prevent his first defeat in a senior international fixture.

Above: Gerrard takes on the Olympiakos defence in the crucial second leg of the Champions League Group A qualifier in December 2004.

Below: Just past the hour mark, Gerrard shoots spectacularly at the Olympiakos goal, only to see his goal disallowed. Later, in a moment of pivotal redress, Gerrard's priceless second (Liverpool's third) strike took the Reds through to the finals.

Above: Heads bowed, staring defeat in the mouth – Gerrard, Sami Hyypia and Steve Finnan look beaten as Liverpool go 3-0 down in the first half of the Champions League final against Italian giants AC Milan in Istanbul.

Below: The fightback starts here! Gerrard celebrates scoring the first Liverpool goal, to kickstart his team on the road to a glorious result none of them dared dream of.

Victory! Gerrard kisses the ultimate club football prize, the coveted Champions League trophy, in what was an emotional climax to an unforgettable career high for the Liverpool boy and man.

Above: Gerrard celebrates with his team mates by lifting the cup he'd worked so hard to win.

Below: The Liverpool team proudly parade the Champions League trophy through the streets of their city.

Above left: Liverpool's captain leaves the Melwood training ground after training with team mates, 4 July 2005. Gerrard had broken off contract talks less than six weeks after lifting the Champions League trophy. He was widely reported to be frustrated with his club's failure to come up with an improved contract.

Above right: After an exhausting but triumphant 2004/5 season, Gerrard looks relaxed, sharing a joke on the bench at Wrexham with fellow team mates, the day after his dramatic decision to remain with his beloved Liverpool.

Below: Gerrard and close colleague Jamie Carragher parade the European Cup in front of their faithful fans, prior to the pre-season friendly between Wrexham and Liverpool on 9 July 2005. Both players signed a new four-year deal to keep the pair at Liverpool until 2009.

Alex Curran – fiancée of Steven and mother to their daughter Lilly-Ella – seen here at a charity event in Liverpool, November 2005. The couple are expecting their second baby later this year.

Steven won UEFA's Most Valuable Player of the Season award in August 2005. Gerrard's stock continues to rise as a young player vital to the footballing hopes of club and country.

CAPTAIN'S HONOUR

matches, and we will need him. But I think he can handle it. He is developing as a player as well, which is why he is so important to us. He can dictate the play now, be the pulse of the team, and his passing is improving all the time.'

Gerrard had opened talks with Liverpool officials over a lucrative new contract having pledged to sign during the summer. Rumours circulated that a five-year deal worth £55,000 a week was on the table as SFX, Gerrard's representatives, met with Liverpool chief executive Rick Parry to thrash out a deal.

Meanwhile, Gerrard helped England qualify for the European Championship finals in their goalless draw with Turkey in Istanbul. Bruised and berated by the Turks, Gerrard rose above them, playing, again, on the left of England's diamond – twenty-one international caps, still no defeat and now a major tournament to look forward to.

More good news quickly followed for the Anfield hero. His outstanding start to the season, his exemplary recovery from criticism and disciplinary woes and his downright passion and love for Liverpool Football Club, was set to be rewarded with, what for Gerrard, must have felt like a knighthood. It certainly would have meant much more than signing a profitable new contract.

Liverpool's 3–2 defeat at Charlton at the end of September, together with a 2–1 home defeat to Arsenal, prompted Gerard Houllier into making a very telling change on 15 October 2003. Sami Hyypia, the club's most successful captain in years, was stripped of the role and the armband was passed on to Gerrard.

'I have thought long and hard about this,' explained Houllier, upon announcing the move ahead of Liverpool's UEFA Cup first-round second-leg tie against Olimpija

STEVEN GERRARD: PORTRAIT OF A HERO

Ljubljana. 'I have decided to move the armband to Steven Gerrard. Stevie will lead the team tonight and in the future. This is not something that should be seen as against Sami. He has been a good captain for us. He has lifted six trophies as captain. I have considered a number of issues. Firstly, I think Stevie has certain leadership qualities that I spotted very early in his career. When he was young, all he needed was time to mature. Now he is twenty-three and he is ready. There has been a maturing in both his game and his personality.'

Naturally, Gerrard, who had clocked up 200 senior matches, led his team to an emphatic victory on the night he captained Liverpool for the first time. Goals from Anthony La Tallec, Emile Heskey and Harry Kewell gave the Reds a 4–1 aggregate win over Olimpija Ljubljana, the Slovenian minnows. After the game, Gerrard revealed:

> Sami was one of the first to congratulate me. He's been a great captain and he'll still lead the team from the back. I have to say I'm thrilled, though. The manager has always said I would be captain one day, but it was still a shock. It is a dream. I was captain of my school side and I used to go along to Anfield to watch the team and I always looked up to people like John Barnes, who captained the team during the 1990s. I'd dream that one day it would be me captaining the team I love.

Gerard Houllier, who had played such an integral role in Gerrard's meteoric rise into one of the most coveted roles in world football, could only recall the wonderful day he first laid eyes on the player, some six years before.

'Stevie was lean, only seventeen, putting his foot in and

CAPTAIN'S HONOUR

shouting like someone controlling traffic,' revealed the paternal French manager, in the *Daily Express*. 'I said to him afterwards, "You can come and train with the first team tomorrow." I could see he was a natural born winner. To me he looked like someone who would captain the club one day... I have watched Stevie develop and grow up and it looks now as if he understands the duties he has regarding his career.'

For Gerrard the duties were very clear. 'A club like this should be playing in the Champions League and we should be challenging for major honours. Nothing else is acceptable,' he told the *Sunday Times*. The reality was that Liverpool – on the field – were not playing like such a side. Gerrard began his reign as captain in the Premiership when Liverpool lost their third league game in a row – 1–0 at Portsmouth. 'The fans' patience can only last for so long,' warned the captain after Liverpool's demoralising loss. 'At some stage they are going to get fed up with us and start dishing out some stick. I think they have been supportive beyond the call of duty.'

There was no doubting that Gerrard knew the magnitude of his new role. 'I'm not going to start having a go at different players just because I'm captain now. But if I feel as though I've got something to say that will benefit the team or a certain individual, I'll say it. There are responsibilities on and off the field. Look at David Beckham. He's brilliant with people, on the pitch and off it. It's all about being a good ambassador. I'm looking to set the right example by performing at a consistent level and helping others on the pitch and also helping them off it – for example, if a player has a problem or needs my assistance to get a point across to the manager.'

STEVEN GERRARD: PORTRAIT OF A HERO

Liverpool's problems were momentarily cast aside with a 3–1 home triumph over Leeds United, but their troubles were far from over. Their disorganised form continued on to Christmas, with Gerrard only managing one goal – a penalty in the Reds' 3–1 home win against Birmingham City. The only cheer for Liverpool's fans came on 11 November with the news that their captain had finally signed a new contract committing himself to the club until 2007 and warding off the attentions of Chelsea, for the time being at least. Announcing the news on Liverpool's official website, Gerrard said:

> I'm absolutely delighted to have signed a new contract. I'm glad it's out of the way so I can concentrate on getting Liverpool back into the Champions League. The club told me they wanted to keep me and I told them I wanted to stay here... I've been here since I was eight years old and there has never been a single moment when I have wanted to move on and play for someone else. I want to win a lot more trophies with the club, get them back into the Champions League and I want to stay here for as long as possible. I have been made captain of one of the biggest clubs in Europe and I'm really proud to have signed an extension to my contract.

Gerard Houllier, toasting five years at the Anfield helm, was equally delighted with the news. 'It shows the players at the club share our vision for the future,' said the Liverpool manager. 'They know we are improving and it's a very good piece of news for everyone who loves the club.'

Gerrard was incredibly proud of his achievements with

CAPTAIN'S HONOUR

Liverpool, but reaffirmed his desire to win more silverware.

'I still take a step back sometimes,' he said. 'Becoming the captain of Liverpool, having twenty-odd England caps and more than 200 appearances for the club at twenty-three is great. But there are still a few medals missing from my collection that I have ambitions of winning. First of all, I want to get the club back into the Champions League. That is the main priority.'

One of Gerrard's main fears remained that his friend, Michael Owen, would be tempted away from the club should they not make it into the Champions League. In the run-up to Christmas, Liverpool were beaten at home by Manchester United, dumped out of the League Cup at home to Bolton and humbled by Southampton at Anfield – results that left many questioning the future of Anfield's biggest names and left their title ambitions in tatters. Gerard Houllier was subject to a constant barrage of interrogation and, to make matters worse, Owen had not signed a new Liverpool contract when he had been expected to. Gerrard responded to the situation by saying:

> He really wants to play Champions League football; it's as simple as that. If we don't make it then he is going to move on. No one can blame him after what he has done for this club. I am desperate for him to stay, but the only person who knows whether he is going to go is Michael himself. He is one of the best strikers in the world and he will not be happy playing in the UEFA Cup. And people who get on the bandwagon and criticise his loyalty are totally unfair – he has been here since he was ten years old!

STEVEN GERRARD: PORTRAIT OF A HERO

In Liverpool's final game of 2003, a 2–2 draw away at Manchester City, Gerrard picked up a thigh injury that forced him to sit out of the Reds' first four games of the New Year.

'You just don't feel a part of things,' the crocked star told the *Sunday Telegraph* after being forced to return to Melwood's treatment table. 'That's what I suffer from most. I feel as if I belong to the physios, and the players and staff are in a different place. You feel so down and lonely. And bored, really. It is, without question, the downside of being a footballer.'

Liverpool didn't fare too badly without their suffering superhero – winning three out of those four matches – including a 1–0 victory away at Chelsea and a 2–0 win over Yeovil Town in the third round of the FA Cup. Gerrard's absence told, however, when Liverpool's mini-revival was halted with a 2–1 defeat at Tottenham.

Fortunately for Gerard Houllier's side, the England star was passed fit for a return to action four days later, in a re-arranged encounter with lowly Wolves at Molineux. Michael Owen had also suffered from some niggling injuries so far that season, and joined Gerrard in a Liverpool line-up for only the twelfth time in the campaign. Tellingly, eight of Owen's nine goals that season had come when Gerrard was with him in the team. Understandably, Houllier saw that as no coincidence:

> When Steven plays for England, they do not lose. Look at the results. They always win or draw when he plays. And you know Michael can always score goals. It is a good partnership. We have certainly missed that, as well as the players individually. There is an

CAPTAIN'S HONOUR

understanding in their game. Stevie knows where Michael will move, and his runs. That is crucial to us.

We have had to play three months without Michael and a month without Steven. That is a lot of talent to lose.

After praising the contribution of his captain, Houllier took charge of his 200th league game with Liverpool at Wolves. Bruno Cheyrou, the young French midfielder, who had been in sprightly form during Gerrard's absence, opened the scoring for the Reds before an ugly late tussle and a last-gasp volley from Kenny Miller afforded the home side a point. The ugly tussle was between Gerrard and former Liverpool captain Paul Ince, playing for Wolves. The rival captains squared up to each other, but with Gerrard restrained, it was Ince, the most experienced player on the field, who ended up in the referee's notebook after pushing the Liverpool midfielder in the face.

With that debacle firmly at the back of Gerrard's mind, he helped Liverpool through to the fifth round of the FA Cup three days later – setting up one of Cheyrou's two goals in a 2–1 victory over Newcastle. The Reds then drew a blank in a goalless draw with Everton at Anfield, a result that did little to alleviate the increasing frustrations of the Anfield faithful.

Gerrard, who had demanded that Liverpool make it into the Champions League upon signing his new contract, was back in goal-scoring mood as Liverpool made the short journey to Bolton. The captain had riled the home side by suggesting, pre-match, that the Reds should be seeing off teams like Bolton with ease. Despite the comments, he was once again Liverpool's driving, engineering midfield enforcer. With Bolton a goal ahead, his splendid delivery from a free-kick allowed Sami Hyypia to head in shortly after half-time. Then, after Sam Allardyce's side had taken the lead for a second time, he emphatically volleyed home a slick assist from Anthony La Tallec to level again, demonstrating his desire to haul Liverpool into Champions League contention. The sad thing about Gerrard's awesome display was that his team-mates were falling woefully short of the high standards he set for them.

'I'm not going to change as a person and start giving bollockings all over the place or being nasty, but if something has to be said to improve the team I'll say it,' Gerrard had told the *Sunday Telegraph*. 'Being captain is also about your role off the field, helping people. If I find out one of the players is not happy for one reason or another, I'll be there for him to talk to – if he wants that. Some people want an arm around them, others prefer to deal with problems their own way.'

The rallying cry was simple: Liverpool had to endeavour to win all their remaining home games. It was all in print, too. Gerrard's captain's column in Liverpool's match-day programme for their game with Manchester City read: 'I don't want to put any more pressure on our shoulders, but beginning tonight we've got to look to win all our home games. That's the way it's got to be. We have played Chelsea, Manchester United and Arsenal here. They are what I call lottery games, ones where anything can happen. But with all due respect to the teams we've still got to play at Anfield, we should be looking to pick up maximum points.'

Leading by example and, as if by magic, Gerrard led Liverpool to their first victory in four Premiership matches,

CAPTAIN'S HONOUR

against Kevin Keegan's side at Anfield. Somewhat fittingly, he also hit the winning goal; capitalising on some errant spillage by City stopper David James to ram home only his third goal of the season.

After being dumped out of the FA Cup in a tumultuous fifth-round replay away to Portsmouth – a game that put Gerard Houllier under increasing pressure – Liverpool headed back into European competition to face Levski Sofia. The UEFA Cup remained the only possible chance of silverware for the Reds, but Champions League qualification meant so much more. Nevertheless, the relief was plainly evident when Gerrard – celebrating becoming a father for the first time following the birth of his daughter Lily-Ella – put Liverpool ahead after 67 minutes of the first leg against the Bulgarians. The Reds skipper reacted to a headed clearance following a corner routine, by sending a thunderous 35-yard volley into the bottom corner of the net. And it was Gerard Houllier, the person that had acted as a fatherly figure to Gerrard for so long, so attentively and so astutely, that the gleeful twenty-three-year-old ran over to embrace in celebration – a defiant message of support for the beleaguered French manager. Harry Kewell scored an equally sublime goal to put Liverpool in a commanding position going into the second leg.

A 2-2 draw away at Leeds followed in the Premiership before the Reds headed to Bulgaria for the conclusion of their UEFA Cup third-round tie. How Sofia felt the wrath of Liverpool's frustrations! Gerrard, whose performances were so evidently coming from the heart, got Liverpool up and running and ended the tie as a contest by rounding the Bulgarians' goalkeeper and squeezing home from an impossible angle. Michael Owen hit another goal soon after and Gerrard set up two more for Dietmar Hamann and then Sami Hyypia as Liverpool cruised into the next round with a 4–2 victory in Bulgaria.

Gerrard's performances remained Liverpool's shining, guiding light. Defeat at Southampton was followed by a 1–1 draw with Marseille at Anfield in their UEFA Cup fifth-round first leg. Two home wins in the Premiership against Portsmouth and Wolves lifted the gloom; with Sami Hyypia hitting a crucial injury-time winner against Wolves to keep the Reds' Champions League dreams alive. Heartbreak was to follow, however, as Liverpool travelled to France for their second helping of Marseille. The French side ejected the Reds from Europe with a 2–1 victory, leaving Gerrard visibly deflated at the end of the game.

Sven-Goran Eriksson's admiration for Gerrard was growing by the game. The incredible determination of the twenty-three-year-old in holding Liverpool together in their darkest hour was something that could not remain ignored by anybody, let alone Eriksson. Gerrard had even gone nearly an entire season without being booked, so with David Beckham absent through injury, the England manager rewarded his efforts by handing him the England captain's armband for a friendly with Sweden.

'On the pitch, he is a fantastic footballer,' enthused Eriksson, upon announcing the news. 'Off the pitch, I remember when I first met him, and if I compare the man now to the young boy then, he has progressed enormously. He is very much more mature now and calmer. He deserves to be the captain and he's practising it a lot this season with Liverpool.'

CAPTAIN'S HONOUR

Gerrard had missed England's previous two games – friendlies against Denmark and Portugal – but he returned to lead them in his twenty-second international appearance.

'It's a dream come true for myself,' said Gerrard to assembled media. 'But it's still a bit surprising, because there are players with more experience than me in the squad. But it's very nice to be the captain – and hopefully I can cap it with a win.'

Gerrard, revelling in his finest international hour, subsequently displayed the kind of natural leadership instincts in the Ullevi Stadium that had been evident in his game since his days as a willowy schoolboy. Despite his own excellent performance, it wasn't matched by his England team-mates and they went down to a second-half strike from Sweden's Zlatan Ibrahimovic. After nearly four years as a senior international, Gerrard tasted defeat for the first time in an England shirt, ironically in his first game as captain.

The most important thing for Gerrard as the season ebbed towards its climax remained, not to stay injury free, but to ensure that Liverpool finished in the Premiership's top four. It was 'the be all, and end all', as he had exclaimed in his programme notes. After a thumping 4–0 victory over Blackburn at Anfield and then a 4–2 defeat at Arsenal – results that epitomised Liverpool's alarming inconsistency – the Reds met Charlton Athletic at home.

Gerrard's insatiable nature and his sincere desire to keep Liverpool in the fourth place came to the fore, in a somewhat devious sense, when, with Liverpool trailing to a Shaun Bartlett header late in the game, he flung himself to the floor under pressure in the Charlton penalty area in a desperate attempt to sway the referee. The incident brought the captain's first booking of the season – a somewhat incredible statistic for even the most cautious of central midfield ball-winners. Defeat to Charlton jammed Liverpool firmly in the proverbial pressure-cooker. Gerrard was clearly feeling it more than most. Having assumed penalty-taking duties from Michael Owen, Gerrard got the chance to put Fulham to the sword at Anfield from 12 yards. Sadly for him, Edwin van der Sar pulled off a stunning save to deny him and the resultant goalless draw left Liverpool clutching at straws and facing a daunting trip to Old Trafford to face Manchester United with only four Premiership games remaining. They could not afford to lose. Ahead of his biggest game of the season and his most important as captain, Gerrard said:

> There is no margin for error and we cannot afford, come Monday morning, to have the same number of points on the board. If we get beaten and Newcastle win this weekend, there is a chance it is all over.
>
> I am just fearing finishing this season the same as last one. Going away in the summer and knowing you are coming back to play UEFA Cup football. I remember Chelsea on the final day of last season. I had been sent off, we finished fifth and it was one of the few low points I have had in my career. The atmosphere in the dressing room was bad that day. There was this terrible feeling of failure. I don't want that again. That's the fear that is driving me on.

Liverpool were set to face Newcastle at Anfield on the final day this time around – the team most likely to pip them to the post.

CAPTAIN'S HONOUR

Come that Newcastle game and the final whistle, I don't want to be walking around the pitch, clapping our fans, having finished fifth again. I want to be clapping those fans knowing that we have qualified for the Champions League. I am thinking about nothing else but Champions League, Champions League, Champions League.

If we finish fifth it will have been a complete washout. And I'd be a liar if I said I was not concerned about our chances of making it, because of our form in the last three results.

This season has shown that United, Arsenal and Chelsea are in a league of their own now. We have fallen short. The players here all need to improve and we need to strengthen as well. I'm the captain, a player but also a fan. I want us to come away with a sense of pride. Okay, it might not have worked out perfectly, but finishing fourth is still massively important.

Thank goodness then for Danny Murphy – one of Gerrard's closest friends on and off the field. The man who had been the tormentor-in-chief to Manchester United in their own backyard, took over penalty-taking responsibilites and obliged his team-mates by giving Liverpool a quite priceless 1–0 victory at Old Trafford after Gerrard himself had been felled by Gary Neville in the second half.

The Reds' momentum from that result saw them beat Middlesbrough 2–0 at Anfield and then teeter on the brink of Champions League qualification away to Birmingham. In arguably Liverpool's finest attacking display of the season, Gerrard shone. After Michael Owen had opened the scoring, the Reds' captain showed outstanding technique to cross for Emile Heskey to score before he wrapped up a resounding 3–0 victory with his first goal in thirteen league matches. Upon chesting down a cross-field past from Danny Murphy, Gerrard, having darted in from the left side, strode forward and smashed the ball clinically past Ian Bennett, the Birmingham goalkeeper. The celebrations said everything. Barring a minor miracle, Liverpool had qualified for the Champions League.

'We just couldn't cope with Gerrard,' said Birmingham manager Steve Bruce after the game. 'I hope he continues that form in the European Championships. He was absolutely awesome today. I think he is the complete player at the moment. He was fantastic.'

Gerrard completed a stunning personal domestic season by setting up Michael Owen's goal as Liverpool ended their campaign with a 1–1 draw at home to Newcastle. In all, the Liverpool captain, who had almost single-handedly earned the Reds a place in the Champions League, received sixteen Man of the Match awards in his forty-seven appearances. That was at least four times as many as any other Liverpool player. He had not been overawed by the extra responsibility lauded upon him by Gerard Houllier, he had only thrived on it. The captaincy had made him a better player too, evident by the fact that he entered the referee's notebook on just three occasions during the season.

Among Gerrard's wealth of worshippers was Sir Alex Ferguson, whose Manchester United side had missed out to Arsenal in the Premiership title race. He revealed in a forthright interview with the *Sunday Times* his admiration for the talents of Liverpool's inspirational captain when asked who he would like to replace Roy Keane with one day.

CAPTAIN'S HONOUR

If you were looking for the player you would replace Keane with, it's Gerrard, without question. He has become the most influential player in England, bar none. More than Patrick Vieira. I think he does more for his team than Vieira does for his. Not that Vieira lacks anything – he doesn't. To me, Gerrard is a Keane; he is now where Keane was when Roy came to us in 1993. When the ball is in their penalty area, he is right there, round their penalty area; when it is in his team's penalty area, he is back there... He's got that unbelievable engine, desire and determination. You can see Gerrard rising and rising. He may be a very big player for England at the European Championships.

Almost as soon as Liverpool signed off for the season, Gerrard, an automatic name in Sven-Goran Eriksson's twenty-three-man squad for the European Championships, was being linked with a move away from Anfield as incessant praise came flooding his way. 'Do you see anyone in world football better than Steven Gerrard at the moment?' asked Gerard Houllier, proudly.

'Steven Gerrard has been incredible this season,' Sven-Goran Eriksson purred, as he gathered his star-studded squad together. 'The development of him as a footballer and even as a man is quite definite. Compared to when we came in three years ago, he is another man, another footballer. He can do everything.'

So sad then for Gerrard to learn that Liverpool had told Gerard Houllier – the man who was, perhaps, solely responsible for making him the footballer he had become – that his services were no longer required at Anfield. The Liverpool skipper was away with the England squad on a training camp in Sardinia and demanded that, as captain, he should be consulted in the search for the next manager. He was already being linked with a pocket-bursting move to Chelsea and the departure of Houllier dealt a blow to Gerrard's future plans.

> I'm sure David Moores, the chairman, and Rick Parry will want to know the team's views and feelings. My mobile is on for them to call me when the time is right. Appointing a new manager is a massive decision for the whole club, not just for Michael Owen and I. For every single player, for the board of directors and for the chairman himself, it's a massive decision. The next three months for Liverpool are going to be really crucial. As important as they have ever been – the appointment of the new manager and the quality of the players they bring in... Everyone knows how desperate I am to win the league. The last few seasons have been very frustrating for myself personally and for the whole club.

Gerrard, of course, had a lot of sympathy for Houllier, who had ended a six-year tenure as Liverpool manager. He continued:

> It is unfair on him. He is the one who has had to take all the blame. It's not just down to him why the team has been unsuccessful over the last few years. It is down to the players. But unfortunately, the way football is, the players do not get the blame. The manager does. That's the sad thing. I feel sorry for Gerard. I have always had a really good relationship with him.

CAPTAIN'S HONOUR

I have spoken to him at length since the decision. It typified what kind of person he is that he never really spoke about himself. He just went on about me and told me to keep doing what I am doing. He was being a father figure to me again, just as he has been for six years. I thanked him for all the things he has done for me. I wished him luck. But we both have to move on now. I wouldn't say he has been the most important figure in my career, but he has been one of them.

Aside from the turmoil that his club found themselves in, Gerrard had to remain focused on his first significant participation in a major tournament at international level. Two years earlier, he had missed an entire World Cup through injury and two years before that, in the previous European Championships, he had figured for only 29 minutes in a Three Lions' shirt. Since then, he had proved his fitness, maturity and enduring talents to the world: now he was set to extend an extraordinary season onto a level he had never experienced before.

'I'm flying and the form is good. I'm happy off the pitch. Everything is perfect. I have had a good season,' said Gerrard. 'Things have gone well for me personally. I think it is well documented that I am not happy with the way it has gone at Liverpool over the past two seasons. But my form has been good. I am very ambitious and I am aiming to have a successful tournament with England. I've got this summer and, hopefully, a World Cup two years afterwards in which to prove to people all around the world that I can play in big tournaments.'

And what did Gerrard make of England's chances? 'I fancy us for the European Championships,' continued the

STEVEN GERRARD: PORTRAIT OF A HERO

Liverpool hero. 'I'll be very disappointed if we don't get to the final anyway. After the Turkey game, I became convinced we could peak earlier. The togetherness and the fighting spirit, the attitude of the players in training and in the dressing room before the match – if we can take those memories into the tournament, we'll be a very difficult side to beat.'

England were all set to face France in their opening group game, after warming up for the tournament by drawing 1–1 with Japan and thumping Iceland 6–1 at the City of Manchester Stadium. 'I'm looking at the midfield battle against Vieira, Zidane, Makelele, Pires and Dacourt,' Gerrard exclaimed in anticipation of the tournament's beginning. 'They are all top class, but I am sure Vieira is saying the same thing about our midfield. We will be right up for it. I am confident we can do really well. We have quality all over the pitch. We have Michael Owen.'

And the Liverpool captain relished another meeting with one of the players he admired most – Patrick Vieira. 'Me and Patrick like to get on the ball and dictate play,' said Gerrard. 'We try to go forward when the time is right and we can both defend. Patrick is the best around and it's nice to be compared to him. Midfield will be a major part of the game. Yet there are key battles all over the pitch and whoever wins most of them will win the match. My current form is the best I've been in. I want to make up for having missed out on the World Cup and, hopefully, it is my time.'

Vieira, himself hoping for success with France in Portugal, lauded Gerrard's talents. 'We have a great respect for each other,' said the Arsenal captain. 'That's the main thing and if on the pitch there is a tackle to give I'll give it to him and

CAPTAIN'S HONOUR

he'll give it to me. That's the way it is and during the 90 minutes we'll both give 100 per cent for the team. He would be in my top three midfielders in the world. I couldn't vote for Thierry Henry for footballer of the year so I voted for Gerrard because I think Liverpool got into the Champions League because of him. I think Steven Gerrard and Paul Scholes are the two best English players.'

The European Championships exploded into life when England met France in Lisbon. Frank Lampard, Gerrard's new partner in crime in midfield, headed Sven-Goran Eriksson's men ahead in the first half. But two minutes of utter madness at the end of an enthralling 90 minutes turned the game in France's favour. David Beckham had missed a penalty and, with England lacking the services of Lady Luck, Zinedine Zidane curled in a brilliant free-kick to bring Les Bleus level. Then, with only seconds left, Gerrard sold David James dreadfully short with a back pass and the England goalkeeper could only bring down Henry for a penalty. Gerrard, no doubt feeling physically sick, watched as Zidane, who was actually sick near the penalty spot, stepped forward to give France the victory. England, and Gerrard in particular, had to pick themselves up.

'It was one of the lowest points of my career,' said Gerrard. 'I had committed an error in a massive game. I was very down on Sunday night, but I was so tired I didn't lose any sleep. The most important thing in football if you make mistakes is to bounce back.'

Having recuperated in their lavish surroundings at the Solplay Hotel in the western suburbs of Lisbon, England and Gerrard bounced back in ardent style against Switzerland. Eighteen-year-old wonderkid Wayne Rooney needed no introduction to the tournament, and headed

STEVEN GERRARD: PORTRAIT OF A HERO

England ahead from Michael Owen's clever pass to settle early nerves in Coimbra. Rooney's thunderous second-half shot made it 2–0 before Gerrard, having teed Rooney up for that goal and with Switzerland down to ten men, scored himself in a major tournament for the first time when he slammed home Gary Neville's pin-point cross. Swiss striker Alexander Frei was later charged and then spared a suspension by UEFA after television footage revealed that he had deliberately spat in the direction of the Liverpool player.

Rooney's performances were overshadowing those of any other player in the tournament. He was England's valiant young hero again as they beat Croatia 4–2 in their final group game to make it through to the quarter-finals. Rooney, the Everton striker, scored two fabulous goals, joining Paul Scholes and Frank Lampard on the goal-scoring roster.

In hindsight, the quarter-final tie that followed with the hosts, Portugal, was nothing short of an epic. England, much fancied and seemingly brimming with vigour and energy, against Portugal, who themselves were brimming with an abundance of enigmatic talent and who would be roared on by a vociferous home support. It was, unequivocally, the biggest international match that Gerrard, and many of the others wearing the Three Lions' shirt that night, had ever taken part in.

It all began so well for England. Michael Owen answered his critics by scoring for them after only three minutes, flicking the ball over Portugal goalkeeper Ricardo after a long kick from David James had evaded the attentions of Costinha. But, after losing Rooney to a broken foot, the Three Lions were pinned back into their own half and were forced to endure, rather than to enjoy, the rest of the match.

CAPTAIN'S HONOUR

Gerrard had little effect on the contest as Portugal pressed and, having been booked, was withdrawn with nine minutes to go, replaced by Owen Hargreaves, the defensive-minded Bayern Munich midfielder. Almost immediately, if not coincidently, Helder Postiga, the Tottenham striker, sent the game into extra-time with a firm header past James. England were then left to curse one of the most contentious refereeing decisions ever seen in a major international tournament. Swiss referee Urs Meier disallowed a seemingly legitimate Sol Campbell header right at the end of the match, citing a foul by John Terry as the problem, but which television cameras cruelly suggested otherwise.

Extra-time brought no England respite. Manuel Rui Costa fired Portugal ahead from 20 yards, before Frank Lampard scored to level the breathtaking contest and send it to penalties. We all know what happened next.

Chapter Ten

Stevie Wonder

On 16 June 2004, Rafa Benitez was confirmed as the successor to Gerard Houllier. The forty-four-year-old Spaniard signed a five-year contract and was immediately charged with reversing fortunes at Anfield and ensuring that Liverpool's prize assets – Messrs Owen and Gerrard – would remain there. Benitez arrived having bid a tearful farewell to his former club Valencia, where he had just won the Spanish League title and the UEFA Cup.

'It is like a dream to be here,' he told the media, upon fulfilling a long-standing ambition to manage a club in England. 'I am very, very proud to be joining one of the most important clubs in the world in one of the best leagues in the world – and I want to win... It is very important that I talk to players like Steven Gerrard and Michael Owen about my ideas. I need players like them with a good mentality and quality.'

With Chelsea ready to smash the British transfer record to

prise Gerrard away from Merseyside, Benitez faced an unenviable beginning to his career in the Anfield hot seat. The Spaniard had big boots to fill when you consider that Gerrard had shared such a concrete bond with Houllier. His own relationship with the Liverpool captain had to be similar. Benitez met his new captain, Michael Owen and Jamie Carragher for the first time at England's team hotel in Portugal – anxious to outline his ambitions for Liverpool.

Gerrard returned from Portugal with speculation over his future ringing in his ears. Jose Mourinho's arrival at Chelsea meant that every player worthy of the tag 'world class' was linked with a move to Stamford Bridge. The riches of Chelsea owner Roman Abramovich promised, more than anything, success – that was what Gerrard wanted, having tolerated two seasons of steady regression with Liverpool. Reds fans hoped and prayed that Gerrard would stay at the club he adored and, on 28 June, the Anfield captain acknowledged their prayers and insisted that he was to remain a Liverpool player. 'I have gone with the decision that is in my heart and that is to stay with Liverpool,' he said. 'I have not been happy with the progression at the club over the last two years and, for the first time in my career, I thought about the possibility of moving on to a different club. But after coming home from Euro 2004 and sitting down with my family and also asking Rick Parry for four meetings in two months and spending all the time with my agent and close family, I have decided that I am staying on with Liverpool Football Club and that I am 100 per cent committed to them.'

Benitez, no doubt, breathed a sigh of relief like everybody else connected with Liverpool. The Spanish boss had only acquired the services of French forward Djibril

STEVIE WONDER

Cisse, who had agreed to sign during Gerard Houllier's reign earlier in the year, so Gerrard's affirmation was integral to his policy for the future. Benitez could start to administer such plans as Liverpool headed across the Atlantic for a pre-season tour of Canada and America.

The break gave Gerrard a chance to reflect on his performances during Euro 2004 and also on his decision to stay with Liverpool, having been on the brink of signing for Chelsea. As he settled at the Reds' New Jersey training camp, he said:

> I've no regrets about not moving clubs and the decision I made. I'm glad I'm preparing for a new season at Liverpool, but only time will tell if I've made the right choice. I want to win trophies and to be successful. I want to win championships. The decision was hard in some respects, and my head was battered for a bit, but [it was] not difficult in others. It's about being successful for me. I believe I can do that at Liverpool. I have worked hard to be captain and I didn't want to throw that away. I can't wait for the season to start after what happened in the summer. The sooner the first game against Tottenham comes the better, because I want to blow away all the frustrations I have felt.

The European Championships had left a bitter taste in his mouth, too. England's quarter-final exit was scant reward for their efforts and Gerrard, by his own admission, hadn't been able to display his true qualities in Portugal. 'I didn't make the impact I wanted,' he continued. 'Going out in the quarter-finals was disappointing and I never played to the level I know I can. There were signs of what I can do, but I was too hot and cold. People will say that was down to the speculation over my future, but I was 100 per cent focused on the tournament. I haven't got any excuses for my form and I'm not going to use that as one. It has gone now and I have to use the World Cup qualifiers and, hopefully, the next World Cup, to push myself. Maybe people will put me under the microscope this season more because of what happened. I don't mind that.'

Rafael Benitez's arrival left Gerrard anticipating a new beginning at Anfield. Expectations remained high, but the intrigue and belief had returned. Benitez was set to bring in Spanish compatriots Xavi Alonso and Luis Garcia; two exciting prospects, and two players that would make an immediate impact. 'It is a fresh start for everyone here,' said Gerrard. 'No favourites; you cannot afford to have an ego and think, "I did well last season. I've proved myself." It would be easy to think that, but that's gone. It counts for nothing. It's exactly the same for me as the next player. Although I'm skipper, I have to put the work in and prove to the manager that he can count on me. I've been impressed with Rafa. I remember playing against Valencia in the Champions League and in a friendly and we never got a kick. He comes across as a very tactical coach. He is hands on in training and he wants individuals to know their jobs before they go out onto the pitch. He has his ideas and it is up to the players to put them into practice.'

During their tour of America and Canada, Liverpool beat an unfamiliar-looking Celtic side 5–1 in their first game, with Gerrard making his first appearance since Euro 2004

STEVIE WONDER

in the second half. A goalless draw with Porto in Toronto and then a 2–1 defeat of Roma in the Giants Stadium completed a promising first work-out for the Reds under Benitez. Gerrard limped off in the game with Roma, having felt tightness in his thigh, but medical checks revealed no lasting damage and the Anfield captain was all set to embark on the season of a lifetime.

On 10 August, Liverpool began their Champions League adventure against AK Graz in, of all places, the Arnold Schwarzenegger Stadium. All eyes in Austria were on Michael Owen, one of Liverpool's own all-action superheroes, who had yet to sign a new Liverpool contract. With speculation rife that Owen was all set to leave, Rafa Benitez named the striker among his substitutes fuelling the rumours that he was bound for one of Liverpool's Champions League rivals. Any involvement for Owen in the match against Graz would have meant that he was cup-tied, thus rendering any imminent move implausible. All focus on that particular pressing matter was cast aside by Liverpool's primary superhero – their captain fantastic, who, once again, proved himself utterly irreplaceable by leading Liverpool to a valuable win and, in doing so, shouldering some of Owen's goal-scoring mantle. After only 23 minutes of the game, of the new season for that matter, Gerrard watched Dietmar Hamann's pass run into his path and unleashed an unstoppable, trademark, first-time, long-range effort into the top corner of the net. And, after having an equally spectacular effort ruled out by the referee, the skipper virtually sealed Liverpool's passage to the group stage of the Champions League when, 11 minutes from the end, he met Harry Kewell's pass to the right side of the area and blasted a low shot beyond Graz's helpless goalkeeper.

Only days later, and on the eve of the new Premiership season, Michael Owen sealed a lucrative multi-million-pound move to Real Madrid. Any hope that the England striker was set to remain at Anfield diminished in Austria and Benitez and the Liverpool fans were left to contemplate life without him. Djibril Cisse, the French striker, who the Reds now had to put faith in to score the goals that Owen wouldn't, got his season off to a flier away at Tottenham on the opening day of the season, scoring with a first-time effort from seven yards out to give Liverpool the lead. Jermaine Defoe equalised for an ill-deserving Tottenham side and the Reds were forced to begin life without Owen with just a solitary point to show for their efforts. After the game at White Hart Lane, Gerrard revealed to the media:

> We were all shocked about Michael leaving. It looked like he would be staying – then Real Madrid called, and everyone knows how difficult that is to turn down. He has gone, and we have to get on without him. It is a good chance for Cisse to get the goals now Michael isn't here. Time will tell whether we will miss Michael and whether my decision to stay was right. It's disappointing to see him go, but I've got to move on and so has the team. He's a massive player and has been for us over the years.
>
> I've no regrets about staying, I'm confident I can be successful here and I won't be changing my mind now or at Christmas. Cisse is definitely going to score goals. He is quick and a threat to any defence, but the pressure is now on. Everyone knows Michael was our goal machine and we're hoping for goals from Cisse and

STEVIE WONDER

Baros to make sure he's not missed. With Michael gone, there is a lot of responsibility on them now.

Gerrard received his twenty-ninth England cap against the side he faced to earn his first. He helped England fill the cracks of Euro 2004 somewhat, with a typically hearty performance in a 3–0 Three Lions victory against the Ukraine at St James' Park.

Three days later, Liverpool followed up their draw with Tottenham by beating Manchester City, as Anfield welcomed Rafa Benitez for the first time. Gerrard was the match manipulator again; this time setting up Milan Baros and then sliding home the winner 15 minutes from the end as the Reds came from behind to win 2–1. Four days later, Liverpool limped, rather than strode, into the Champions League, earning a £17 million cash windfall after being beaten 1–0 at home in the second leg of their qualifier with AK Graz. Thankfully, and as if Liverpool needed any more reminders of Gerrrard's worth, the captain's brace two weeks earlier proved enough to give the Reds a 2–1 aggregate victory. Defeat to the Austrians, however, did little to suggest that Liverpool would be contenders to win the competition.

New boys Xavi Alonso and Luis Garcia were handed their debuts when Liverpool travelled to the Reebok Stadium to face Bolton Wanderers in the Premiership. Rafa Benitez moved Gerrard onto the right-hand side of midfield to accommodate the new pairing, and with the captain's overriding influence lost from the middle, Bolton, and their own midfield talisman, Jay-Jay Okocha, flourished. Kevin Davies scored the only goal of the game to condemn Liverpool to a premature first Premiership defeat of the season.

STEVEN GERRARD: PORTRAIT OF A HERO

The proverbial microscope that was seemingly following Gerrard on his travels for both club and country, returned to Austria for England's first World Cup qualifier as the Three Lions embarked on the long road towards Germany 2006. The Liverpool captain overcame a fitness test on a slight groin problem nine hours before kick-off to take his place in central midfield in Sven-Goran Eriksson's starting XI. With England already leading courtesy of a goal from Frank Lampard, the Liverpool star took it upon himself to score his fifth international goal midway through the second half in the Ernst Happel Stadium. Gerrard's old club team-mate Michael Owen set him up, nudging the ball into his path in anticipation of his next move. The twenty-four-year-old subsequently struck an unerring, dipping, looping rocket into the top corner to put England 2–0 ahead. Unfortunately, Gerrard's sparkling display was let down by an Austrian comeback aided by a calamitous error by goalkeeper David James and then a misunderstanding between him and the England coaching staff. Having signalled to the bench that Wayne Bridge was injured, Gerrard was hauled off with Eriksson and company believing it was he, and not the Chelsea full-back, who needed treatment.

'It was a bit of a misunderstanding,' said Gerrard after the game. 'Wayne Bridge had a kick on his Achilles and I signalled to the bench to change him – and they changed me. I thought the manager wanted me to come off, but he thought I had signalled to come off. It's one of those things and I can't do anything about it.'

A 2–1 victory in Poland the following Wednesday relieved England's Austrian woes, with Gerrard again superb in orchestrating a hard-fought victory given to them by Jermaine Defoe's classy strike in Katowice.

STEVIE WONDER

The Liverpool captain's noteworthy early-season form continued to bear fruit as Liverpool returned to Premiership action at home to newly promoted West Bromwich Albion. With England's finest daily newspapers fast running out of superlatives for him, Gerrard scored another vintage goal to get Liverpool, and the Benitez revolution, up and running. The midfielder's fourth goal in six games owed much to a clever one-two with Luis Garcia, which allowed him the space to crack home a low, left-footed effort from 12 yards. Goals from Steve Finnan and Garcia himself, after another exchange of passes with his captain, handed Liverpool a 3–0 victory, but it was Gerrard's box-to-box, tackle-to-tackle, pass-to-pass performance that left the lasting impression.

'I've had a few chats with the manager and he told me he wants more goals from midfield,' emphasised Gerrard after the game. 'That's what I'm trying to give him. It's all about me getting forward at the right times and making the right runs. I don't want to go forward all the time and risk leaving gaps behind me, but I'm happy with four goals so far.'

Gerrard's appetite for goal-scoring provided more fuel to rumours that Real Madrid had cited him as a potential acquisition. It seemed as though no pronouncement of loyalty would suffice in dispelling the speculation that the midfielder's Anfield exit was imminent. Liverpool's appetite for success in Europe was no secret, and Monaco, beaten finalists from the previous season, provided the Reds with their first test in the Champions League group stage. Inspired by their captain and by the return of former manager Gerard Houllier to Anfield working for French televison, Liverpool cruised to victory. Gerrard's precision pass set up a goal for Djibril Cisse, before Milan Baros completed a 2–0 win. The victory may have been one positive, but perhaps the most potent aspect of the game to have emanated from inside the Bill Shankly gates that night was Gerrard's instant midfield bond with Xavi Alonso; the pair conducted proceedings with admirable assurance and suggested that they could be paramount to any impending success.

The peering eyes of Europe descended on Old Trafford for Liverpool's next game, a meeting with Manchester United on a Monday night that promised to expose their credentials. Gerrard, once again, lined up alongside Alonso in Liverpool's new-look midfield, but an almighty blow was to hit Rafa Benitez and his team. With Liverpool trailing to a Mikael Silvestre headed goal, Gerrard grimaced in pain in possession of the ball and, after receiving on-the-field treatment to the source of his discomfort – his left foot – he limped off ominously down the tunnel.

'Xabi Alonso passed to me, my foot turned but my studs didn't and I felt a crack in my foot. There was a lot of pain, and I couldn't run,' Gerrard later revealed after Liverpool had lost the game 2–1. 'I'll have a scan tomorrow and, if it is broken, I'll try and remain positive, but I'll be devastated.' The biggest fear harboured by Liverpool was that their captain, who left Old Trafford on crutches, had broken a metatarsal bone – an injury that had haunted three other England internationals in previous seasons – including David Beckham and, during Euro 2004, Wayne Rooney.

Upon receiving the results from the scan, medical staff confirmed that Gerrard had fractured the fifth metatarsal bone in his left foot. Early prognosis did not read well for Liverpool's aspirations – their leader was set to be

STEVIE WONDER

sidelined for at least two months – the longest injury lay-off of his professional career. He was immediately ruled out of England's crucial World Cup qualifiers against Wales and Azerbaijan and at least three of Liverpool's Champions League dates, not to mention some crucial Premiership games.

The Liverpool captain had broken the tiny bone midway down his little toe – and the fifth metatarsal was a notoriously slow healer. After learning the results of his X-ray, Gerrard said:

> This is a bad blow for me. I want to be out for as short a time as possible. It was such an innocuous thing. I don't really know how it happened. There was no one near me. I was just stretching to take a pass from Xabi Alonso and my foot stuck in the turf. I heard a crack and it hurt like hell. What is disappointing is that I will miss the Champions League games... It's bad timing. We are starting again with a new manager, who is working on different things, and it is a bit of a learning process for the players.
>
> As far as I'm concerned, this injury will keep me out for two months and no longer... I'm still the captain and have a big role to play, even if I can't be out there with the lads.

Liverpool were forced to continue their development under the stewardship of Rafa Benitez without their crocked skipper. With Sami Hyypia taking the armband on the field, the Reds showed no ill-effects from Gerrard's absence by beating Norwich City 3–0 at Anfield. But as their club captain set his sights on a return to action in November – at the climax of Liverpool's Champions League group-stage matches – the Reds' form remained unconvincing – particularly away from home. In early October, Gerrard had surgery to insert a metal pin into his injured foot.

'In a way it's good and bad news for me. No one likes to have to go into the hospital for an operation, but if it's going to get me back playing on schedule it's better for me,' Gerrard explained. 'By having a screw inserted in my foot, the bone will set in place and heal a lot quicker. I'm desperate to get back, but I've just got to rest. I'll be watching the England versus Wales match at home like everyone else.'

The torture of having to endure his longest-ever spell on the sidelines was helped a little by news of a nomination for the FIFA Player of the Year award. Gerrard joined a list of thirty-five players up for the prestigious accolade, a roster that included his Liverpool team-mate Milan Baros, who had been top scorer at Euro 2004. The Anfield captain, having undergone an operation that he hoped would speed his recovery, watched his England team-mates on television as they defeated Wales 2–0 at Old Trafford and won 1–0 in Azerbaijan to bolster their World Cup qualification bid.

By the end of October, Gerrard was out of plaster and walking on his injured foot, sparking rumours of a swift return to action. Having been told that the injury could rule him out until Christmas, a visit to see the surgeon who performed his operation confirmed that the bone was healing quicker than expected. Subsequently, the twenty-four-year-old earmarked a return to action in Liverpool's Premiership match with Middlesbrough on 20 November. 'I had a meeting with the specialist today and everything

STEVIE WONDER

was really positive,' Gerrard told the Liverpool *Dail Post*. 'I have been given the go-ahead to start running again and all going well I could be back training with the lads in two weeks. It was music to my ears and I am delighted with the news. It has been difficult, but the physios here at the club and the doctor have been brilliant. I am happy with the way things are going and I can definitely now see light at the end of the tunnel.

'If I really pushed it I could probably be back for the Palace game on 13 November, but I think a more realistic target would be Middlesbrough away the week after. I do not want to rush things unnecessarily and I will probably play in a practice game beforehand. If there are no complications along the way I should definitely be involved in the trip to Boro.'

Gerrard's rehabilitation on Merseyside continued as Liverpool prepared for a crucial Champions League tie away to Deportivo La Coruna, a game that they could ill afford to lose. 'I've got every faith in the lads getting a good result out in Spain,' continued the Reds' captain. 'Unfortunately, I won't be there with them. I'll be working hard at Melwood then going home and tuning into the television like the majority of fans.'

Liverpool won 1-0 in Spain – their first victory in that country for twenty-one years – by virtue of an own goal by Deportivo's Jorge Andrade. The victory made for a tantalising crescendo to the group stage for Rafa Benitez's side – but they still needed their captain back – desperately.

On 15 November, Gerrard, a surprise omission from a fifty-strong shortlist for the European Footballer of the Year award, made his playing comeback in a reserve match. Quite incredibly, a crowd of 6,280 turned out at Telford's tiny New Bucks Head stadium to see the Liverpool captain play the second half of the Reds' reserves clash with Wolves. The bumper crowd brought the Shropshire town to a complete standstill, with most travelling down from Merseyside to catch a glimpse of their fit-again hero. Gerrard was taken off moments before full-time, invoking suspicion that he would make the bench for Liverpool's forthcoming match with Middlesbrough – the game that the twenty-four-year-old had targeted as his comeback match. After his 40-minute work-out, Gerrard said to the assembled journalists:

> It's good to be back. It's been a very frustrating two months for me because I hate watching football. It's even more frustrating with the injury past I've had. Hopefully that's all behind me now and I can have a good run like I have done for the last two years and push on until the end of the season. I've tested it out and it feels 100 per cent. The boys have done really well without me but, hopefully, I'm looking to get on the bench for the Middlesbrough game. We've got some big games coming up... We're still in the Champions League and all the other competitions, so hopefully the future's bright.

After a week of vigorous, unceasing exercise at Melwood, Gerrard was, as expected, named as a substitute for Liverpool's trip to the Riverside Stadium on 20 November, after missing twelve domestic and European Liverpool matches. The midfielder was given a rapturous ovation as he began a pitch-side warm-up with Liverpool trailing to a goal by Boro's Chris Riggott. And, with the Reds' midfield

STEVIE WONDER

faltering and with Dietmar Hamann anonymous, Rafa Benitez chose to withdraw the German and thrust his captain back into action just short of the hour mark, charged with galvanising his team. Gerrard, despite spraying some delightful passes right, left and centre to road-test his foot, could not help prevent a demoralising 2–0 defeat for Liverpool on Teesside. In the realisation that a Premiership title challenge was already eluding them after their fifth league defeat of the season, the Reds had to make sure of progression in the Champions League.

'The Champions League is the ultimate. We are still in it and I am confident we can qualify,' said Gerrard as he prepared for Liverpool's penultimate group-stage match against Monaco in the Stade Louis II. Didier Deschamps, the former Chelsea midfielder and manager of the French side about to meet Liverpool, delivered his own assessment of exactly what having Gerrard back from injury meant to Liverpool. 'He is the leader of their team, a charismatic player who has a huge influence on Liverpool's game. Without Steven Gerrard, Liverpool are not the same,' he said. 'He is someone who encapsulates the whole energy of the team with his style and he sets the tempo. He can be one of the best players in Europe and the world. He is a typical modern player, a complete footballer.'

With their captain back in their starting XI, Liverpool were confident of gaining the win they needed to confirm their passage into the knock-out stage of the tournament. However, bereft of any luck in Monte Carlo, Liverpool lost to a solitary goal by Javier Saviola, after the Argentinian had looked to have controlled the ball with his hand.

As the Reds faced up to the prospect of having to beat Olympiakos by two clear goals in their final Champions

STEVEN GERRARD: PORTRAIT OF A HERO

League group game to progress, Gerrard announced his return to action as Liverpool recorded their finest victory of the season in the Premiership. A resounding performance by the Reds captain and his team-mates saw them beat reigning champions Arsenal 2–1 at Anfield. Goals from Xavi Alonso – delightfully teed up by Gerrard – and then youngster Neil Mellor – from long range in the final minute – gave Liverpool a stunning victory.

During Gerrard's injury lay-off, Rafa Benitez's side had been making steady progress in the League Cup and, having seen off Millwall and Middlesbrough earlier in the competition, the Reds made the journey south for a quarter-final tie with Tottenham at White Hart Lane. Benitez, with the Champions League match against Olympiakos in mind, decided to give Gerrard, and a number of other first-team players, a rest. Nevertheless, the youthful team that he deployed in the capital sent Liverpool through to the semi-final by winning a penalty shoot-out after the game had ended at 1–1.

Gerrard, enjoying a new lease of life after injury, played in a more advanced forward role in Liverpool's Premiership match at Aston Villa. The Reds warmed up for their monumental Champions League encounter with Olympiakos with a 1–1 draw at Villa Park.

'I don't know if that could be Steven's future position, but he is superb in it,' said defender Jamie Carragher after seeing his captain run Villa's defence ragged. 'In central midfield he is as good as anyone in Europe, but in this role, I haven't seen many better in Europe either. When he gets that ball in between the midfield and defence, he can run at people, he can shoot, he's got creativity and he sees a

STEVIE WONDER

pass. I spoke to some of the Villa defenders who said, "When Steven runs at you he is virtually unstoppable." I know from training. People don't realise how much pace he has got. He is one of the quickest around.'

Such boundless energy and such eternal brilliance boded well, as Liverpool squared up to one of their biggest European games in years with their whole future at stake. The night of 8 December 2004 will live long in the memory of all Liverpool fans – it was the night that defined a remarkable season. Failure to qualify from the group stages of the Champions League would have spelled disaster for the Reds, with perhaps the most significant of repercussions being the exit of Gerrard in the January transfer window. The Anfield captain had made no secret of what he wanted – and it all rested on the game with Olympiakos, with Liverpool already a long way adrift from the lead in the Premiership. He delivered a chilling ultimatum on the eve of the game.

> I can't wait for three or four years for the club to be turned into a title-winning side. If I left at any time in the next few years, I'd get certain fans who would maybe understand the decision and some who would turn against me, but that's normal. I'm a fan and I'm the captain and it would hurt the fans more if I did decide to leave.
>
> I want a big family by the time I'm thirty-five and to be able to show medals to my children. It would mean a lot for me to be successful with the club I've supported all my life. Hopefully, from now to the end of the season, they can show me they're as ambitious as I am. If the club is moving forward and

doing well, I won't have to be looking anywhere else. But if it isn't looking as good, I'll have to think again in the summer.

It will be a disaster for the club and myself personally if we end up in the UEFA Cup. I have already won it. It plays second fiddle to the Champions League and I don't settle for second best... I wouldn't say it's win or bust, but it is a massive game for me personally and everybody associated with Liverpool – we will show what being in the Champions League means to everyone here.

Ironically, Gerrard even claimed during one of his most honest and lengthy press conference responses: 'I have to be realistic and say we're not going to win the Champions League this season, but I do think we can improve on the quarter-finals, which we achieved a few years ago.'

Whether or not Liverpool fans agreed with Gerrard's forthright comments, they could only hope and pray that their team would prevail against Olympiakos at Anfield – a football stadium that has seen so many awe-inspiring European games down the years. Little did they know that they were about to witness one of the best; one of the most evocative. 'You'll Never Walk Alone', resonated around Anfield as ever, but with adding meaning, added purpose. Liverpool had to win 1–0 or by two clear goals to make it through. If not, they would have to face far greater consequences than just Champions League elimination. 'Make us Dream', said one banner, held aloft in the Kop end – a message that held so much truth at the end of the subsequent 90 minutes.

Olympiakos, the group leaders, had beaten Liverpool on

STEVIE WONDER

their own patch in late September and fancied their chances of another scalp. The Greeks had a match-winning midfielder of their own in Brazilian superstar Rivaldo and it was he who shook Liverpool to the core with a curling first-half free-kick that deceived goalkeeper Chris Kirkland and put the visitors into the lead. Gerrard, who had already clipped an improvised effort against a post, was immediately charged with igniting a Reds fightback.

At the beginning of the second half, Rafa Benitez threw on rookie forward Florent Sinama Pongolle and, almost instantly, the Frenchman squeezed home Harry Kewell's low cross to bring Liverpool level. Just past the hour mark, with time beginning to ebb away, Gerrard saw a long-range shot squirm under the Greek goalkeeper into the net only to see it ruled out for a foul by Milan Baros. With 12 agonising minutes remaining, Baros was replaced by another young centre-forward brimming with enthusiasm – Neil Mellor. Two minutes later, Liverpool's last role of the dice paid dividends. Antonio Nunez aimed a header goalwards from Pongolle's cross, that was repelled only to be gobbled up and slammed into the net by the lurking Mellor. With the wind firmly in their sails, Liverpool rolled out the stage for a moment that proved utterly priceless. With three minutes to go, the desperate home side launched another raid on the Olympiakos goal. Jamie Carragher crossed from the left-hand side and Mellor, aware of the position his captain would be in, cushioned a well-directed and inviting header into Gerrard's path 22 yards from goal. Without hesitation, and with awesome technique, the talismanic midfielder thundered a wonderful half-volley across the goalkeeper into the corner of the net. Anfield went berserk as Gerrard savoured a moment of pure emotion in front of the adoring Kop.

Having been so perilously close to Champions League elimination, Liverpool were through to the knock-out stages of the world's premier club competition thanks to a moment of sheer spellbinding brilliance conjured by the right boot of their captain. In one moment, Gerrard rose from being an Anfield great to becoming an Anfield legend. He told the waiting press:

> Thank God for that strike. I don't think I've ever scored a more important goal for Liverpool. But I am not going to take the credit for the win on my own. You have to credit the substitutes and it was a great performance by the team. I'd be a liar if I said I thought we could do it when we went behind. At half-time, I thought we had a mountain to climb. It was a massive night for me. It was not one of my best performances, but it was one of the best goals I've ever scored. The ball was taking ages to come down and was spinning, and I thought this one is going into the stands. It was about time I caught one sweet – and I have not caught one as sweet as that for a long time.

The goal, and Gerrard's all-round contribution, had the man who presided over it purring. 'Steven can win all he wants with us and we need him,' Rafa Benitez said. 'He has seen that we have a good team and we can do more things in the future. But if we want to win more games, important games, we need Steven in the team. We need his strength, the strong mentality he has and his quality. I think he likes, and wants, the responsibility of leading this team.'

STEVIE WONDER

Gerrard's astonishing, money-spinning goal sparked wild celebrations on Merseyside. To Liverpool fans it was the best early Christmas present they could wish for. They could continue to dream at least until the resumption of the Champions League in February – and that was worth much more than the £10 million the win over Olympiakos earned for the club.

Celebrations did not last long for the Reds. The 200th Merseyside derby completed an incredible week for them, but the result at Goodison Park did little to replenish their faltering form in the Premiership. Rafa Benitez broke up the Alonso-Gerrard midfield partnership that had performed so well, by dropping the Spaniard to the bench. Consequently, Everton's Real Madrid-bound midfield general, Thomas Gravesen, kept Gerrard on a leash all afternoon and Lee Carsley scored with a rather tame shot to give high-flying Everton their first victory over their city rivals in five years.

Three days later, Liverpool met Portsmouth at Anfield. By now, T-shirts illustrating Gerrard as a gladiator with the slogan 'At my signal, unleash Hell' were being sold by street vendors all around the stadium. This garment of choice for many a Liverpool fan, young and old, exemplified the true meaning of the Reds' captain. Critically, however, Gerrard was showing himself to be the Reds' only true gladiator and, on too many occasions, was he relied upon to 'unleash hell' on opponents all on his own. As much as the Liverpool fans wanted to believe it, Gerrard was not superhuman. With 20 minutes to go against Portsmouth, and with the game heading for stalemate, the twenty-four-year-old accepted a short pass from a free-kick by Xavi Alonso and lashed a vicious rising drive into the net via a post. Sadly, the other Liverpool players could not adhere to his rousing commands to hold onto the lead and a mistake by Jerzey Dudek late in the game gifted Pompey a point.

Rafa Benitez's side went some way towards healing open Premiership wounds by beating Newcastle 3–1 at home – a result which began a run of three-successive victories over the Christmas period. Gerrard's integral form continued to attract plaudits as the January transfer window drew ever nearer.

'He is their driving force, hammering his men forward as if he has a one-man crusade to make certain they play attacking football and win,' Alan Shearer told the press ahead of Newcastle's clash with the Reds. 'He is a fantastic footballer, absolutely magnificent. He has picked Liverpool up by the scruff of the neck and dragged them through games. He is an outstanding figure in the English game, a top player and someone I have the utmost respect for. I watched him in midweek against Portsmouth. And I watched him in their last Champions League game against Olympiakos – his sheer range of passing and his overall ability is outstanding. He is scoring goals as well. It is not just his passing but also his shooting. From 20 to 25 yards when he has got the ball, he really can be deadly.'

Shearer could, at least, empathise with Gerrard's desire to win silverware with his hometown club, having signed for Newcastle for that very reason.

'I know he has had offers to leave, but he is a hometown kid and wants to win things for his club,' continued Shearer. 'I have the greatest respect for him wanting to stay and to do that for his fans.'

Liverpool followed up their fine win over Graeme

STEVIE WONDER

Souness' side by beating West Brom 5–0 on Boxing Day at the Hawthorns. Gerrard scored the Reds' third goal of a convincing win, ramming home a low free-kick to register his seventh strike of the season before being afforded the luxury of a rest for the final half hour. A 1–0 home victory over Southampton quickly followed, as the Reds ended 2004 beginning to show signs of overdue consistency.

New Year's Day, however, dealt a stark reminder to Liverpool that they were far from being Premiership title contenders. Joe Cole's deflected effort handed champions-elect Chelsea a 1–0 win at Anfield and Gerrard hardly allayed fears of a summer transfer by trading a 'high five' handshake with their manager Jose Mourinho at the end of the game.

The Reds bounced back with a 2–1 win at Norwich City before meeting championship outfit Watford in the first leg of their Carling Cup semi-final at Anfield. The Hornets frustrated the Reds until Gerrard side-footed home the only goal of the night after good work from Milan Baros to put Liverpool in command of the tie.

A home defeat to bitter rivals Manchester United left Rafa Benitez's side all at sea in the Premiership. With Roy Keane imperious in midfield for Sir Alex Ferguson's men, Gerrard and his failing team-mates were powerless to prevent their side from losing to a goal from Wayne Rooney. That misery was compounded when a youthful Liverpool side, minus its captain, lost 1–0 at Burnley in the FA Cup third round after an unfortunate Djimi Traore own goal.

Benitez had answered Gerrard's calls for fresh faces up front by acquiring the services of Real Madrid hitman Fernando Morientes. His arrival seemed certain to signal an upturn in fortunes, but Liverpool's woes only continued as they hit rock-bottom with a 2–0 defeat at Southampton. With all title ambitions now extinguished, Gerrard, yet again, came to the Reds' rescue to put to bed any growing fears of a crisis. Playing with a slight thigh problem, the captain sealed Liverpool's passage into the League Cup final by slotting home from the edge of the area 13 minutes from time at Vicarage Road to complete an unconvincing 2–0 aggregate win over Watford.

'This was always a potential banana skin and Watford made it hard for us. People try to put this competition down, but there will be 70,000 at the final and those are the games you want to play in,' said Gerrard, after ensuring that Liverpool would take part in their third League Cup final in four years. He continued:

> We're in a cup final, still fighting for a top-four finish in the Premiership and in the last sixteen of the Champions League. If you look at the bigger picture, it's not too bad. I'm sure I speak for everyone when I say we'd like things to be better, but when so many changes are made at a club, things are going to take time. This is Liverpool, one of the biggest clubs in Europe, so when you lose three games in a week, you expect a bit of stick. Losing to Manchester United and Southampton in the Premiership and going out of the FA Cup at Burnley was possibly one of the worst weeks I've had since I've been at this club. In the aftermath we needed to regroup, make sure we stuck together and played as a team, because we were not doing it in those games. We were playing as individuals, not passing the ball well, not keeping possession and not

STEVIE WONDER

fighting enough. These are the basics, but we showed them against Watford and that sent out the right message. It was a massive result.

We've all had a difficult time lately, fans and players alike, so it was important to get people smiling again.

Indeed, Liverpool kept their fans smiling with comfortable wins against Fulham and Charlton before Gerrard returned to action with England, gaining cap thirty-four of his career in the Three Lions' goalless draw with Holland at Villa Park. And despite Liverpool's renewed appetite in the Premiership, a 2–0 defeat to Birmingham tainted their hopes of finishing in the top four. The Reds real hunger remained for the Champions League.

Gerrard, having picked up his second booking of the competition against Olympiakos, was then forced to sit in the stands as Liverpool recommenced their European adventure against Bayer Leverkusen at Anfield. The Reds shirked his absence to win 3–1 in front of their home fans and put themselves on the brink of qualification for the quarter-finals. Goals from Luis Garcia, John Arne Riise and Dietmar Hamann were the difference on another night of pulsating theatre at Anfield, but a late Leverkusen goal silenced the jubilation and kept the Germans in the tie.

Only five days later, Liverpool were back in their second home for their Carling Cup encounter with Chelsea. Cardiff had been a happy hunting ground for the Reds in recent years and, following their victory over Leverkusen, they were brimming with confidence, despite the daunting prospect of facing Jose Mourinho's rampant Chelsea.

The game was already shrouded in intrigue with most in the media adamant that Gerrard was bound to sign for

STEVEN GERRARD: PORTRAIT OF A HERO

Chelsea at the end of the season, having come close to doing so the previous summer. But the Liverpool captain was only looking forward to leading his side out in a major cup final for the very first time. Ahead of the Cardiff showdown, he told the press:

> I've already won two League Cup-winner's medals in Cardiff and I want a hat-trick. The boys are really looking forward to causing an upset. I've scored in a League Cup final already against Manchester United. Hopefully it will happen again. Confidence is high. All the lads are buzzing after the Champions League victory over Bayer Leverkusen.

Gerrard's winning mentality made a welcome return to midfield as he locked horns with his equally gifted England team-mate Frank Lampard. Amazingly, John Arne Riise scored inside 45 seconds; superbly volleying home a Fernando Morientes pass. Liverpool held that slender lead until one of the most humiliating moments of Gerrard's career.

With only 11 minutes remaining, Paolo Ferreira lofted a free-kick into the Reds' penalty area and the captain, jumping higher than Riise and Jamie Carragher, inadvertently guided a glancing header past his own goalkeeper into the net. The first own goal of his professional career left Gerrard visibly distraught. In one misguided instant, he had, or so it seemed, squandered his final chance to realise his boyhood dream and lift a trophy for Liverpool. From that moment on, there was only one winner. With the game in extra-time, Chelsea, having dominated the entire match in the face of some dogged Liverpool defending, made the trophy their own

STEVIE WONDER

with goals from Didier Drogba and Mateja Kezman. Antonio Nunez made for some last-minute nerves with a late header, but Chelsea held on to their 3–2 lead to lift the Carling Cup at Liverpool's expense.

Gerrard's torment was clear for all to see. His world had collapsed around him. Slumped on the turf, with tears filling his eyes and the Chelsea fans ironically chanting his name, the crestfallen skipper sat alone contemplating a bleak future. The Monday morning newspapers offered little sympathy either, with most choosing to acclaim Gerrard's unfortunate own goal as his 'first goal for Chelsea'. For the Liverpool captain, there was no escape from the speculation that his Anfield career was plummeting to its end. After all, it was he who, well before the League Cup final, had stated that his Liverpool future rested on the potential for them to win silverware the way Chelsea were threatening to do. The Champions League was now the be all and end all for Rafa Benitez's side and surely they couldn't win that, could they? Even Gerrard, with all his bookish football knowledge, had laughed off that very suggestion.

'It was very painful,' grimaced Gerrard after his Cardiff nightmare. 'Losing any game of football is painful, but to lose a cup final and score an own goal made it a really bad day for me. But I have to be strong, pick myself up and look forward to the next game. We have other things to play for, but that was a tough night.'

The twenty-four-year-old remained defiant after the 'worst day' of his life and was desperate to make a lasting mark as Liverpool captain. 'It'll be tough for us to win anything, but we'll give it our best shot in the Champions League,' he continued, in the *Guardian*. 'Our hopes are still alive and if we get through and Chelsea get through, I'd like us to meet them again – I fancy our chances. I said before the Carling Cup final that it would either be the best day of my life or the worst. It was the worst. I really felt we were going to hold on to the win. I'm gutted for the lads and the supporters, but we've now got to try and stay focused on qualifying for the Champions League. If we come fourth in the Premiership it will feel like we've won a cup final, because Everton have a big lead over us. I haven't given up my dream of lifting a trophy as Liverpool captain.'

More determined than ever, Gerrard led his team out for a crucial Premiership match away at Newcastle United. For him, there would be no respite; no chance to hide away from the limelight. His Carling Cup heartache received little remedy, however, as Liverpool lost to Laurent Robert's free-kick at St James' Park.

Liverpool now, more than ever, with everything else falling apart, had to make efforts in the Champions League count. Gerrard's passion-fuelled and interminable efforts, at least, deserved to be rewarded with something big. The Anfield captain, back from suspension, returned to grace Europe's premier competition as Liverpool crushed Bayer Leverkusen 3–1 in the BayArena to make it through to the quarter-finals in style. Where Liverpool were failing domestically, they were more than making up for it with their outstanding performances on the continent. Gerrard's display in Germany, like Liverpool's, was astounding. A delightful sweeping cross allowed Luis Garcia to nose Liverpool ahead, before another goal from the Spaniard and a strike from Milan Baros afforded the Reds a famous victory.

STEVIE WONDER

'We knew we could punish them on the counter,' said a delighted Gerrard after the game. 'That is what we planned to do – we had seen the videos. We played well, the best we have played for a while. That was the gameplan – we never came here for a draw or a 1–0 defeat.'

Those final ten Premiership games began with a dour goalless draw with Blackburn at Anfield as Liverpool suffered another hefty hangover after a dizzy night in Europe. That result meant that the Reds would go into their next game, the 201st Merseyside derby, with three points absolutely mandatory. Everton, flying high and favourites to claim the last Champions League qualification berth in the Premiership, came to Anfield with high hopes of virtually ending Liverpool's chances of overtaking them. Ahead of the colossal clash, Gerrard said:

> It's going to be a massive game for us, one that will tell us a lot about where we're going to finish. You always know what's at stake going into these games, but this one's about a lot more than just local pride. There might be millions resting on the result. They're very emotional matches anyway, but this might just be the biggest Merseyside derby I've ever played in... This is when we really do need to stick together, roll up our sleeves and get rid of the inconsistencies that we've suffered from at times.

Gerrard's rallying cry seemed to rub off on his team-mates; haunted by the fear of failure. Even after their fine win against Bayer Leverkusen, any suggestion of winning the Champions League was being met with howls of laughter but, as Gerrard stated after, the 'real' Liverpool turned up to take on Everton. After 27 classic minutes, Gerrard chose placement and not power to put Liverpool ahead from a free-kick – his tenth goal of the season. Soon after, Luis Garcia headed home to catapult Anfield into ecstasy. Tim Cahill pulled a goal back to set up a nervy second-half ending, but Liverpool, led so imperiously by Gerrard again, held on to move within four points of their Merseyside rivals in the Premiership. At the game's conclusion, the Liverpool captain could be seen kissing the badge on his shirt – just the pronouncement of loyalty and sheer love that the Kop wanted to see.

On the international front, Gerrard helped England see off Northern Ireland with a 4–0 triumph at Old Trafford before the Three Lions met Azerbaijan at St James' Park. Sven-Goran Eriksson's side were made to wait for a breakthrough by their inferior opponents but, when it did come, it was worth waiting for. Wayne Rooney swung over a cross from the right-hand side; the ball was deflected to the edge of the area where it met the hungry, agile, right boot of Gerrard. The twenty-four-year-old's fierce volley smashed into the ground before finding its way into the net off the crossbar in the blink of an eye. The Liverpool star's sixth international goal, coupled with a classy strike by David Beckham, gave England a 2–0 win and pushed them further towards World Cup 2006.

Gerrard returned from international duty to help Liverpool to a narrow 1–0 home victory over Bolton ahead of their Champions League quarter-final first-leg tie against Juventus.

'It's a massive game. The last eight. We have done well to get there and we're the underdogs. But we will give it a go,' said Gerrard, who had meticulously run the rule of

STEVIE WONDER

the Italian giants, to the *Daily Star*. 'If Juventus were to score at Anfield, it would be a mountain to climb. A clean sheet is vital... I'm up for it.'

It was the first meeting between the two European household names since the Heysel disaster that had borne so many repercussions. Both Liverpool and Juventus made public declarations to honour the memory of the victims, hoping to heal the wounds left open by the 1985 tragedy. From the emotion, came the electrifying energy for Liverpool to take the game to their much-fancied opponents – and how! Within ten minutes, Gerrard's corner had been flicked on by Luis Garcia for defender Sami Hyypia to wallop home a wonderful left-foot volley and send Anfield loopy. Fifteen minutes later, Garcia, already a star of Liverpool's sparkling campaign in Europe, lofted a dazzling, swerving 25-yard volley over Gianluigi Buffon and into the net. It was a telling moment – a special goal that told the Liverpool fans that, yes, they could win the Champions League. From that breathtaking instant on, Liverpool, escorted by the diligence of Gerrard, dug deep to contain Juventus and prevent the away goal the captain had warned against. Their resistance proved agonisingly futile, however, as a header from Fabio Cannavaro squeezed past deputising goalkeeper Scott Carson in the second half to hand the Italians a sturdy lifeline.

'That was easily the best we've played all season. I would put it beyond the Arsenal and Olympiakos performances,' said Gerrard after the game, reflecting on a night of unbridled passion and belief on the part of his team. 'Given the calibre of opposition, the first-half performance may even be as good as anything I can remember in the last few years. You have to look at what we've done. We've beaten one of the best teams in Europe. Juventus and AC Milan were everyone's favourites and not many would have given us a chance.... A lot of us are going to have to put in the performances of our career in Turin.'

Liverpool only had to wait a week before their trip to northern Italy. In the meantime, they saw their hopes of qualifying for the Champions League in the Premiership all but diminish with a 1–0 defeat at Manchester City. The Reds' anguish at the City of Manchester Stadium extended well beyond the result of that match. Gerrard sustained a groin injury; one that cast serious doubt over his involvement in the looming Champions League quarter-final second leg.

The Stadio Delle Alpi, in all its splendour, had been the scene of Manchester United's most impressive performance in their Champions League-winning crusade of 1999. Six years on, another British hopeful set foot in Juventus' backyard hoping to defy the odds and progress to the semi-finals. But where United had had their own talismanic hero, Roy Keane, to guide them forth, Liverpool were dealt the cruel blow of having to do it all without theirs. Gerrard was ruled out of the tie and was left at home as his side toiled for the right to face Chelsea in the semi-finals.

'Without Gerrard's leadership, Liverpool could have a few problems,' were the words Fabio Capello, the Juventus manager, used to assure himself that it would be his side that would progress. His expression seemed justified in reflection of previous games where Liverpool had struggled without their captain. That was not to be the case this time – in the Reds' biggest European game for twenty years. Buoyed by their hunger, Rafa Benitez's 'weakened' side made it through, holding the Italian 'Old Lady' to a goalless draw to win 2–1 on aggregate.

STEVIE WONDER

Having had intensive treatment on his injured groin at Melwood while his side were battling against probability in Turin, Gerrard returned to action in Liverpool's home game against Tottenham. He left Anfield wishing that he hadn't. The Reds had to win the game to keep alive any realistic hopes of qualifying for the following season's Champions League via their league position. With Spurs leading 2-1 in the second half, Gerrard was sent sprawling by Michael Carrick inside the penalty area. Referee Mark Halsey immediately pointed to the spot. Liverpool's captain picked himself up, but blasted his penalty high and wide to the dismay of the Kop. Sami Hyypia did manage a goal to salvage a draw for the Reds, but the reality had dawned that, domestically, their season was destined to end in failure.

'I should have scored and I'm so sorry I missed,' said a downcast, but sincere, Gerrard after his penalty nightmare. 'I would like to apologise to the fans, my team-mates and the club – I blame myself for us not winning. That's me finished with penalties.'

With Liverpool adrift in sixth place, Rafa Benitez decided it best to use his captain only as a late substitute in the Reds' 2-1 victory at Portsmouth – affording him a well-earned rest ahead of the Champions League semi-final. Gerrard did return to play at Selhurst Park three days later, but he could not prevent Liverpool from losing their tenth away outing of the season at Crystal Palace. The 1-0 defeat in South London did little to inspire, and more to suggest, the thought that Liverpool were about to be sent crashing from their European pedestal by the might of Chelsea.

Gerrard took more than enough incentive with him to Stamford Bridge. Where he craved success with his hometown club, he was also feverishly desperate to avenge his own goal in the Carling Cup final.

'If you look into Stevie's eyes you can see a determination to put things right,' said Rafael Benitez, as he prepared his team for another epic night in Europe. 'Talking to him, watching him in training, he so clearly wants to do well.'

Liverpool were a staggering thirty-one points behind Chelsea in the Premiership going into the tie: a true measure of exactly how inconsistent the Reds had been domestically; a mere shadow of themselves in European competition, where they seemed unstoppable. Once again, Gerrard's future was thrust under the spotlight, with many suggesting that the two-legged semi-final would ultimately decide which of the two clubs the midfielder would be signing for in the summer. The only thing on his mind, however, was a place in the most coveted cup final of them all and a chance to put his story on the bookshelf alongside the great Liverpool captains of yesteryear.

A dental operation in the days leading up the match didn't deter the Reds' captain as the dogged spirit that Benitez had instilled in his side told again at Stamford Bridge. Chelsea missed their fair share of chances as fate began to swing in the direction of Merseyside and only a fine save from Petr Cech denied a laborious Liverpool an away goal after Milan Baros had met an appetising Gerrard cross with his head.

With even the most prudent of Liverpool minds now focused on the all-or-nothing second-leg encounter against Chelsea, the Reds' domestic season, naturally, looked set to end without cheer. Nevertheless, Gerrard, for all his prudence and diplomacy as captain of Liverpool, could not help but score one of the finest goals of his career in

STEVIE WONDER

their penultimate home Premiership match against Middlesbrough. With the Reds trailing to a first-half strike from Boro's Slizard Nemeth and facing their fifteenth defeat of the season, Gerrard embraced the ball to the right of centre, 30 yards from goal. Sensing an opportunity like nobody else would tend to do in such a position, he fired an outstanding, swerving, plummeting volley into the top corner. It was the kind of breathtaking moment rendered perfect to warm Anfield up for its biggest night on the European stage for twenty years.

'It's the biggest game of my life,' exclaimed Gerrard, as he prepared to shoulder the responsibility of continuing Liverpool's Champions League fairytale, with them now only 90 minutes away from the final. So tantalising was that prospect; so high were the stakes resting upon it. In a whimsical sense, it was almost as if fate had decided, amid all the rumours, that Gerrard was destined to leave Liverpool and sign for Chelsea, that the two English giants would meet in a match that had so much riding on the outcome. The Reds' captain continued:

> We need eleven gladiators out there to beat Chelsea, and the fans have to be ready for an incredible night. Anfield is the best place for big European nights by a mile. It is an incredible atmosphere, and we need that – we know exactly what role the fans can play, and we know how the team must play. The confidence running through us on these types of nights is incredible. It is going to be a great spectacle for everyone, I just hope, come the final whistle, we will be celebrating. This season, we have had incredible nights at Anfield against Olympiakos and Juventus,

just unbelievable occasions, but this will surpass that. During your career not many chances come along to get to the European Cup final like this. European nights at Anfield are something special and the fans will be up for it. It could be awesome.

Gerrard's foresight rang true as Anfield trembled with unrestrained passion as Liverpool's moment of truth finally arrived. The Kop choir bellowed out the angelic words of 'You'll Never Walk Alone' as the atmosphere mirrored the excitement on such a huge occasion. Chelsea, who had been crowned Premiership champions three days earlier, strode out to a deafening, intimidating roar. Liverpool's gladiators proceeded to roar into battle. After only three minutes, and in front of the Kop, the Reds scored the decisive goal that catapulted them to the final, with Gerrard inevitably involved; his supreme vision, accuracy and creativity summed up by an impudent flick over Chelsea's defensive line. Milan Baros latched on to the invitation only to find his run blocked by the impeding Petr Cech. With the Czech striker floored, Chelsea's startled defence scrambled to clear the ball, but Luis Garcia, personifying determination, darted forwards to nudge it goalwards. William Gallas made one last attempt to prevent a goal, but a combination of the referee and his assistant decided that the French defender's clearance was too late – the ball had crossed the line.

Anfield rocked on its foundations. For those old enough, the hysteria evoked memories of Liverpool's 1977 European Cup quarter-final encounter with St Etienne – widely regarded as Anfield's most exhilarating night. Before the eyes of their adoring fans, Rafa Benitez's

STEVIE WONDER

modern-day superheroes, led by a local boy, were rolling back time to those heady days of glory. Everything Chelsea threw at them, from Garcia's goal onwards, the Reds resisted like men possessed. For any Red, the second half felt like an eternity, especially when the fourth official declared six minutes of stoppage time with Liverpool on the brink of glory.

The Kop fell eerily silent as Eidur Gudjohnsen, right at the end, seized to pounce on Chelsea's best chance of the match, but he could only lash his close-range shot past the far post to the rampant relief of pumping Red hearts. The referee's final whistle signalled wild celebration on Merseyside as Liverpool declared their date with destiny set for Istanbul. Gerrard's joy was clear for all to see; he was the last player off the pitch, having been so overcome by the achievement of leading Liverpool back to the European Cup final. After the game, the proud captain told the *Liverpool Echo*:

> This is the best night in my life by a million miles. The ground was shaking 50 minutes before the game when we were warming up and I have never known anything like it. At the end I felt like jumping in and celebrating with the fans. They are the best in the country by miles and I just hope they enjoy the final as much. It will be the proudest moment of my career when I lead these incredible men out in Istanbul. We haven't been good enough in the league, but we have been awesome in the Champions League.
>
> Chances to win the European Cup don't come along too often and we have to grasp the moment and make sure that in Istanbul we have no regrets... We have a great chance now to make history and become legends.

STEVEN GERRARD: PORTRAIT OF A HERO

Before their trip to the Turkish capital to face the mighty AC Milan, their Champions League final opponents, Liverpool had to conclude their terribly disappointing league campaign. Having seen Everton virtually assure themselves of fourth place a day earlier, the Reds' staggering alter-ego reared its ugly head at Highbury. Rafa Benitez's side felt the full force of yet another European hangover, losing 3–1 to Arsene Wenger's Arsenal; their only joy derived from a deflected Gerrard free-kick – his fortieth Liverpool goal. With all hope of qualifying for the Champions League via the Premiership now gone, the captain was given a complete rest while a 2–1 victory over Aston Villa at Anfield brought the curtain down on the domestic season. Liverpool's hopes of playing Champions League football the following season subsequently rested on the outcome of the final, and even then qualification would have to be decided by the governing bodies.

Where Liverpool had failed in the Premiership, Gerrard had flourished for the whole season. He ended the campaign with his highest-ever score count and another pristine disciplinary record; thirteen goals that owed much to him being employed in a more advanced midfield role by Rafa Benitez, but also to his ever-improving ability and authority. He only picked up a total of six bookings in his forty-four appearances. Gerrard, like his team in Europe, had surpassed all that was required of him. Of course, there was still more to come. Following his meteoric rise from scanty Huyton schoolboy to the captain of his beloved football club, the twenty-four-year-old stood poised for the real crowning moment of his career.

Chapter Eleven
Turkish Delight – The Champions League Final: 25 May 2005

'The Champions League has brought out the best from this side; there is great belief and confidence among us all. We have gone all the way to the final and beaten some fantastic teams and we are now really confident. There's a tough task ahead, but we are not going to Istanbul just to enjoy the experience, we are going there to win it.'

There was no doubt that Gerrard, in the build-up to the Champions League final, went to bed dreaming of joining the company of the legendary Anfield captains who had lifted the European Cup before him during Liverpool's golden age. He knew that achieving such immortality was going to be tough. Having meticulously examined AC Milan's own imperious march to the final, Gerrard was under no illusions that the Italians posed a huge, if not overwhelming, hurdle. But then, Liverpool had thrived on being the underdogs on too many occasions before to have any qualms about being up against the odds again. Belief and desire, two of the midfielder's best qualities, had rubbed off on his team-mates in their hours of need against Chelsea, Juventus and before that, of course, Olympiakos. Rafa Benitez's gallant heroes were more than equipped with the attributes needed to topple Milan, who had suggested that Liverpool were too defensive and would merely be pushovers. Liverpool's captain said to press assembled days before the game:

> We have always been the underdogs and we will be the underdogs in Istanbul. Everyone thinks Milan will just have to turn up to beat us, but they will be in for a really big fight; we are up for it and we are confident that we will be able to surprise everyone again. I don't care what their manager or players say about us. All I am interested in is that we are all spot on for the final. If we were a defensive team, we would not have scored all the magnificent goals in this competition.
>
> I hope Milan underestimate us and I hope they just think they have to turn up to win it because we will be ready to prove them wrong. We will show them respect but no fear; we have watched the tapes of them and we know they are beatable.

As the biggest moment of his career and the conclusion of an exceptional, extraordinary journey drew ever nearer, Gerrard boarded a plane at Liverpool's John Lennon Airport, joining his team-mates and an estimated 40,000 Liverpool fans from across the globe on their pilgrimage to Turkey.

'To lose would be criminal after the great season we have had. We need to make sure we come off that pitch with the

TURKISH DELIGHT – THE CHAMPIONS LEAGUE FINAL: 25 MAY 2005

cup and winner's medals,' reiterated the Liverpool captain, hoping to hold aloft the Reds' fifth European Cup in their first final in twenty years.

The overwhelming pride of realising a childhood dream and captaining his hometown club in the European Cup final – a dream he never thought would come true – had Gerrard thinking about nothing else other than leading out his team in the Ataturk Stadium.

'Since my mates started leaving for Turkey, I've not been able to sleep,' said the twenty-four-year-old, who had publicly denounced his side's chances only three months before. 'My family left for the game and that's when it all started sinking in. I've not been able to think about anything else. I have been dreaming of lifting the trophy, don't worry about that. I haven't stopped thinking about it and it has been in my head 24/7. I want to bring that trophy back for all our fans. They have been with us right the way through and they deserve it.'

Gerrard also promised the Liverpool suburb that first witnessed his awesome talents a lavish celebration, should he bring the trophy home.

> I will be taking the trophy to my local for one hell of a party. If we win it and I get permission from the club, I'll take the cup to Huyton to show my friends and family. I should get plenty of opportunities, too, because we get to keep it this time if we win. I'd organise a big party so that everyone who has supported me could come along and see it. There aren't too many players from the city who have had the honour of winning the European Cup – I know all the stories about 1977, where there were a lot of Liverpool lads in the team.

STEVEN GERRARD: PORTRAIT OF A HERO

This final will be the club's best because it will be me holding the trophy. That's selfish I know, but it will be dedicated to the fans because they have waited a long time for such success. This time will be special and different because the Liverpool sides of old always dominated. But we have been the underdogs all through and have proved a lot of people wrong. But if I come back empty-handed now it will be a disaster. We haven't done it in the league, but in Europe everybody has been dying for the badge and we need to do that again.

Liverpool's first poignant victory of the Champions League final came with the news that they would line up in their famous red shirts, with Milan wearing their alternative white strip. It was a good omen considering the fact that when they had played Roma in the 1984 final – the last time they had won the competition – it had been the same colour coordination. Indeed, Liverpool had worn red and beaten a team playing in white on each of their four previous European Cup-winning nights.

'I am glad we are in red – it's our colour,' enthused Gerrard. 'Don't they say that teams in red always win? There is a real belief in this team that we can do the business. The one thing we must make sure of is that we have no regrets when we walk off the pitch. We will have plenty of time to rest over the summer, so let's make sure that we give it everything on the night.'

The Liverpool captain knew only too well the stakes riding on the game. In demanding times, he had, more often than not, been the man to shoulder, and then to thrive on, the responsibility of guiding his team on. In the

TURKISH DELIGHT – THE CHAMPIONS LEAGUE FINAL: 25 MAY 2005

Ataturk Stadium, he faced the biggest task of all. To assembled journalists, Gerrard stressed:

> There will be a lot of pressure on us to perform, but that is what we are paid for – it's what we're here for. What's the point of being a footballer and not wanting pressure? It only comes in big games and this is the ultimate. I am looking forward to the pressure. I have said all along that this is what I want and now I am getting it. Maybe there is even more pressure on Milan. There is so much expectation on them as favourites and perhaps we can relax a little. They have more experience than us, but they are older. We are a lot younger, which could actually be an advantage. It will be crazy if we win and getting a winner's medal in the biggest competition would mean the world to me.
>
> I can't even bear to think about losing this game, not for one second. It's not on the agenda. The prospect of losing a Champions League final doesn't bear thinking about. This is the dream; this is the big one. For all of us, this is the biggest game we can play, and I will make sure we all realise that. For me, personally, what could possibly be better than being the captain who leads Liverpool out for the Champions League final? Well, lifting the trophy, obviously.
>
> Put it this way, we are not going to Istanbul just to turn up and enjoy the night. We are going there to win it, believe me. We need everyone, the eleven players and all the subs, to be prepared to die for the club in Istanbul. We need that mentality when everyone has to put everything on the line for Liverpool, because that is what it will take to win.

STEVEN GERRARD: PORTRAIT OF A HERO

In the game against Olympiakos at half-time, we thought we were out. We sat there in the dressing room and everyone was gutted, because we really thought that was it. No one said anything; we were just staring at the floor, because none of us believed that we could get three goals in the second half. But we did and from that moment there was a belief about us. I will remind the players of that feeling at half-time against Olympiakos, and I will tell them that there's no point going out just to enjoy the occasion, it will be a disaster if we lose. A disaster.

Five days short of his twenty-fifth birthday, Gerrard, having dreamt of the moment for almost all of those twenty-five years, escorted his team out into the cauldron of noise created by the masses of Liverpool fans convened in the Ataturk Stadium. As the emotion of 'You'll Never Walk Alone' hollered from all four corners of the stadium with all its sincerity, the Reds captain gathered his team in a huddle to deliver those promised final words of encouragement.

Just over a minute later, and barely 50 seconds into the fiftieth European Cup final, Milan caught Liverpool off guard as Paolo Maldini, their veteran captain of four winners' medals, skilfully swept home Andrea Pirlo's right-wing free-kick. In the blink of an eye, the novelty of the occasion had worn from Liverpool's gaze. Here were Milan, the clear favourites to win, ahead with not even a minute of the final played – even the most ardent of Reds' fans feared the worst. Rafa Benitez's side, though, as they had shown in previous rounds, were not about to lie down and allow Milan to maul them. They duly responded vehemently.

Sami Hyypia forced Milan goalkeeper Dida into action,

TURKISH DELIGHT – THE CHAMPIONS LEAGUE FINAL: 25 MAY 2005

planting a firm header goalwards from Gerrard's cross before Rafa Benitez's plans were hampered by an injury to Harry Kewell. The Australian, who had been a surprise selection in the starting XI, limped off to be replaced by Vladimir Smicer. And, with Liverpool in disarray after having had a legitimate penalty appeal turned down, Hernan Crespo – on loan to Milan from Chelsea – converted Andrey Shevchenko's low cross to put the Italians two goals ahead. Shevchenko himself had seen a goal disallowed for offside beforehand as the Serie A side dominated. Moments before half-time, Crespo impudently finished from Kaka's incisive through-ball, stabbing the ball over Jerzy Dudek and leaving Liverpool with a mountain of staggering proportions to climb.

The half-time whistle brought rapturous cheers from the pocket of Milan fans; from the hordes of Liverpool followers it brought only ghastly silence. The Reds' deflated stars wandered from the pitch believing that their dream was over. 'At half-time I thought it was going to be impossible,' said Gerrard, later. 'I thought that there were only going to be tears of disappointment and frustration at the end. We were outclassed in that first half.'

Rafa Benitez gathered his players in the small dressing room deep in the bowels of the Ataturk Stadium to deliver the most difficult half-time pep talk of his career. 'I just remember the manager getting his pen out and writing down the changes he wanted on the board,' recalled Gerrard. 'He also said to try and get an early goal as that could make them nervous. But, to be honest, I just couldn't concentrate. There were all sorts of things going through my head; it was weird. I just sat there with my head in my hands. I thought it was over, I really thought it was over.'

STEVEN GERRARD: PORTRAIT OF A HERO

Benitez's inspiring words – whatever they were – coupled with the echoes of Liverpool's famous anthem emanating from their resolute fans and the unscrupulous noise of premature celebration from Milan's dressing room, rejuvenated Liverpool. Rumours also circulated after the game that Milan had tempted fate by opening boxes of custom-made garments to wear underneath their shirts for the post-match celebrations. Having been persuaded not to wear them by one player who clearly didn't believe that they had the right to be toasting victory so soon – said to have been Crespo – the Milan players left the T-shirts blazoned across the floor of their dressing room. As Liverpool strolled out for the second half, an open door revealed the truth of Milan's disrespectful mentality.

Benitez withdrew right-back Steve Finnan at half-time, replacing him with Dietmar Hamann as the Reds sought recompense – it was a decision that proved a masterstroke. Liverpool kept their composure and, following a smart stop by Dudek to deny Shevchenko's free-kick, came the Reds' impetus to initiate the most extraordinary six minutes in their history.

Gerrard, who had begun to grab a firm hold on midfield – something that had eluded the England star in the first half – started another patient Liverpool attack from the edge of his own penalty area. Just over 20 seconds later, the Liverpool captain, having ghosted forwards unchecked, rose majestically to loop John Arne Riise's delightful cross from the left into the net. Not renowned for scoring headed goals of such quality – it was only the third of his professional career – Gerrard's goal evoked the magic – the belief – that would turn the 2005 Champions League final on its head.

TURKISH DELIGHT – THE CHAMPIONS LEAGUE FINAL: 25 MAY 2005

The twenty-four-year-old sprinted back to the halfway line furiously gesturing with his arms, knowing that his side were still in with a chance – the momentum his strike gave Liverpool was quite profound. Scarcely two minutes later, Vladimir Smicer, making his final appearance for the Reds, took aim from 25 yards and crashed an unstoppable shot into the far corner to send the red sections of the Ataturk Stadium delirious. Rafa Benitez's side had gone from being a beaten team at half-time to being on the verge of a comeback labelled nothing short of miraculous. Almost inevitably – and roared on by their disbelieving fans – that revival read complete as Gennaro Gattuso tripped Gerrard inside the penalty area and Xabi Alonso stepped forward to shoulder the enormous responsibility of nudging Liverpool level. The Spaniard saw his effort saved by Dida, but he gleefully accepted the rebound to hurtle the ball into the roof of the net to make the score 3–3. It was, for all watching, simply unbelievable.

Exhausted, after such an astonishing explosion of courage and determination, Gerrard and his heroic team endeavoured to contain Milan for the final half hour. Buoyed by their devoted following, who were constantly chanting the words of their endearing anthem, the Reds succeeded in slowing the frantic pace of the contest and held out for extra-time and a chance to re-charge their drained bodies.

Gerrard played most of extra-time as a right-back, manfully aiding his unwavering side in stifling all that Milan dared to conjure. At the end of the first half in extra-time the Liverpool captain even put his arm around Andriy Shevchenko, seeming to utter the words 'all the best'; it was a gesture that exemplified the mutual respect the pair – two of the world's most decorated players – had for each other in such spell-binding, earth-shattering circumstances.

Liverpool's fans fell silent in the second 15 minutes, as Milan laid siege to the Reds' goal. Shevchenko came the closest to breaking their hearts, but found Dudek, the Reds' much-maligned goalkeeper, in irrepressible form. The Ukrainian powered a downward header against the flailing legs of the Polish custodian and then, incredibly, saw his instantaneous follow-up somehow turned over the bar. Dudek leapt to his feet nodding his head in disbelief, if not satisfaction. Milan's match-winning chance had gone and penalties ensued – the only way to end such an enthralling game of football.

Rafa Benitez, as he had done both at half-time and at the end of 90 minutes, visited the mind of each of his five designated penalty-takers as the Liverpool fans, and the majority of those watching on television, held their breath, whispering words of encouragement. The Reds' destiny now rested in the lap of the gods – they had not practised penalties in the days leading up to the final.

Gerrard, designated as Liverpool's fifth penalty-taker, stood in the middle of a line of bodies – arms linked – on the halfway line ready to watch the conclusion of the season, unable to help his side anymore. Having lost the second coin toss of the night, Gerrard could be seen bowing his head, still trying to fathom all that had gone before, as Serginho walked forward to take Milan's first penalty. Amid a cacophony of whistling from the Liverpool support, the Brazilian placed his penalty high over Dudek's crossbar. The whistles turned to cheers as Serginho turned away in despair.

Dietmar Hamann was Liverpool's first taker, coolly

TURKISH DELIGHT – THE CHAMPIONS LEAGUE FINAL: 25 MAY 2005

slotting his kick to the right of Dida, before the Reds were propelled into dreamland by Milan's crucial second miss. Jerzey Dudek, the hero of the hour, flung himself to his left to deny Andrea Pirlo and then Djibril Cisse put Liverpool two in front. Dudek proceeded to remind Liverpool fans of Bruce Grobbelaar's goal-line stance that helped the Reds win their last European Cup twenty-one years before, wobbling his knees in an attempt to put off Milan's third penalty-taker. Jon Dahl Tomasson scored, and Liverpool's hearts were forced into overtime again as John Arne Riise saw his effort saved by Dida and then Kaka slammed his kick past Dudek. Vladimir Smicer, with his last-ever kick for the Reds, sent Milan's goalkeeper the wrong way to induce match point.

Andriy Shevchenko, Milan's most celebrated player – one of the world's most potent stikers, who had seen his penalty win the competition for Milan two years before – stepped forward knowing that he had to score, or else the European Cup was heading back to Merseyside. In what seemed like slow motion, the Ukrainian opted to clip his penalty towards the centre of the goal. As Dudek fell to his right, he read Shevchenko's intentions perfectly and repelled the ball with his left hand, crowning Liverpool with their fifth European Cup. Cue unreserved, adrenalin-fuelled exhilaration.

Almost every single television camera and photographer courted Gerrard, knowing that it would be his face that painted the best picture of Liverpool's remarkable triumph – never had there been a cup final like it ... anywhere. The Reds' captain embraced everybody in his path as he made his way on a lap of honour to thank the fellow Liverpool fans who had accompanied him on such an amazing, magical journey. Shortly before becoming only the second Scouser after Phil Thompson to lift the European Cup as skipper of the Merseysiders, Gerrard acclaimed the contribution of his manager as he embraced him on the world's television screens.

Talking to ITV, Gerrard pointed to a beaming Rafa Benitez, saying hoarsely: 'We didn't believe we could do it at half-time, but all credit to this man, he never let us put our heads down. We carried on fighting and every one of us deserves credit for that. I'm just made up for the fans: they've saved up for weeks and months to be here – just look at them – 35,000 of them.'

Liverpool's Man of the Match then stepped forward for the proudest moment of his career. The words of his song – the one the Liverpool fans cry in appreciation of his many talents – reverberated around the stadium. To the tune of Que Sera Sera:

Steve Gerrard, Gerrard.
He'll pass the ball 40 yards,
He's big and he's f***ing hard,
Steve Gerrard, Gerrard.

And the man who had just become the second youngest captain to win the Champions League paused as his valiant team-mates were presented with their medals. Then came his moment: stepping onto the stage, UEFA president Lennart Johansson presented Gerrard with his medal before the twenty-four-year-old saw his reflection in Europe's most-coveted prize for the first time, waiting impatiently for his signal to hold it aloft. He kissed the huge gleaming trophy with all the affection in the world, before Johansson, obviously bewildered by all the excitement, very nearly deprived him of the moment by making to hand the trophy to Jamie Carragher. All was forgiven, however, as Carragher pointed fervently towards Gerrard and amid the fireworks, the noise and the tickertape, the Liverpool captain clasped the trophy in both hands and raised it to the sky. It was, undeniably, the proudest, most significant moment of his career to date.

There followed more celebrations as Liverpool paraded the trophy around the Ataturk arena. The stadium's public address system relayed the immortal tones of 'You'll Never Walk Alone' sung by Gerry and the Pacemakers – as if Liverpool's exultant fans needed any enticement to sing it with such emotion, together as one, in commemoration of the five-time winners before them. To a man, with scarves aloft, it was a tear-jerking image that will live forever in the memories of all who revelled in the greatest football match of all time.

Back on Merseyside, there was no time to prepare for the biggest party Liverpool had ever seen. Within seconds of Dudek's final, momentous, penalty save, the streets of the city were flooded with rapturous fans waving flags, beeping car horns and still disbelieving of events in Istanbul. Back on the outskirts of the Turkish capital, a weary Liverpool hero, still wearing his red shirt, was thrust before the world's media, who were intent on draining more insight from the man who had seemingly written the script for football's greatest show.

> There were a few heads down at half-time; the manager made a few changes and put a belief in the side. The important thing at half-time was to try and get back in

the game and make it respectable for the fans. We were a different side in the second half; I think the early goal changed it. To be honest, though, when Jerzy made that double save from Shevchenko I started to believe it was going to be our night. Just before he hit the ball I thought 'Goal'. Then, when it went over the bar, I realised it could be ours. In extra-time we were running on empty and playing for penalties.

We were massive underdogs at the beginning of the competition and I'll hold my hand up and admit that I didn't think we were going to go all the way, but we've fought all the way through, played well, defended well and scored some good goals. As you've seen tonight, we were never beaten. We've beaten some fantastic sides in the competition and nobody can say that we don't deserve to be winners. I just hope that those above let us defend it. It's called the Champions League, so the champions should be able to defend it.

The Liverpool fans are crazy and unbelievable and they were the twelfth man again tonight. I would like to dedicate this victory to them because they deserve it – I'm really happy for them.

All the Liverpool fans that Gerrard cared for so much wanted to hear, however, were the answers to lingering doubts about his imminent future. 'I'm just glad because, after the Carling Cup final, a lot of people were questioning my commitment,' exclaimed the captain. 'How could I leave after a night like this, together with all the nights I've experienced throughout the season? This is the greatest night of my life. It still hasn't sunk in yet, I'm sure it will do. We can go and have a few drinks now.'

TURKISH DELIGHT – THE CHAMPIONS LEAGUE FINAL: 25 MAY 2005

Soaked in champagne, Gerrard returned to the team's hotel and took the giant trophy to his bedroom, emulating the great Liverpool captains – such as the late Emlyn Hughes – who hadn't been able to let go of the trophy for fear of waking up from their dream.

'I woke up with my winner's medal on and I managed to get Shevchenko's shirt as well, I am buzzing,' said Gerrard. 'I slept with the trophy in my room. I just didn't want to let it go. When someone took it away from me on Thursday morning, I felt as though I had somehow lost a part of me. It was an incredible night, just ridiculous really, and I didn't want to let it go.'

It is not often that a cup final can be accredited to one player. Only Blackpool's 1953 FA Cup triumph springs to mind – that being the 'Stanley Matthews' final. And where Liverpool had benefited from so many heroic performances in Istanbul, from Dudek through to Alonso, it would be hard to certify the 2005 Champions League final as the doing of one player in particular. But had Gerrard not been playing – say injured or suspended – it is almost certain that Liverpool would not have won, let alone recovered from a three-goal deficit against one of Europe's best sides. Without being unfair to Dudek, or indeed any other of the Reds' heroes, their chivalrous contributions paled in comparison to Gerrard's monumental efforts. Throughout the six-and-a-half years of his professional career leading up to the final, the local boy with the strongest heart had proved his significance. On so many occasions Liverpool had faltered without his invaluable presence and, conversely, profited from it when he had been in the side. Like the heroes of days gone by – Ian Rush, Kevin Keegan, Graeme Souness, to name but a few – Gerrard had earned the right to become King of the Kop. The 2005 European Cup final was, for every Liverpool fan, the 'Steven Gerrard' final.

The victorious Liverpool squad returned to John Lennon Airport with the sun shining down on Merseyside. Displaying the pride of the city, thousands lined the streets to welcome their heroes home. Newspaper stands across Liverpool tried their best to tell the full story of the night before – but could anyone really put it all into words and make sense of it all?

Gerrard joined his team-mates on a victory parade around his home city; perching at the front of an open-top bus alongside the Champions League trophy. An estimated 750,000 people swamped the streets as the packed bus made its way past Anfield and through the city centre. It seemed as though the entire population of Liverpool wanted a glimpse of their legendary team and the trophy's glorious return to Merseyside. Gerrard said to media assembled afterwards:

> It was unbelievable. None of the players imagined there would be so many people here, waiting to cheer us on. The scenes were incredible. I was sitting on the plane coming home with my medal and thinking 'life can't get any better than this', and then you saw those fans everywhere. Someone told me there were about a million people on the route and it was just so special. I can remember the celebrations following the cup Treble in 2001, but this was something else. The lads were just buzzing. For some of the foreign players it was a real eye-opener, but this is Liverpool Football Club and that's why we never gave in against Milan

TURKISH DELIGHT – THE CHAMPIONS LEAGUE FINAL: 25 MAY 2005

when it looked like a lost cause. The fans in Istanbul were brilliant and the welcome home topped off the greatest night of my life. I'd just like to say thank you to everyone who turned out on behalf of all the players. Those supporters are the best.

With laborious celebrations destined to persist long into the night, Gerrard and the rest of Liverpool's players and staff retired to a private venue. Only then could they begin to piece together the amazing, unforgettable events of 25 May 2005.

Gerrard's efforts in bringing the European Cup back to Anfield failed to go unnoticed later in the year as he was voted the Champion League's most valuable player by EUFA. More tellingly, Gerrard came third in the European Footballer of the Year award voted for by Europe's top journalists. Only Chelsea's Frank Lampard and Barcelona's Ronaldinho – the outright winner – finished above the Liverpool captain in the rankings. The Ballon D'Or trophy is widely regarded as the highest accolade available to a player plying his trade in Europe. Gerrard's name stood proudly amongst those of Europe's finest – and rightly so.

Chapter Twelve
Personal Professional

The personal life of Steven Gerrard is rarely thrust into the spotlight. He has never been embroiled in any off-the-field scandal, neither has he ever sought such attention, as many modern-day footballers are often accused of doing. If Gerrard's name does make the national newspapers anywhere else other than the back pages, it is most likely to be the fault of his beautiful girlfriend-turned-fiancée, Alex Curran, who frequently enjoys perusing north-west fashion boutiques clad in the latest designer attire. The couple have been together since 2001, having met in a Liverpool nightclub. Before Alex, Gerrard dated another stunning blonde, Jennifer Ellison.

The Liverpool star's relationship with the former *Brookside* actress was a turbulent one. She was seventeen and he was nineteen, when they met in a city-centre nightspot in March 2000. The meeting was a blind date planned by friends of the couple. Gerrard invited Jennifer to watch Liverpool play

STEVEN GERRARD: PORTRAIT OF A HERO

Sheffield Wednesday – the game in which he scored his first goal for the club. Thereafter, they had appeared to be getting serious before an acrimonious split in October of the same year amid speculation that she had, instead, fallen for her *Brookside* co-star and on-screen boyfriend Philip Oliver. However, that separation was short-lived. The Liverpool lovebirds reconciled their relationship in January 2001, publicly announcing that they were back together at a gala dinner for the Liverpool International Supporters' Club player of the year. The reconciliation also did wonders for Gerrard's on-the-pitch form. At the time, he overcame a back injury to play starring roles in Liverpool victories over arch-rivals Manchester United and Arsenal.

Gerrard was suffering physical pain of a different kind in those early months of 2001 – his wisdom teeth. In February 2001, he visited a specialist French dentist recommended to him by the then Liverpool manager Gerard Houllier. The French football authorities are firm believers in healthy teeth. Nothing strange about that, but they also believed that healthy teeth meant an injury-free football player. They had the theory tried and tested on the successful French national side and Jean Tigana also ushered his Fulham players for check-ups before they marched to the top of the First Division that year.

'Always when a player has trouble, you look at the teeth.' The French national squad's doctor Dr Franc Logall explained to the *Daily Express*. 'We recently checked our top twenty players and six of them had infections in the mouth. It can lead to tendonitis and problems with muscles or even the heart. We don't know precisely how one thing leads to another, but it is nerve-related.'

Gerrard promptly had his troublesome wisdom teeth

PERSONAL PROFESSIONAL

removed and duly returned free from injury to help Liverpool to their 2001 Treble success.

In the meantime, he was still getting his teeth into Jennifer Ellison, but his relationship with the blonde temptress was ill fated. Gerrard didn't want any distraction from a football career that was rapidly bearing fruit. His one-track mind saw him ditch the beautiful actress in February 2001.

Rumours of city-centre nightclub brawls and revenge attacks had also blighted the soap star's personal life. She revealed that jealous attacks on her had made the relationship intolerable. 'We craved a normal relationship, but the only time we felt comfortable was when we were at his mum and dad's house eating Chinese takeaways and watching videos,' she told the *News of the World*. 'I know that's the price of fame and, believe me, I'm grateful for everything I have, but we just couldn't take any more hassle, so we sat down and decided that we had no option but to call it a day. We didn't argue. It was just a sad realisation that if we continued to be together we'd never have any kind of normal life. Everywhere we go, we get hassle because of who we are. It's impossible.'

Gerrard soon met Alex Curran – a girl who, quite literally, became a model girlfriend for him, but he remained defiant that he wasn't about to let anything, including his personal life, get in the way of the sport he lived for or of his passion for Liverpool.

'It's about living for football and being a professional. It means staying in and sacrificing nights out,' he told the *Daily Mirror*. 'I have to make sure I give myself the best chance of being in peak shape when matches come around. Everyone has a drink and a burger now and then, but it's all about doing it at the right time. I can't afford to relax for one moment. I have to keep a low profile, eat the right things and not drink. There's a long way to go before I'm where I want to be. There are a million things I still need to learn, but if I'm going to progress, Anfield is the best place for it. If I keep listening to the coaching staff here, I'm sure I'll become a better player.'

In hindsight, Gerrard's hunger for his first taste of glory with his hometown club had deflected him away from the frenetic showbiz lifestyle that Jennifer Ellison embraced – and evidently it worked wonders, as Liverpool romped to domestic and European glory later that year.

Gerrard briefly dated a girl who he had met at Manchester Airport in the summer of 2001 before he met Alex Curran. Stacy Barnes, an eighteen-year-old blonde beauty, went out with him for five months following his split from Ellison. But she was another attention seeker who, upon splitting with him, promptly sold her story to the tabloids. Although once again the Liverpool ace was fancy-free, soon after he met his perfect match.

Curran, a nineteen-year-old student from Aintree on Merseyside, met Gerrard in a Liverpool city-centre nightclub in the winter of 2001 and the couple began a less-publicised romance. The Liverpool-born beauty accompanied Gerrard on a post-season break to Dubai the following summer as the couple announced their affection, soaking up the sun at the Arabian hot spot's six-star Jumeirah Hotel. Gerrard's joy of finding new love was tempered with the realisation that he would not being taking part in the World Cup following an operation to cure a persistent groin injury. Crucially, though, the couple stayed away from the headlines and their relationship

PERSONAL PROFESSIONAL

blossomed. Only photographs of them out shopping together made the tabloids.

Curran became firm friends with Michael Owen's partner Louise Bonsall and the other partners of Gerrard's Anfield team-mates. Close friends of the couple claimed that they were deeply in love as the Liverpool star confirmed his affection with a series of ravishing gifts for the blonde bombshell, including driving lessons and a Mercedes SLK to learn with.

July 2003 brought the news that Curran was pregnant. And shortly after 8.30pm on 23 February 2004, the couple were celebrating the birth of their first child. Gerrard had missed England's match with Portugal to be at her bedside at the Liverpool women's hospital. Weighing 7lb 1oz, the couple's new baby daughter was named Lilly-Ella.

Only three months after the birth, Gerrard asked Curran to marry him. His friend and team-mate Michael Owen had proposed to his childhood sweetheart on Valentine's Day and, without wanting to be outdone, Gerrard wrapped a huge diamond ring in the baby's blanket to surprise his girlfriend. She accepted instantly. The following summer, the newly engaged couple prepared for Euro 2004 while they accompanied the rest of the England players and 'wags' (wives and girlfriends) to Sardinia for a pre-tournament break. Alex and baby Lilly-Ella then accompanied the England star to Portugal to see him take on France and Switzerland in the two opening matches of the tournament.

Curran's love of designer trends and hair extensions became a target of the tabloids, as did her admission that she did not know that England were facing France in their first game. In fact, all of the 'wags' – a name given to them by the tabloids – on tour in Portugal almost managed to outshine their partners with some dazzling off-the-pitch displays. Curran made good friends with Victoria Beckham too, and no doubt the Queen of 'Wags' gave her some tips on motherhood along the way.

There was no doubting Alex Curran's beauty, style and love for Liverpool's adopted son. Gerrard was soon in need of some solace after a back-pass blunder contributed to England's downfall against France: he found the perfect place – on the shoulder of his new fiancée.

Curran was also by Gerrard's side as Chelsea came knocking that summer – pleading with him to stay with Liverpool. Her magic worked and he celebrated by buying a brand new Aston Martin to drive his young family around in and jetted off to Dubai for another break ahead of the football season that would change his life forever.

Gerrard went on to lift the European Cup with Liverpool before the couple and their daughter relaxed on a break at the Portuguese villa they had bought the previous Christmas as rumours of Gerrard's seemingly imminent move to London circulated. Having helped to persuade him to stay on Merseyside a year earlier, Curran had a hand in doing so again, possibly even Lilly-Ella, too.

Gerrard revealed his affection for his young daughter to *OK!* magazine and also told them that he planned to get married after the 2006 World Cup.

'Lilly is the most important thing to happen to me,' he said. 'I really want more kids, three or four. I'd like a big family. I want to go through the buzz I get with Lilly again. When she sees me on the telly she shouts "Daddy!" and tries to kiss the TV. She's definitely a daddy's girl, but that's probably because I go away a lot.'

Having already seen Michael Owen and Louise Bonsall

PERSONAL PROFESSIONAL

tie the knot, the couple's appetite for a lavish wedding ceremony can only have been enhanced as they attended the wedding ceremony of Jamie Carragher and his childhood sweetheart Nicola Hart in July 2005 at Weston Park, a seventeenth-century stately home in Shropshire. A few months later, pals of Curran revealed that the stunning blonde was pregnant with the couple's second child. Gerrard could have his hands full in summer 2006, in more ways than one.

Gerrard's material possessions are rather like those of other Premiership football stars – he has the archetypal big house, an array of flash cars and a designer watch – but he still makes sure that his elder brother, Paul, and parents, Paul and Julie, don't go without.

'I have only got one brother and I will not let him work,' he told *GQ* magazine. 'It would be weird, wouldn't it? I'm earning good money and don't want to see him going out and working nine to five, breaking his back for a couple of hundred quid a week. I look after him because I know that if the boot was on the other foot, and he was a football player, he would not let me work.'

Gerrard is also incredibly close to his parents. Having had his dad watching him in almost every game he has ever played, the Liverpool star marks him out as one of his role models.

'He thinks he knows more about the game than me. I see him every day. And he gives me an honest opinion of how I played,' Gerrard said. 'He's watched near enough every game I've been in since I was eight, so I suppose he knows the way I play. If I played crap, he always tells me. I usually put the phone down before he really gets going.'

STEVEN GERRARD: PORTRAIT OF A HERO

Until early 2001, Gerrard was living with his parents in Huyton, close to his other family members, his grandfather and his cousins. His first car, at the age of seventeen, was a red Volkswagen Golf 1.4, but as he began to cash in on his career with Liverpool, he sought a move to Southport, a more affluent area on the periphery of Merseyside. He splashed out on a Mercedes and a BMW X5 and took residence in a luxury bachelor pad on the town's promenade – a £1.4 million penthouse apartment in a renovated Victorian hospital. Gerrard's football friends, Dominic Matteo and Gareth Farrelly, also shelled out at the same time for one of the thirty trendy homes in the Marine Gate complex. The Grade II-listed building gave Gerrard privacy and security, as well as marble floors, a sauna and a steam room in addition to a stunning view across Southport's elegant marina.

Gerrard acquired more cars to add to his stunning collection, but just over a year after he made residence in Southport, he bought another house in order to move in with Alex Curran. In October 2002, he acquired the former home of Robbie Fowler, who had left Liverpool to sign for Leeds United. The huge detached home at Blundellsands in the Crosby area of northern Liverpool, was thought to be worth a cool £600,000.

Gerrard's team-mates Jamie Carragher and Stephane Henchoz lived close by and the beautiful home seemed like the perfect setting for the Liverpool hero to start a family with his girlfriend. The four-bedroomed house on the idyllic Briarwood estate had two bathrooms, a conservatory and a snooker room with generous thick woodland to its rear. The mansion was the venue for hours of deliberation in the summer of 2005, as Gerrard pondered leaving Liverpool.

PERSONAL PROFESSIONAL

Upon his decision to stay on Merseyside, he decided to move again. He celebrated the signing of his new contract, worth an estimated £100,000 a week, by moving into a £2 million mansion in leafy Formby, a place most favoured by affluent footballers and celebrities. His new home on the town's desirable Victoria Road is said to have nine bedrooms and bathrooms, three living rooms, a cinema, an indoor swimming pool and landscaped gardens. The road was named the region's most expensive street in March 2005, when a survey by Mouseprice.com found the average house price to be £553,324. Everton striker Duncan Ferguson, snooker star John Parrott and former England centre-forward Alan Shearer all have houses there.

However perfect his personal life seems, Gerrard has not totally escaped trouble away from the football field. In January 2004 he was charged and later fined £1,000 and handed five penalty points after being caught speeding in the Liverpool suburb of Bootle in his Audi A4 turbo cabriolet. Apart from the odd rumour about gangland threats as his Liverpool future hung in the balance and the exposure of his rocky relationship with Jennifer Ellison, plus some understandable warnings regarding late-night cavorting, Gerrard has found near-perfect succour in his private life, putting his beloved family first and remaining mature and undeterred by the modern-day pressures that rest on the shoulders of young footballers.

Outside of a Liverpool shirt, Gerrard is the master introvert. He is a keen golfer and, with the glorious Birkdale club close to his home, he is never too far from a few rounds with his friends. He is also keen on snooker, having played it from a very young age and enjoys getting one over his friends and team-mates whenever he can.

STEVEN GERRARD: PORTRAIT OF A HERO

He revealed to Liverpool Football Club's official website, www.liverpoolfc.tv, that his interest in music ranges from Phil Collins to Coldplay with the former's 'Greatest Hits' his most favourite album. He also rates the *The Office* as his favourite comedy programme and *Scarface* as his favourite movie. Armani and Hugo Boss are among his favourite fashion labels and pasta, fish and chicken are his favourite foods. Indeed, Gerrard's favoured restaurant is The Warehouse Brasserie in Southport, where he regularly dines.

Wherever he goes, Gerrard can be considered a model professional off the field. He has steered clear of trouble since he was caught on a night out in 2000 prior to an England match. Gerard Houllier, the Liverpool manager of the time, warned him and told him that it could affect his career. From that moment on, Gerrard vowed not to indulge in late-night drinking. He became a better footballer for it. Gerrard is now set to marry Alex Curran in summer 2007.

Chapter Thirteen
A Story Only Half Told

For any average footballer, winning the European Cup as captain of his hometown club would be seen as the pinnacle of a career – a climax that nothing could possibly surpass. That is not the case for Steven Gerrard. Eternally insatiable, Liverpool's favourite son wants for nothing. Yet, having acquired the latest medal of an already-enviable collection and having duly put pen to paper on a lucrative new Anfield contract, he set about pursuing new dreams.

'I've only one medal left to win at Liverpool and that's the Premiership,' he says, referring to the title that is, perhaps, the hardest one to achieve of them all. 'That's what I want more than anything and Liverpool is the only place I've ever wanted to win it. I love Liverpool so much. This is my club. My heart is with Liverpool. I don't need to tell anyone that.'

Gerrard's dream is tempered by the fact that Liverpool, the most successful English side of all time, have not been crowned domestic champions since 1990. Nor have they come within true, touching distance of doing so ever since. The naked truth is they have plenty of work to do before they can convince their fans that they are ready to mount a serious challenge again.

The captain's decision to remain at Anfield – presumably into the twilight years of his career – leaves question marks over whether he will ever be able to hold the Premiership trophy aloft. Had he uprooted from Merseyside and signed for Chelsea then it is highly likely that he would have been able to raise it above his head as early as 2006, given the Londoners' current stranglehold on the title. There would, however, be no satisfaction; in his head, maybe, but certainly not from his heart.

That is probably what Gerrard came to realise in those dark summer days of decision-making during the summer of 2005. Imagine the scene: Chelsea have romped to another victory that confirms them as champions and are set to be presented with the trophy at Stamford Bridge. Gerrard, having been deployed as an unused substitute, stands clad top to toe in a blue tracksuit. He joins in with the celebration that bears no resemblance to the wild scenes of Istanbul a year earlier; he is far from being the centre of attention. The Chelsea fans don't chant his name, only that of John Terry, who struts forth to be the first to hoist the gleaming trophy. Gerrard has to wait a good while before he gets his hands on the trophy, and even when he lifts it high above his head, his stance lacks the pride and gusto of the very same act after Liverpool's Champions League success. He gazes around a stadium landscape still alien to him. There is no Kop end; there isn't a smidgen of red, anywhere. The Chelsea fans can't

A STORY ONLY HALF TOLD

associate with him; neither can he associate with them. He has the Premiership medal he so dearly wanted around his neck, but where is the magic? Where is the pride and adulation? Where is the hearty satisfaction? You see, none of it would be there. Gerrard would probably never be able to achieve the kind of iconic status he will forever encompass at Liverpool while playing for Chelsea.

However, as Jose Mourinho's side threaten to dominate on English soil for years to come, it seems that any player wanting a Premiership-winners' medal will have to first make sure they are on the Stamford Bridge roster and then hope that they feature in ten or more games to qualify for it. But where there are no guarantees in West London, there are certainly none on Merseyside.

At the end of the 2004–05 season, Liverpool finished a perplexing thirty-seven points behind Chelsea – a gap that the Reds must endeavour to narrow if they are even to be considered as likely title contenders in the next few seasons. Unquestionably, it is Rafa Benitez's toughest assignment as manager; it is, equally, Gerrard's toughest as captain. If he is to realise his dream, then Liverpool will have to continue to defy the odds and show determination in the very same, inimitable way they did in 2005. And Gerrard has proved on countless occasions in the past that he can inspire things to happen on his own – even in the most extreme circumstances. His ability to do that will never diminish.

Gerrard's renewed loyalty to Liverpool already reaped its first reward when he scored his 50th senior goal for the club in a League Cup defeat away to Crystal Palace on 25 October 2005.

And as the 2006 season got under way, Gerrard had

surpassed 300 appearances in a red shirt. These achievements alone will move him further up on the rostrum of Liverpool's greatest midfield players. And then will follow the proudest moment of his international career to date.

The 2006 World Cup in Germany, God forbidding he sustains an injury beforehand, will be Gerrard's first appearance at the most prestigious football event on the planet – a chance finally to lay to rest the memories of his injury heartache in 2002. The World Cup is the most likely stage where Gerrard could emulate, if not better, his achievements at club level, with England among the favourites to win the competition.

The Liverpool star has – when fit – been a near ever-present for the Three Lions under Sven-Goran Eriksson, but he is yet to make the same kind of peerless impression he makes with Liverpool while on the international stage. In truth, Gerrard's opportunities to make such an impact have been hampered by the fact that he has often been deployed in a role less suited to his authoritative game. For example, the long spell where Eriksson played him on the left of his infamous 'diamond' formation, moved Gerrard away from his favoured central role. Then there is his partnership with Chelsea's Frank Lampard – Eriksson's current weapon of choice in central midfield. Many critics argue that the pair, for all their divine qualities, are too similar – too attack-minded – to form an effective midfield engine room. That argument is likely to go on, given that Eriksson seems intent on continuing to pick the duo.

Gerrard will be desperate to avenge the doubts over his worth to England and to ensure that he gives himself the

A STORY ONLY HALF TOLD

best chance of glory in Germany, whatever role he is chosen to play in. And, by the end of the World Cup, the midfielder will most probably be on the verge of gaining his fiftieth England cap. He has already enjoyed a career jam packed with defining moments, and Germany 2006 will certainly be another of those – and possibly the most prominent.

The World Cup is only Gerrard's immediate future, of course. His long-term outlook is even more intriguing. He may decide to remain with Liverpool for the remainder of his career; that depends on the success Liverpool have as he sees out his current contract but, of course, nothing in life is certain and clearly not the career of a footballer. If he does remain on Merseyside, he could even go beyond the greatest Anfield record of them all – the league appearance record held by the legendary Ian Callaghan MBE.

During a glittering career spanning eighteen years on Merseyside, Callaghan clocked up an incomparable 856 first-team appearances. Even as Gerrard overtakes the 700 game barrier, his career bears so many comparisons to that of Callaghan. Liverpool-born, Callaghan was the original local hero – plucked from the streets of the city, he took the place of his hero, Billy Liddell, when the Reds were languishing in the old Second Division in 1960. Playing mainly as right-sided midfielder during the entire Anfield reign of Bill Shankly, he served to inspire an incredible revival, claiming five league titles, two FA Cup-winners' medals and two UEFA Cup honours before lining up as a thirty-five-year-old as Liverpool won the European Cup for the first time against Borussia Moenchengladbach in Rome in 1977. The archetypal footballer, he was only booked once in his career.

Callaghan left Anfield in 1978, leaving behind a lasting

legacy and a record he himself believes will never be beaten. In 2000, when Gerrard was still rising to prominence at Anfield, Callaghan told www.thebootroom.net: 'I can't see the record being broken. Players don't stay that long these days, its different now with the transfer system we have. You can't see players getting into the team as a seventeen-year-old and staying there for eighteen years and not missing many games.'

Callaghan may have to eat his words if Gerrard continues his own momentous Liverpool career while continuing to win trophies and remaining free from serious injury. Indeed, of all of Liverpool's talismanic midfield heroes of yesteryear that Gerrard may be compared to, Callaghan bears the most striking resemblances. A gentleman off the pitch, workmanlike and influential on it, he was loved so dearly by the Liverpool fans who warmed to the type of Scouse charm and enthusiasm that Gerrard possesses now. Callaghan, who began his working life as a central-heating apprentice, was only capped four times at international level but he was, interestingly, a member of England's 1966 World Cup-winning squad when he was only twenty-four – two years younger than Gerrard will be if he plays at the tournament in 2006. That may be a good omen, perhaps, given all the similarities between the two Anfield heroes. Regardless of whether or not Gerrard can inspire England to glory in Germany, if he ever topples Ian Callaghan's record it will, almost certainly, crown him as Liverpool's greatest-ever player – and that has to be the most appealing honour of them all.

With Gerrard's playing career likely to last long into his late thirties, maybe more if he takes a leaf out of Teddy Sheringham's book, he is not likely to have thought too

A STORY ONLY HALF TOLD

much about what he would like to do when he does hang up his boots. But is that really true?

As a teenager Gerrard was so eager to win that he often accompanied his dad to games involving other schools. Since then he has always studied football intently, both in his role as Liverpool captain and through his sheer undying enthusiasm for the game. He has openly admitted to watching more matches than he would ever care to remember on television, much to the annoyance of his fiancée. But it all marks him out as a future manager. Indeed, it may be true that he secretly wishes to manage Liverpool one day, should he decide not to cut the umbilical cord that attaches him to the club.

Shortly after making his 300th appearance in a Red shirt, Gerrard told the Red's official website of his thoughts about the future.

'I'm always thinking about what I'll do after football,' he said. 'It's always been my idea to stay involved with this football club for as long as I can. I've been here since I was eight years of age and it would be wonderful to think I could still be here after hanging up my boots. Whether that'd be in a managerial or coaching capacity I'm not sure. Of course, I'm still only 25 and the end of my playing career is still a long way off, but the future is something that is constantly on my mind. Whatever happens I hope it is something linked with Liverpool... I learn things from the manager and coaching staff at Melwood every day and if I did ever become a boss then they'd influence me greatly, as would all the other fantastic managers and coaches I have worked under. My ideas and tactics would be based on theirs.

STEVEN GERRARD: PORTRAIT OF A HERO

Gerrard's appetite to pursue a career in management may be enhanced if the player he rates as his favourite decides to do so before him.

'Being a Liverpool fan and a Scouser, I'm not supposed to admit this, but Roy Keane has been my favourite player over the past ten years or so,' says Gerrard. 'When he was in his prime, he was the best midfielder I have ever seen or played against. Even now, I love the way he approaches the game. I love how he plays every game as though his life depends on it and I'd love to have the same passion and hunger for success that he's still got when I get to his age.'

The end of Gerrard's career remains distant. There will be more goals, more trophies and perhaps even more heartache, too. However, wherever he goes, whatever he does in the future, anything is possible.